Saint Patrick's City
The Story of
Armagh

SAINT PATRICK'S CITY
THE STORY OF
Armagh

ALF McCREARY

THE BLACKSTAFF PRESS
BELFAST
2001

DEDICATED TO THE PEOPLE OF ARMAGH

First edition published in 2001 by
The Blackstaff Press Limited.

Designed by Corporate Document Services Ltd, Belfast.
Printed in Northern Ireland by W&G Baird Ltd, Belfast.

A CIP catalogue record for this book is available
from the Bristol Library.

ISBN 0 85640 711 9

www.blackstaffpress.com

Cover and Frontispiece: Painting by Timothy Lennox, at present on loan to the
Armagh County Museum

Back cover: Detail from a stained glass window in St. Patrick's Church of Ireland
Cathedral, Armagh.

CONTENTS

Preface   vii

Foreword   ix

I	The Real St. Patrick	3
II	Patrick and Armagh	15
III	Saints and Sinners	29
IV	Victors and Vandals	43
V	Turbulent Times	53
VI	The Seeds of Wrath	65
VII	Splendour	81
VIII	Catholic Emancipation - A New Cathedral	99
IX	Good Times - and Bad	109
X	More Upheaval	127
XI	City of Learning	141
XII	A Tale of Two Cities	165
XIII	Different Traditions - One God	185
XIV	The Legacy of St. Patrick	205

Appendix I
     St. Patrick's *Confessio*   223
     St. Patrick's *Letter to Coroticus*   233

Appendix 2
     Succession of Abbots, Bishops and
     Archbishops of Armagh   237
     Comharbaí Phádraig
     (St. Patrick and his successors)   241

Selected Reading List   244

Acknowledgements for illustrative material   246

Index   247

Down through the ages the example of St. Patrick has been a challenge to succeeding generations of people on this island and overseas, and not least in the city of Armagh, the ecclesiastical capital of Ireland where he established his main church.

In this timely book, which was commissioned by Armagh City and District Council as a Millennium project, the author Alf McCreary takes a fresh view of the life and work of St. Patrick and traces how his example has been followed by the people of his adopted island and the ecclesiastical city of Armagh, which was so close to his heart. The author also outlines the story of Armagh, and the resilience and ingenuity of its people who are well-known for their kindness and hospitality. It is particularly fitting that the book is dedicated to them.

The success of St. Patrick's mission led to the flowering of Irish Christianity and education, which gave this land the deserved reputation as the island of saints and scholars. However, there has also been a dark side to our history, and during the centuries of turbulence and unrest right to the present day, the response to St. Patrick and the Christian message and challenge has been at times very dim.
 In more recent years, the so-called Troubles have caused untold misery among our people, and the degree of suffering and animosity would grieve the very heart of our Patron Saint, as it has the hearts of all modern-day Christians who strive to follow his example.

On a more positive note, however, there has been a greater awareness among all the great strands of Christendom of those elements of the Christian faith and its practice which unite, rather than divide, us. The year-long celebrations to mark the 1550th anniversary of St. Patrick in Armagh was called appropriately Armagh Together, and it showed how the religious traditions and cultures in our city and Province can work together in harmony and peace.

Much remains to be done to bind together and to heal the wounds of our society that has suffered such great hurt for so long. Both traditions can look legitimately to the example of St. Patrick, whose Christian witness and reconciling values remain a personal challenge to us all. As St. Patrick himself stated in his moving and revealing Confession: "I have cast myself into the hands of God Almighty, who rules everywhere, as the prophet says: Cast thy thought upon God , and He shall sustain thee."

This important book "St. Patrick's City: The Story of Armagh" is required reading for all those who want to learn more about the real St. Patrick and about his reconciling message for our world of the 21st century. He is an important historical figure, but at the beginning of the Third Millennium, he remains a real person for our time, saying real things to all of us. We thank God for his work and example, and pray that his message and challenge will continue to find a place in all our hearts.

✝ Robert Armagh

Robert Armagh, Church of
Ireland Archbishop

✝ Seán Brady

Most Rev. Sean Brady DCL
Archbishop of Armagh

ACKNOWLEDGEMENTS

The author wishes to acknowledge the help of many people who made the production of this book possible. They include Archbishop Eames and Archbishop Brady and their colleagues; Desmond Mitchell, the former Clerk and Chief Executive of Armagh City and District Council, David McCammick, Corporate Services Director and associated staff, and Council members; Roger Weatherup, former Curator of Armagh County Museum; Pauline Allen for help with typing the manuscript; William McConnell, freelance photographer, and all other photographers credited in the text; members of staff of The Queen's University Library, The Linenhall Library, The Armagh Public Library, the Cardinal Tomas O'Fiaich Library and Archive and other centres of information credited; the editors of all newspapers and other publications mentioned; those whose scholarly and literary sources are quoted and duly acknowledged; and all others, too numerous to mention but not forgotten, who gave freely of their time and skills to help with the production of this book.

In particular, the author would like to thank Anne Tannahill and the staff of The Blackstaff Press; Bryan McCabe of W&G Baird, the printers; and most of all Mrs Hilary McCreary for her unwavering support in the preparation of yet another time-consuming book.

Alf McCreary is an award-winning journalist and author who writes extensively on Irish affairs, and on a wide range of other subjects. He is an Honours Graduate in Modern History from the Queen's University of Belfast, and for more than two decades he was a reporter, columnist and senior feature writer with the *Belfast Telegraph*, where he is currently the Religion Correspondent. He also writes a column for the *Belfast News Letter*, and contributes as a freelance to other publications.

He has won two British National Press Awards, and several Regional Press Awards, for his reports on the conflict in Northern Ireland. In mid-career he became Information Director and Head of Information at Queen's University, and in 1998 he relinquished this senior post to return to full-time writing. This is his twenty-third book.

Other titles by Alf McCreary

The Troubles
 Corrymeela
 Survivors
 Profiles of Hope
 Tried by Fire
 Marie –
  A Story from Enniskillen
 An Ordinary Hero –
  The Biography of Senator Gordon Wilson
 All Shall be Well (with Joan Wilson)

Travelogues
 An Ulster Journey
 This Northern Land

Third World
 Up With People
 Peace in Our Time

Corporate and Institutional History
 The Story of the Royal Belfast Hospital for Sick Children
 Spirit of the Age –
  The History of Old Bushmills
 By All Accounts –
  The Story of the TSB
 Degrees of Excellence –
  Queen's University from 1845 – 1995
  (with Professor Brian Walker)
 Making a Difference –
  The History of Ulster Garden Villages
 On With The Show –
  The Centenary History of the Royal Ulster Agricultural Society
 A Vintage Port – Larne and its People
 A Passion for Success – The Story of Coca-Cola

Essays and Collected Journalism
 Princes, Presidents and Punters
 The Good, the Bad and the Barmy

Autobiographical
 Remember When

FOREWORD

It has been both a privilege and an honour to have been asked to write this book about St. Patrick and the City of Armagh. A great many books and articles on St. Patrick have been published, and also about various aspects of life in the city and surrounding area.

However, there have been remarkably few general histories of the city itself, and this publication, to my knowledge, is the first such volume in more than a century since the Reverend Ambrose Coleman's revision and up-dating in 1900 of James Stuart's seminal work *Historical Memoirs of the City of Armagh,* published in 1819.

Like previous authors including- among others- Father Coleman and the seventh century writer Muirchu, I found the task daunting because of the breadth of the subject, and also because of the practical constraints, as well as the many deadlines, associated with the production of a volume of this nature. It is my hope that I, like those before me, have added something to the general broad knowledge of the subject, on which later generations may wish to build.

I found this project particularly absorbing, partly because of my fascination with St Patrick since my boyhood days, and partly because I was born and brought up near the City of Armagh for which I have long held a special affection. During the lengthy research and preparation involved in this publication, I have encountered great helpfulness and kindness from the Armagh people. Accordingly it is to them that I dedicate this book *St. Patrick's City-The Story of Armagh.*

Alf McCreary

Bessbrook, 26 September, 2001

'The name of St. Patrick is among
the most famous in history. It is
inseparable from Ireland and the Irish
people. Thousands of men, places,
churches and institutions are named
after Ireland's Patron Saint, but
surprisingly few people have any more
than a slight understanding
of the man himself.'

J.M. Holmes
The Real St. Patrick
1992
Irish Hill Publications

'*I am Patrick, a sinner, most unlearned, the least of all the faithful, and utterly despised by many...*'

These opening words of St Patrick's *Confession*, written in rudimentary Latin in his old age, provide an insight into the mind and heart of this extraordinary Christian from ancient Britain who became the national saint of Ireland, North and South. So much has been written, and conjectured, about his life and times that a search for the real St Patrick becomes a literary and ecclesiastical adventure story. There are many false trails, historical minefields and documentary dead-ends, and anyone who embarks upon such a search must do so at his or her own peril.

There are numerous scholarly disputes about the broad sweep as well as the details of Patrick's life and ministry, and so much time, scholarship and effort have been taken up with such differences of opinion that there is a danger of burying the Saint under layers of historical irrelevancy. The real St Patrick was a humble and deeply religious man, full of concern about his fellow human beings. He had enormous fortitude and courage, and a tenacious will to spread the Gospel and to honour the God who was at the very core of his being.

One of the major difficulties in trying to find the real man is that the relatively few details that are known about his life and work have been interlaced with later traditions written about him, where legend and fact are woven together in a virtual reality. Some of these traditions, handed down as oral and copied history, are reminiscent of part of the ills of certain kinds of modern journalism where the facts are rarely allowed to spoil 'a good story'.

Therefore, when people ask "What was St Patrick really like?", there are historical records which paint a broadly accurate picture of the man, and of his character and beliefs. But when they ask if St Patrick drove the snakes out of Ireland, or used the shamrock to teach his people about the Holy Trinity, or a host of similar questions which stem from the popular concept of St Patrick, the answer lies in the realms of legend and conjecture, rather than of historical accuracy.

What might seem relatively simple and basic facts are a matter of opinion - for example, where he was born and where he spent his captivity. To add to the complexity, some commentators claimed that there were two Patricks, while some believed that he never existed. Indeed, some others have claimed that he was confused with another missionary called Palladius, who was thought to have laboured for a short time in Ireland - possibly around Leinster - broadly within the lifetime of Patrick, though he does not mention any immediate predecessor or successor by name.

Opposite: A detail from one of the nineteenth century stained glass windows in the Church of Ireland Cathedral in Armagh depicting St Patrick laying the foundation stone of his church in AD 445.

It is against such a background that the search for the real St Patrick should begin, with a cautionary observation from the late Bishop RPC Hanson, formerly Professor of Historical and Contemporary Theology at the University of Manchester, who points out that historians cannot even give accurate dates about his life and work. Hanson suggests cautiously that he was born about 390, was kidnapped around 406, that he escaped in 412, that he returned to Ireland as a Bishop between 425 and 435, and that he died about 460.

Significantly, Hanson emphasises;

> "It is impossible to reconstruct Patrick's movements in Ireland. That is why we cannot today write a Life of Patrick, as has been done too confidently and too often in the past. ...We can only come to one positive and several negative conclusions. Patrick probably did make his headquarters at Armagh... That Patrick did not die at Armagh and was not buried there is quite certain; and later tradition is unanimous about him at this point. Whether he was buried at Saul instead ... or at Downpatrick ... cannot be determined. Patrick did not visit Slemish, for this had not been the scene of his captivity, and he did not climb Croagh Patrick, however much later tradition and custom may have hallowed these places. This is not, of course, to say that all authentic memory of Patrick died out soon after his death."[1]

It is the mixture of fact and "authentic memory", later developed into a tradition, that helps to build the picture of St Patrick which many people visualise today. Patrick was a real man, and the reality of his life and mission is captured in his own writings - his *Confession* and his *Letter to Coroticus*. These writings of Patrick not only give a self-portrait of the saint, though they were not meant to be autobiographical, but they also mark the beginning of recorded history in Ireland.

The 'legendary' material and 'later traditions', are to be found in a number of documents, but significantly so in the remarkable *Book of Armagh*, written in the 9th century by a scribe called Ferdomnach, which also contains a collection of different works, including the authentic words of Patrick from his *Confession*.

The site of St Patrick's main church.

THE CHURCH OF IRELAND
ANGLICAN ✝ EPISCOPAL
ST. PATRICK'S
CATHEDRAL
FOUNDED BY THE SAINT 445 AD
TIMES OF DIVINE SERVICES IN PORCH
→

The *Letter To Coroticus*, written earlier in his career, is a scathing condemnation of a British war-lord whose raiding troops murdered, raped and carried into captivity a large number of young men and women whom Patrick had baptised the day before. Patrick is furious about the savage brutality of such acts, and also deeply shocked that such cruelty should be condoned by Coroticus who claimed to be a Christian.

Though he is a God-fearing and saintly man, Patrick pulls no punches - partly due to his sense of injustice, and partly because he had sent emissaries to Coroticus asking for the return of the captives and "some of the booty" Unfortunately, his "holy presbyter" and his companions were spurned. Patrick writes "They only jeered at them."

His despair and anger give rise to impassioned prose.

"I am hated. What shall I do, Lord? I am most despised. Look, Thy sheep around me are torn to pieces and driven away, and that by those robbers, by the orders of the hostile-minded Coroticus. Far from the love of God is a man who hands over Christians to the Picts and Scots. Ravening wolves have devoured the flock of the Lord, which in Ireland was indeed growing splendidly with the greatest care; and the sons and daughters of kings were monks and virgins of Christ - I cannot count their number. Wherefore, be not pleased with the wrong done to the just; even to hell it shall not please".

Patrick has no doubts about the Divine retribution that will follow;

"Where, then, will Coroticus with his criminals, rebels against Christ, where will they see themselves, they who distribute baptised women as prizes - for a miserable temporal kingdom, which will pass away in a moment? As a cloud of smoke that is dispersed by the wind, so shall the deceitful wicked perish at the presence of the Lord; but the just will feast with great constancy with Christ, they shall judge nations, and rule over wicked kings for ever and ever. Amen."

The ferocity of his language here is reminiscent of the full force of an Old Testament prophet. Patrick was no doubt hoping that such a strong condemnation of a heinous crime would lead to the excommunication of Coroticus by the British Church, but he was also agonising about the suffering of the relatives of the murdered victims and those captured, including the young men and women who were doomed to a life of servitude and sexual abuse by their captors. Patrick was writing not just as a deeply-concerned observer, but as someone who had experienced at first hand the horrors of the capture and slavery which he had endured as a youth, and which he described so eloquently in his *Confession*. Those painful memories had stayed with him for nearly half a century, as his *Confession* was written when he was more than 60 - described in his own words as "my old age".

He begins by naming his father "Calpornius, a deacon, son of Potitus, a priest of the village Bannavem Taburniae; he had a country seat nearby, and there I was taken captive." There is general agreement among scholars that his father was a local government official who collected taxes for the Roman administration. This was a dubious honour, because the collector was deemed responsible for the debt of tax-evaders, who were probably as prevalent then as they are now! To escape such a burden, many of the tax-collectors took Holy Orders which exempted them from paying taxes. Patrick's father, a deacon, and his grandfather, a priest, had done just this, so in his upbringing he would have been clearly aware of the interaction of Church and State, a knowledge that would serve him well in Ireland.

Although he refers to his parentage and early background, there is much speculation about Patrick's birthplace and the region where he was taken prisoner by an Irish raiding party. A number of places are mentioned, including Boulogne, South Wales, Anglesea, yet another district close to the sea and some distance south of Hadrian's Wall, Glastonbury, Kilpatrick in Scotland and other areas. The uncertainty is well-documented by Father John Walsh and Thomas Bradley in their book "A History of the Irish Church 400-700 AD,"[2] and summarised thus;

"All we can say is that the place of Patrick's capture was probably on the west coast of Roman Britain in a region subject to incursions from Ireland and that Patrick's dual background (the fact that he was both a member of the Celto-Roman gentry and also a deacon's son) was very important to him. Loyal to the Church, he was nevertheless fiercely proud of his imperial roots. In fact ... 'Roman' and 'Christian' were for Patrick almost synonymous terms."

Patrick describes how at the age of 16 he was "taken into captivity to Ireland with many thousands of people - and deservedly so, because we turned away from God, and did not keep His commandments, and did not obey our priests, who used to remind us of our salvation. And the Lord brought over us the wrath of His anger and scattered us among many nations, even unto the utmost parts of the earth, where now my littleness is placed among strangers."

Once again, however, there is no scholarly agreement about his place of servitude. Patrick mentions only one Irish place name - Silva Focluti - and the speculation about its identity ranges from Co. Mayo in the west of Ireland to Slemish, Magherafelt, Strangford Lough and Faughal, near Cushendall in the north-east. One ingenious attempt to link both the west and the north-east of the island is made by Walsh and Bradley;

"While a northern location for Silva Focluti is distinctly possible ... a solution to the problem can be arrived at without rejecting the traditional location of Silva Focluti in the west of Ireland, or the Slemish tradition of the saint's captivity. Patrick may have been in both areas, either because he was sold by a master in one area to a new owner in the other, or because, after his six years of captivity in County Antrim, he escaped to Britain or the continent through a port in Co Mayo. Such an escape would, admittedly, have been unlikely, but would not have been impossible."[3]

However, we are on firmer ground when Patrick describes the hardships of his six years as a shepherd "in the woods and on the mountains", in all kinds of weather "through snow, through frost, through rain" and, in all probability, with hunger and thirst as his constant companions. It was on this severe testing-ground that Patrick, the youth who, by his own admission, had not known "the true God" discovered his real spiritual identity and prepared himself for something greater, which later became his Divine mission to the Irish.

"But after I came to Ireland - every day I had to tend sheep and many times a day I prayed - the love of God and His fear came to me more and more, and my faith was strengthened. And my spirit was moved so that in a single day I would say as many as a hundred prayers, and almost as many in the night, and this even when I was staying in the woods and on the mountains; and I used to get up for prayer before daylight, through snow, through frost, through rain, and I felt no harm, and there was no sloth in me - as I now see, because the spirit within me was then fervent."

Then, literally in the next sentence of his *Confession*, Patrick describes his vision when a voice came to him in his sleep telling him that "soon you will go to your own country". Again a voice told him "See, your ship is ready", but he still had a considerable distance to travel, "perhaps two hundred miles, and I had never been there, nor did I know a living soul there". But the young slave-boy took off, and travelled the two hundred miles where a ship was waiting. Patrick does not tell us how he travelled, but a great deal of the journey must have been on foot. Nor does he describe how he found food and lodging on the way. Spurred on by his intense faith he "went in the strength of God who directed my way to my good, and I feared nothing until I came to that ship." Thus in an almost matter-of-fact way he describes his long journey taken in faith, and totally without fear.

When he approached the ship, it had already been "set afloat." In other words it had most probably been untied from its moorings, prior to setting out to sea. Somehow, Patrick managed to attract the attention of the crew, and he told the vessel's captain that he was able to pay for his passage - again he does not tell us how he got the money to do so. The captain was not best pleased and told him brusquely "It is of no use for you to ask us to go along with us." So what did Patrick do then?

As in every tight corner of his life, he asked for God's guidance. "I began to pray; and before I had ended my prayer, I heard one of them shouting behind me 'Come, hurry, we shall take you on in good faith; make friends with us in whatever way you like'." They invited him to suck their nipples, a somewhat intimate and bizarre method of sealing friendships in those days, but he refused to indulge in such pagan practices and "rather hoped they would come to the faith of Jesus Christ."

The sea-journey lasted three days, and then for 28 days they travelled through deserted country. No place-names are mentioned by Patrick, so it is not clear whether they had landed at another part of the British Isles or on the continent. Some commentators speculate, however, that because they were transporting a cargo of Irish hounds it was possible that they had travelled to Gaul, where such animals were in great demand. The main point about Patrick's story at this point, however, was the fact that he and the sailors were starving.

The captain challenged him directly "Tell me, Christian, you say that your God is great and all-powerful; why, then, do you not pray for us?" Patrick, clearly put on the spot, had no doubts about the guidance of God.

"I said to them full of confidence 'be truly converted with all your heart to the Lord my God, because nothing is impossible for Him, that this day He may send you food on your way until you be satisfied; for he has abundance everywhere.'

Suddenly a herd of pigs appeared on the previously deserted road, and the sailors promptly killed them and fed themselves and the dogs until they all had their fill. This would appear to have been the only authentic "miracle" described by Patrick in his own words, in comparison to the many "miracles" attributed to him by later writers who recorded legend and tradition. The sailors rested for two nights until they had fully recovered their strength. They even found wild honey, and offered some of it to Patrick as a sacrifice. But he replied, perhaps a little haughtily for such a humble man "Thanks be to God, I tasted none of it."

Unfortunately, his trials were not over.

"That same night, when I was asleep, Satan assailed me violently, a thing I shall remember as long as I shall be in this body. And he fell upon me like a huge rock, and I could not stir a limb. But whence came it into my mind, ignorant as I am, to call upon Helias? And meanwhile I saw the sun rise in the sky, and while I was shouting 'Helias, Helias' with all my might, suddenly the splendour

In a verse from the 'Tripartite' Life of Patrick he shows his fondness for Armagh.

Doroega port n-eiseirgi
Ard Macha mo chell
Niba coimsech mo-soiri
Is doire co cend

I had chosen the harbour of my resurrection
Armagh my Church
I am not free to do my own will
I am bonded to the end

but he proceeds to emphasise,

Yet it is Armagh that I love
Pleasant are her thorpes, pleasant
her burial mounds;
A dun that enthrals my soul.

of that sun fell on me and immediately freed me of all misery. And I believe that I was sustained by Christ my Lord."

Once again, his faith had proved unshakeable. Then, in a brief and somewhat obscure passage of his *Confession*, he tells us that he was captured again and that "on the sixtieth night thereafter, the Lord delivered me out of their hands." He then relates, matter-of-factly, that he returned home. " ...after a few years I was in Britain with my people, who received me as their son, and sincerely besought me that now at last, having suffered so many hardships, I should not leave them and go elsewhere."

Such sentiments from his parents were understandable, but Patrick was not allowed to rest in his newly-found freedom and comfort. He tells us of his turmoil when, in another vision, he was approached by a man called Victoricus, "coming as it were from Ireland" with countless letters which were "the voice of the Irish" and "thus did they cry out with one mouth 'We ask thee, boy, come and walk among us once more'." Patrick was "quite broken in heart, and could read no further, and so I woke up. Thanks be to God, after many years the Lord gave to them according to their cry."

After further heart-searching Patrick heeded the call to Ireland, but he was clear about the ultimate source of that invitation, which was, in effect, a Divine command. "I did not go to Ireland of my own accord, not until I had nearly perished; but this was rather for my good, for thus was I purged by the Lord; and he made me fit so that I might be now what was once far from me - that I should care and labour for the salvation of others, whereas then I did not even care about myself."

There is much academic speculation about the time-lapse between Patrick's escape from Ireland and his return as a missionary, just as there is speculation as to whether he received further education in Britain or on the continent. Later writers claim that Patrick planned to go to Rome but stayed at Auxerre, whereas Bishop Hanson remained sceptical about any continental connection with Patrick.

"A preoccupation with his alleged formation in Lerins or Auxerre has hitherto prevented a proper appreciation of Patrick as a figure genuinely representative of the British Church of the first half of the fifth century. Patrick's works were, of course, written on Irish soil, but they are characteristic of the British Church in a way in which no previous or contemporary literature that has survived is, nor any for the next century after his day. ... One could almost go further than this and say that Patrick is the first British personality in history whom the historian can know. ... This can be said of very few other personalities in the ancient world, and of absolutely no other British persons in the whole of ancient history."[4]

However, lest Bishop Hanson's concentration on the "Britishness" of

Patrick might offend those who want to see him as an essentially Irish figure, they may find comfort in the interpretation of Thomas Cahill who claims in his book How the Irish Saved Civilization that "Patrick was a Romanized Celtic Briton - not an Englishman."5

Patrick, however, rises above narrow nationalism in the sense that he saw himself as God's messenger doing His will at a specific time in history. Indeed, Patrick and his contemporary Christians believed that the world was about to end, a view reinforced no doubt by the quickening demise of the Roman Empire which, to many of them, was the known world. Hanson, as ever, puts the point well;

> "It is typical of the fifth-century Church that it should be laying the foundations for the vigorous and intense spread and development of Christianity over the whole of Europe during the next thousand years while the men who were doing the work of foundation-laying imagined that civilisation, the very fabric of society and the course of history itself, were about to collapse, perhaps before their work was completed."6

It is clear from his *Confession* that Patrick himself believed that the Ireland of his day was at the ends of the earth - "Indeed, we are witnesses that the Gospel has been preached unto those parts beyond which there lives nobody."

A large part of his *Confession* is devoted to his missionary work in Ireland, partly as a riposte to those in the British Church who were sceptical of his mission.

> "For many tried to prevent this my mission; they would even talk to each other behind my back and say 'Why does this fellow throw himself into danger among enemies who have no knowledge of God?' It was not malice, but it did not appeal to them because - and to this I own myself - of my rusticity. And I did not realise at once the grace that was then in me; now I understand that I should have done so before."

Patrick is also troubled because his critics made accusations against him concerning a sin of his youth which he, in troubled mind, had confessed to a friend. Patrick does not relate what the misdemeanour was. Some commentors claim that it might have been sexual, and one even alleges that it could have been murder, but clearly it weighed heavily on Patrick's mind for the rest of his life. "In the anxiety of my troubled mind, I confided to my dearest friend what I had done in my boyhood one day, nay, in one hour, because I was not yet strong." Whatever the short-coming, it underlines Patrick's human failures, just as he could understand the frailties of his flock.

He writes about the many dangers he faced, almost daily. There were "twelve dangers in which my life was at stake - not to mention numerous plots". Later in his Confession he admits "Daily I expect murder, fraud, or captivity, or whatever it may be; but I fear none of these things because of the promises of heaven." Even in his darkest moments, his faith in God is rock-solid; "I have cast myself into the hands of God Almighty, who rules everywhere, as the prophet says; 'Cast thy thought upon God and he shall sustain thee'." In this context, Patrick shows that despite his embarrassment at his lack of education, he has read his Bible thoroughly and that its teachings are a constant inspiration and comfort to him.

He is at pains not to place himself in compromising circumstances, and he

is particularly careful about receiving unsolicited gifts.

"For although I be rude in all things, nevertheless I have tried somehow to keep myself safe, and that, too, for my Christian brethren, and the virgins of Christ, and the pious women who of their own accord made me gifts and laid on the altar some of their ornaments; and I gave them back to them, and they were offended that I did so. But I did it for the hope of lasting success - in order to preserve myself cautiously in everything so that they might not seize upon me or the ministry of my service, under the pretext of dishonesty, and that I would not in the smallest matter give the infidels an opportunity to defame or defile."

On the other hand, he was not above spending money to keep in with the local power-brokers. He gave "presents to the kings, besides the fees I paid to their sons who travel with me." Yet even that did not protect him from harm. "Even so they laid hands on me and my companions, and on that day they eagerly wished to kill me; but my time had not yet come. And everything they found with us they took away, and me they put in irons; and on the fourteenth day the Lord delivered me from their power, and our belongings were returned to us because of God and our dear friends whom we had seen before." Patrick may not have been able to express his views in flawless Latin, as classicists point out, but he had the knack of telling a story well.

His lack of literary sophistication actually adds to the richness of his text. "He does not write a line simply for effect. He never exaggerates, never distorts. ... There is no barrier between him and his reader. He is one of the most honest men who ever wrote Latin, perhaps the most honest of all who ever wrote Christian Latin."[7]

The picture of Patrick which emerges from his writings is that of a strong, resolute, determined, and deeply spiritual man with attractive qualities of kindness and humility. He is every inch a good Bishop, tending to his flock, evangelising, baptising, educating and looking after his people in every way possible. He is not class-conscious, though he seems unduly flattered that the sons and daughters of the Irish aristocracy are among his converts. He is acutely conscious of the social evils of his day, and he is one of the first senior figures in the Christian Church to rail publicly against slavery, whereas the Apostle Paul merely exhorted Christian masters to be kind to their slaves, whom he told to obey their masters. Patrick also has time to pay attention to the administration of the church, thus demonstrating that those who are heavenly-minded can also be of earthly use.

Bishop Hanson states "In St Patrick we have a full-length picture of a British bishop, and it is a most attractive one."[8] The late Dr George Simms, the former Church of Ireland Archbishop of Armagh, and himself a scholarly, gentle and saintly prelate, wrote of Patrick "He is more than a name, more than a legend, more than a symbol of Ireland and the Irish wherever they live. He is a saint and, as has been said, 'saints are not made by accident'. They are part of history. Indeed someone said that saints were those who did ordinary things extraordinarily well."[9]

Much of his spirit lives on in the beautiful St Patrick's Breastplate, which was not his own work. It was written several centuries after his death, but it is Patrician to the core.

St Patrick's name adorns great Cathedrals and Churches all over the world, including St Patrick's Cathedral in New York, seen here with the sky- scrapers of Fifth Avenue as a backdrop.

Christ be within me,
Christ be beside me,
Christ be behind me,
Christ be before me.

Given the many outstanding qualities which Patrick demonstrated, his greatest legacy to his adopted island and to the city of Armagh, where he established the centre of his mission, is three-fold. First, he places major emphasis on the growth and the witness of the Church itself. He continually delights in his *Confession* on the success of the Church. He states "... it was most necessary to spread our nets so that a great multitude and throng might be caught for God, and that there be clerics everywhere to baptise and exhort a people in need and want, as the Lord in the Gospel states, exhorts and teaches, saying 'Going therefore now, teach ye all nations, baptising them in the name of the Father, and the Son and the Holy Spirit, teaching them to observe all things whatsoever I have commanded you'."

Secondly, Patrick whose early education had been cruelly cut short by being taken into slavery, is ever conscious of the importance of learning. Again and again he is aware of his lack of education, to the point of acute embarrassment.. He admits that "I have not studied like the others". He states with painful frankness "Hence today I blush and fear exceedingly to reveal my lack of education; for I am unable to tell my story to those versed in the art of concise writing." For Patrick, education was an absolute priority, and his ministry led to the greatest possible blossoming of learning in the island of "saints and scholars", who brought that light of learning to the greater Europe of their day.

Thirdly, Patrick left an example of greater social awareness about the welfare of others and what might be described broadly as better community relations. He exhorted people to eschew violence and un-Christian practices and to base their lives on the tenets of the Gospel. One could argue that such an example had a more dramatic effect in the years of his mission and afterwards, than in the increasingly secular world of today. But his challenge remains as daunting as ever.

He never forgot the trauma of his capture and slavery, and even in his old age the pain remained. "He could never quite lose this image of himself as utterly helpless, utterly defenceless and abandoned. That is why we feel an inextinguishable sympathy with Patrick. He has managed to convey to us so movingly his own feeling about himself, not what he would like us to feel or to think, but what he really felt himself. But we never imagine that he is indulging in futile self-pity. Patrick does not pity himself, because, as he himself tells us, in his moment of helplessness and extreme need he found a helper and a friend in God."[10]

As he said himself "Whence I, once rustic, exiled, unlearned, who does not know how to provide for the future, this at least I know most certainly that before I was humiliated I was like a stone lying in the deep mire: and He that is mighty came and in his mercy lifted me up, and raised me aloft, and placed me on top of the wall."

The last paragraph of Patrick's *Confession*. typically, underlines his humility and his conviction that the vision for his mission and the strength to sustain it, came directly from God;

> " I pray those who believe and fear God, whosoever deigns to look at or receive this writing which Patrick, a sinner, unlearned, has composed in Ireland, that no-one should ever say that it was my ignorance if I did or showed forth anything however small according to God's good pleasure; but let this be your conclusion and let it so be thought, that -as is the perfect truth- it was the gift of God. This is my confession before I die."

Having studied Patrick's own writings, as opposed to the legends and tradition which came later, he reminds me strongly of St Peter, the ill-educated, transparently honest and simple yet profound man on whom Christ promised to build His Church. Patrick was a worthy rock and foundation for the Irish Church, and a patron Saint of whom all those living on the island of Ireland - and those of Irish extraction all over the world - can justly be proud. In modern parlance he was, and is, a hard act to follow. How far his people of all ages have followed his example is a somewhat different story.

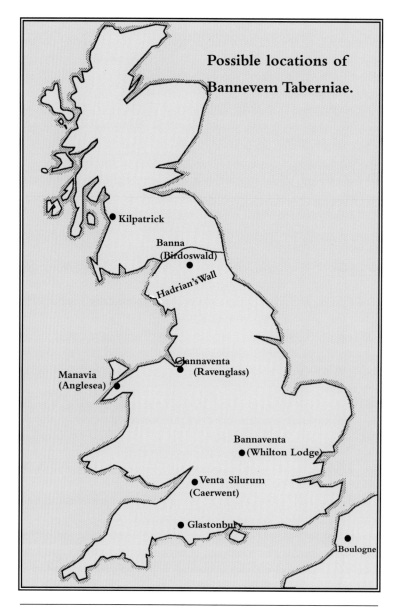

Possible locations of Bannevem Taberniae.

NOTES

1	*Saint Patrick – His Origins and Career,* Page 188 and pp 197–8, published by the Oxford University Press in 1968.
2	Published by Columba Press Dublin (Permission Sought) 1991 pp 13–14
3	Op. Cit. pp 17–18
4	Hanson. Op. Cit. pp 198–200
5	Page 158, published by Doubleday, New York.
6	Hanson Op. Cit. page 201
7	Ibid. page 206
8	Ibid. page 200
9	*The Real Story of Patrick*, page 8, published by The O'Brien Press Dublin, 1991.
10	Hanson Op. Cit. pp 208–9

> *'Although I am imperfect in many things, I nevertheless wish that my brethren and kinsmen should know what sort of person I am, so that they may understand my heart's desire'*
>
> St. Patrick's *Confession*

Once we leave the comparatively firm ground of St Patrick's own writings to gain a picture of the saint, we enter the world of speculation and of conjecture - however persuasive many of these claims may appear. These stories add flesh and blood, plus excitement and drama, to the story of St Patrick, but so long as we remain aware of the questions hanging over their historical veracity, we will not be carried away by the later portraits of the saint, however fascinating and colourful they may be. That is not to deny that there may be more than a grain of historical truth in some of the later stories - the problem is in trying to assess how significant that grain might be. This is particularly important in our age when perception is sometimes more important than reality, and in extreme cases, when perceived reality threatens to become reality itself.

Much of the significant source material is to be found in the *Book of Armagh*, to which reference has been made already and to which we will return later on. However it is important, at this stage, to ask why Patrick established his major church at Armagh, rather than, say, at Saul or Downpatrick which are closely associated with Patrician legend and tradition. Again, many scholars have speculated as to Patrick's motives in choosing Armagh. Did he deliberately decide to establish Christianity at the heart of an area of pagan worship or is the answer more simple? Perhaps Patrick, like any shrewd evangelist, instinctively established his headquarters at the seat of secular and religious influence which in his day was Emain Macha, now called Navan Fort.

Though scholars speculate about the details of Emain Macha and Patrick's motives for establishing his church in that area - as they do about much else in this distant period of history - "Emain Macha was the ancient capital of Ulster, its first historical place, the seat of its ancient kings when the power of Ulster was at its greatest, the pagan, spiritual and political centre of the Province, the geographical focus of its greatest works of literature and the first archaeological site in Northern Ireland to be nominated ... to UNESCO as a site of international importance."[1]

Emain Macha derives its title from a legendary war-goddess Macha, whose name is also perpetuated in Armagh - that is Ard Macha, the Height of Macha. Even this is not as straightforward as it seems. Roger Weatherup, the former Curator of Armagh County Museum, claims that traditionally the focus of the city "is the hill on which the Church of Ireland Cathedral stands where Macha, conscious of its steep-sided security, built her palace which was then named Ard Mhacha or Macha's Height." Writing in the book *The Buildings of Armagh*, which was published in 1992 by the Ulster Architectural Heritage Society , he states that "After about three hundred years, the hill was abandoned in favour of the townland of Navan three miles to the west where a later Queen Macha constructed a new fortress called Emain Macha."

A stone carving of the mythological goddess Macha, from whom the city of Armagh takes its name, in the Chapter Room of St Patrick's Church of Ireland Cathedral.

There are two well-known legends about the war-goddess Macha which are nothing if not colourful. In the first she ruled Ireland, married one of her rivals and lured her other enemies into the woods one by one and defeated them. According to the *Annals of the Four Masters*, she then forced them to build the great Fort of Emain, so that it might be the capital of ancient Ulster. She marked off the territory with a brooch - in Old Irish called eo-mhuin-hence the word Emain. According to the Annals, Macha and her successors kept their headquarters at Emain Macha for more than 800 years.

In the other legend, Macha married a man who boasted to the King of Ulster that his wife could outrun his horses. The woman, though pregnant, was forced to run against the King's chariot, otherwise her husband would be executed. Naturally, she won the race and immediately gave birth to twins - a boy and a girl, and the old Irish word for twin was emain, which once again leads us to Emain Macha. Equally significant, this version of the legend claims that Macha, quite understandably, cursed the Ulstermen for making her run in such condition, and for nine generations the Province's warriors had a debilitating disease for nine days whenever a crisis arose[2]. (This may also explain the Ulster debilitation of failing to agree on peaceful co-existence in a Province that has been wracked by violence and dissension almost, it would seem, since time began.)

The name of Emain Macha is also perpetuated in the *Ulster Cycle of Tales*, dating from roughly the 7th to the 12th centuries. These tell the daring deeds of the legendary heroes like Cuchullain, and the constant battles with their mortal enemies in Connaught under the leadership of their warrior Queen Medb. In all of these tales, Emain Macha is the legendary capital, just like Camelot in the tales of King Arthur, and the stories describe, with exaggeration, the magnificence of the great palace that once stood at the centre of power in Ulster.

Although we derive the name of Emain Macha from the twilight world of legend, we move beyond legend to the scientific work of archaeologists who found evidence of human activity at Emain Macha for as far back as 5,000 years ago. Scientists working under the leadership of Dudley Waterman of Queen's University, Belfast from 1963-71 confirmed that it had been a Bronze Age settlement, and their discovery of the remains of a Barbary ape there would suggest that only a kingly class would own such an exotic pet in those days. The scientists further believe that Emain Macha was the site of a huge pagan temple, around 100 BC. "This structure - formed by a ring of large posts, probably roofed, and dominated by a gigantic central totem pole - was forty metres across. Shortly after its construction, it was filled with stones, purposely burned and then covered with sods and earth, possibly so that it would continue forever as a focal point in the other-world."[3]

It seems clear, therefore, that Emain Macha was a significant centre in the early history of Ulster, and it would seem obvious that Patrick would have wished to establish his church near such a focus of power. Yet again, there is no scholarly consensus. As the late Cardinal Tomas O'Fiaich, a noted historian and a former Roman Catholic Archbishop of Armagh, writes tongue-in-cheek "The saint who proclaimed himself 'the most unlearned of men' must surely be enjoying the battles of the scholars in pursuit of him."[4]

Navan Fort, Emain Macha, the ancient capital of Ulster.

A reproduction of the Navan Fort site, in St Patrick's Trian, Armagh.

Part of the answer to the question as to why Patrick chose Armagh lies in the turbulent history of the times. An ancient people called the Ulaid held power in Ulster until roughly the middle of the 5th century when they were pushed eastwards by the northern Ui Neill, who reputedly created the Airgialla - a buffer state of satellite kingdoms between the two peoples, probably in mid-Ulster. Around the same time, another group - the southern Ui Neill - displaced the Laigin in Leinster and set up kingdoms in Meath, Westmeath and Longford, as well as in parts of Louth, Dublin and Offaly.

Although this significant new disposition of territorial power and boundaries was being implemented, uncertainty remains about the date of the defeat of the Ulaid. Did this occur around 332 AD, as some people claim, or was it much later around 450 AD by which time Patrick would have had an opportunity to establish his church at Armagh, only a hill away from what was left of Emain Macha? And if the Ulaid lost control of their territory in the middle of the 5th century, did Patrick move with them as they were being pushed further back eastwards, and ended up in the area of Downpatrick, with which his name and tradition are so closely associated? Historians cannot provide definitive answers to such fundamental questions, so it is no surprise to discover than in the absence of hard facts on such matters, the field is once again open to speculation.

This brings us back to the *Book of Armagh*, that priceless 9th century manuscript. In pre-Christian times the only written communication was through Ogham, a language carved in stone, but the arrival of Christianity and the written word, as we have come to understand it, was revolutionary. The *Book of Armagh* is, in effect, a collection of different works, including the complete New Testament, the earliest complete copy to survive from the

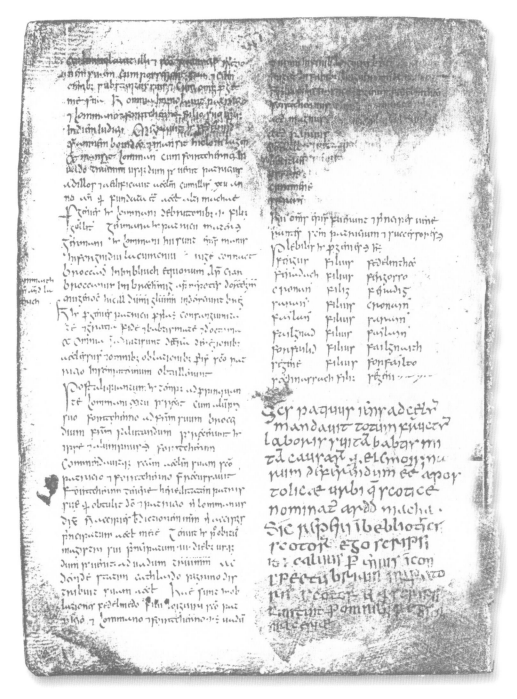

An entry from the "Book of Armagh" referring to Brian Boru. This addition to the original manuscript was made in the presence of Boru himself and on the King's orders affirmed the ecclesiastical supremacy of Armagh. Brian Boru died at the battle of Clonrarf in 1014.

ancient Irish Church. It also contains a *Life of St Martin of Tours* by Sulpicus Severus.

The Book also contains Muirchu's *Life of St Patrick*, and another Life of the saint by Bishop Tirechan, with a number of his miscellaneous Additions or Dicta. There is also the *Book of the Angel*, which purports to tell the story of Armagh as a Christian centre, but many scholars regard it as special pleading for the city - perhaps the ancient version of putting a "spin" on a story - centuries before our modern politicians developed this into a fine art.

Though the *Book of Armagh* is the work of a number of writers, it was compiled by the Master Scribe Ferdomnach. He worked in the Scriptorium of the Monastery at Armagh. This picture is a detail from a window in St Patrick's Church of Ireland Cathedral, Armagh.

Though the *Book of Armagh* is the work of a number of writers, it was compiled by the Master Scribe Ferdomnach who worked in the Scriptorium of the monastery which had been founded at Armagh as a result of St Patrick's mission. To people of our generation who marvel at the technology of the Internet and the fax machine, as well as suffering the endless intrusion of the ubiquitous mobile phone, it is almost impossible to comprehend the painstaking craftsmanship and hard work which went into the creation of a 9th century manuscript.

First, there was the preparation of the vellum, made from calf-skin which was placed for several days in a bath of dung or lime to loosen the hairs. The hide was scraped with a blunt knife to remove the loosened hairs, and the skin was dried and stretched. Then it was dampened and smoothed with a pumice stone to provide a smooth surface. Finally, it was soaked yet again, and left to dry.

The scribe used a kind of ink made from local materials, including plants and copper and iron, as well as imported lapis lazuli. His quill was made from goose or swan feathers, and it was trimmed and hardened by being dipped into hot sand, so that it would move smoothly across the vellum. The preparation of the materials took a long time, and the art of copying required great patience and precision. Sometimes the inspiration was slow in coming, as many writers know. The demands of this slow but, of necessity, accurate work were described delightfully in a poem written by an Irish monk:

> *'I and Pangur Ban, my cat,*
> *Tis a like task we are at:*
> *Hunting mice is his delight.*
> *Hunting words I sit all night.'*

The detailed work in the *Book of Armagh* may not be immediately obvious to the untrained eye, but Giraldus Cambrensis, the 12th century Norman historian who had access to a similar manuscript, wrote appreciatively thus; "... if you take the trouble to look very closely, you will notice such intricacies, so delicate and subtle, so close together and well knitted, so involved and bound together ... that you will not hesitate to declare that all these things must have been the result of the work, not of men, but of angels."

A sculpture of an Irish monk and his Cat Pangur Ban, by the Irish sculptress Imogen Stuart, who presented it to Cardinal Tomas O'Fiaich (O'Fiaich Library and Archive).

The beauty of the *Book of Armagh* is underlined in the *Liber Ardmachanus* by John Gwynn, published in 1913. It is described as "a small, square volume, measuring in height 7³/₄ inches; in breadth 5³/₄; in thickness 2¹/₄: consisting originally of 222 leaves of vellum, on each side of which the writing is arranged mostly in double columns. ... The penmanship is of extreme elegance, and is admirable throughout for its distinctness and uniformity. The character is a minuscule of the type described as 'pointed Irish', which is employed alike for the Latin and the Irish documents and notes."[5]

While production of the *Book of Armagh* makes a fascinating story in its own right, so too is the adventure associated with its survival. The Book was greatly revered, and because it was thought by ordinary people to have been written by Patrick himself it was known as "St Patrick's Testament." It was also held in esteem by the Kings and nobility. In 937 it was specially encased by Donnachadh, son of Flann, the King of Ireland, and in 1004 an addition to the manuscript was made in the presence of Brian Boru himself, the High King of Ireland.

Brian Boru, however, had his own agenda which was to gain the approval of the Church for his military ambitions. It is recorded that he placed a golden ring of twenty ounces as an offering on the altar of St Patrick's Church, perhaps as a down-payment for his final resting-place in such turbulent times! Less than a decade later, his corpse was laid to rest on the hill of Armagh, in the precincts of St Patrick's Church, following the Battle of Clontarf.

From the earliest times within the monastery, the *Book of Armagh* was kept by a special steward, the last one being Florence MacMoyre. His stewardship was less than impressive, for in 1680 he pledged the *Book of Armagh* for £5, to help pay his expenses to London to give evidence against Dr Oliver Plunkett, the Roman Catholic Bishop of Armagh. On his return he was unable to buy it back, and this sacred relic of the Armagh church became available for purchase on the open market.

Then in 1707, in a state of ill-repair, it passed into the possession of the Brownlow family in Lurgan where it remained until 1815 when the Reverend Francis Brownlow sent it on loan to the Royal Irish Academy in Dublin. There it excited interest among academicians who appreciated its true worth. In 1853 it was purchased by Dr Reeves for £300, who later sold it, without profit, to the Lord Primate of Ireland, Lord John George Beresford, Chancellor of the University of Dublin. He, in turn, presented it to the University library where it remains to this day. Its survival, through such a period of dubious adventures, is nothing short of miraculous.

Though the *Book of Armagh* provides valuable insights into the early Church, it is worth noting that scholars have found it particularly difficult to reconstruct the *Life of Patrick* by Muirchu, because no complete manuscript survives.[6] Versions survive in four manuscripts, including that in the *Book of Armagh*, but there is enough material to provide a vivid portrait of the saint from legend and tradition.

Muirchu Moccu Machteni, a 7th century priest in the Armagh archdiocese, had access to a version of Patrick's *Confession* when he was writing the Life in a period somewhere between 661 and 700, but he admits, somewhat touchingly, his shortcomings as a biographer. Later writers in the Patrician debates are somewhat less modest, with sometimes questionable justification, about their literary abilities.

Muirchu was conscious that he was writing a long time after Patrick's death, and that his source material, apart from the Confession, was less than reliable:

> "I have taken my little talent - a boy's paddle-boat as it were - out on this deep and perilous sea of sacred narrative, where waves boldly swell to towering heights among rocky reefs in unknown waters ... However, far from giving the impression that I want to make something big out of something small, I shall (merely) attempt to set forth, bit by bit and step by step, these few of the numerous deeds of holy Patrick, with little knowledge ('of traditional lore'), on uncertain authority, from an unreliable memory, feebly and in poor style, but with the pious affection of holy love, in obedience to the command of your sanctity and authority."

Despite his shortcomings, Muirchu writes with much more fluency than the subject of his biography, though - as we have noted earlier - there is an endearing directness and compelling modesty about Patrick's own words. In the style of medieval hagiography , Patrick is depicted as a kind of superman and as a saint who performed miracles. He is decidedly ascetic, he has the power to confront evil, and to impart holy curses, he is good with animals, and totally committed to bringing the light of the Gospel to the darkness of a pagan land.

In the early part of the Life, Muirchu writes about Patrick's background, his kidnap, servitude in Ireland and his return home - most of which corresponds broadly to the *Confession*. However, Muirchu goes well beyond Patrick's relatively brief outline and claims that the saint set out for Rome to study there, but stayed for several decades with Germanus in Auxerre, where he heard of the mission of Palladius to Ireland and of his death, that he himself was ordained as a Bishop by Amathorex, and that, with others, he was sent back to Ireland by way of Britain.[7]

According to Muirchu, Patrick landed on the coast of Wicklow, then re-embarked and sought out his old master Miliuc at Slemish. He also makes contact with the heathen King Loeghaire at Tara, and also founds his main church at Armagh. A good example of Muirchu's colourful style is this story about Corictic.

> "I shall not pass over in silence a miraculous deed of St Patrick's. News had been brought to him of a wicked act by a certain British king named Corictic, an ill-natured and cruel ruler. He had no equal as a persecutor and murderer of Christians. Patrick tried to call him back to the way of truth by a letter, but he scorned his salutary exhortations. When this was reported to Patrick, he prayed to the Lord and said: 'My God, if it is possible, expel this godless man from this world and from the next.' Not much time had elapsed after this when (Corictic) heard somebody recite a poem saying that he should abandon his royal seat, and all the men who were dearest to him chimed in. Suddenly before their eyes, in the middle of a public place, he was ignominiously changed into a fox went off, and since that day and hour, like water that flows away, was never seen again."

Muirchu also tells of an evil man's land being turned into a marsh, of an angel offering the saint direction from a burning bush (the parallel with Moses is obvious) and of the crucial contest of strength with the druidic forces of paganism. He writes about the journey to the great plain of Brega, near the royal palace at Tara. Patrick and his companions pitched their tent and offered Easter devotions to God. Meanwhile the King and his retinue, compared by Muirchi to the Babylon of Nebuchadnezzar, saw Patrick's 'divine fire'. The druids warned the King that unless this fire "is extinguished on this night on which it has been lit, it will never be extinguished at all."

This striking figure, the "Tandragee Man", was found in a garden in Tandragee near Armagh. Dating from the Iron Age (some 1000 years BC), the figure represents King Nuadha who lost an arm and his throne in battle to Bres. Nuadha had an artificial arm made of silver and in a return to power overthrew Bres. The figure which stands in St Patrick's Church of Ireland Cathedral in Armagh depicts Nuadha holding his artificial arm.

The Royal retinue was driven out in chariots to witness this challenge to paganism, and the druids advised the King not to approach the fire. Instead, Patrick was summoned to come forward, and he did so with a Psalm on his lips. Patrick blessed the only one of the King's company who believed in him, but the others hurled curses and abuse at the saint. Once again he prayed, and a druid was struck down, fatally cracking his skull on a stone. Then there was darkness, and an earthquake, and chaos ensued.

Everyone retreated in confusion. Later on, the Queen implored Patrick not to destroy the King, who had pledged himself to accept Christianity. However he was only pretending to do so, but as Patrick and his followers approached the Royal presence, they avoided all danger and disappeared out of his sight in the form of eight deer and a fawn heading for the wilds. The King did not give up, and the next day he invited Patrick to a feast, where another druid tried to poison him. However, Patrick blessed the cup , the liquid froze, and the poisoned drop fell to the ground when the cup was upturned. To underline his power, Patrick blessed the cup again, and the liquid returned to its natural state.

The druids used all kinds of magic to try to destroy Patrick but, with prayer, he thwarted all their efforts. Eventually the King gave up and came to the sensible conclusion "It is better for me to believe than to die." Patrick had the last word, however. He told Leoghaire that "your own reign shall run on" but because he had resisted the Christian teaching and had been so offensive to Patrick personally, "none of your offspring shall ever be king." Muirchu relates this story in great detail, and it is not difficult to imagine the impact he hoped to create by his tales of the triumph of good over evil and the miraculous powers demonstrated by this holy man of God.

Muirchu states that Patrick died on 17 March "as it is celebrated throughout Ireland every year", so the tradition establishing St Patrick's Day goes back to at least the 7th century. Muirchu further claims that darkness was suspended for 12 days, that angels singing psalms kept vigil over his body for the first night, and that Patrick died at the age of 120. Again this may be an attempt to link him to the patriarchal figures of the Old Testament who were described as having lived to a very old age.

Bishop Tierchan, who was thought to have been a contemporary of Muirchu, also writes about Patrick's early life. He claims that the saint returned to Ireland from continental Europe with a large band of "bishops, presbyters, deacons, exorcists, ostiaries, readers and boys whom he had ordained"; that he ordained some 350 bishops during his ministry, that he travelled round most of Ireland founding churches and performing miracles.[8]

Scholars note that Tirechan's account is more a collection of memoirs than the more structured life of Muirchu, and that his writings are much less valuable concerning Patrick, though they do convey an important flavour of the times in which they were set down. But both writers contribute to what has been called "the cult of St Patrick." Tirechan, a native of Co Mayo stressed Patrick's supposed connections with the west of Ireland, and he was at pains to link Patrick with Armagh, as was Muirchu, who stated that it was the place "he loved more than any other."

The historian Dr Charles Doherty has summarised well the difficulties associated with the early writings. "Patrick's ancient biographers were not simply writing the 'life' of their saint. They were engaged in expanding the cult of Patrick, so their writing tells us more about the churches fostering the cult and their relationship with the other great churches of seventh century Ireland: St Brigid's at Kildare, St. Colum Cille's at Iona and St. Ciaran's at Clonmacniose."[9]

Doherty claims that the cult of Patrick developed from the midlands of Ireland and later extended to the east of Ulster. He states "by the time Tirechan is writing in the late seventh century there was a deliberate policy of searching out churches which 'ought' to belong to the Armagh federation, and of claiming back those that had been appropriated by the other great churches of the period - Clonmacnoise, Kildare, Iona, Clones and Devenish. Armagh's greatest rival for ecclesiastical headship of the country was Kildare, but by the late seventh century political circumstances dictated that she could not match the power of Patrick."

The so-called "cult of Armagh" may be further reflected in the origin of Muirchu's *Life of Patrick*, which he was encouraged to write by Bishop Aed of Sletty, originally from the Irish midlands. The Bishop had moved to Armagh, possibly bringing with him some of the traditions of the cult which had originated in the midlands area..

Muirchu states that Patrick founded his church at Armagh on land given to him by the local chieftain Daire, and not surprisingly, he elaborates the

Symbols of the Evangelists,
from the *Book of Armagh*.

story considerably. He claims that the chieftain gave Patrick land not on the top of the hill which he had requested, but lower down. Some time later the chieftain grazed his horse on Patrick's land, which displeased him greatly because, he said, Daire "has behaved foolishly in sending brute animals to disturb the small place which he has given to God." The horse was found dead the next morning, and when the chieftain sent out two men to kill Patrick, he himself was struck down. Patrick, according to Muirchu, blessed some water which then brought the chieftain and his horse back to life.

Daire, understandably after such a powerful show of Christian strength, gave Patrick his first choice, namely the land on the top of the hill. When they both went out to inspect it, they saw a fawn and a doe lying on the hill. Patrick's followers wanted to catch the fawn and kill it, but Patrick forbade them, carried the fawn on his shoulders to a safe place, with the doe following. This "safe place", according to tradition, is the hill of Armagh on which the Roman Catholic Cathedral was eventually built, thus maintaining a direct link with the tradition of St. Patrick.

Bishop Hanson, however, takes an altogether more worldly view. He challenges the historical accuracy of the story, and asserts that if it were true it depicts Patrick as over-bearing, truculent and irritable - a picture which is distinctly unlike the evangelist in alien territory who is anxious not to cause offence or to create persecution for the Church. He believes that the story is a typical piece of folk-lore and "that there lies behind it a (quite possibly authentic) local tradition at Armagh that Patrick founded a church there and that Daire gave the land for it."[10]

Another document, *The Book of the Angel*, states boldly that the claim of Armagh to precedence over all the other churches was due to the fact that an angel had announced to Patrick that God had established his main church there. This announcement was made allegedly to Patrick during a conversation with the angel at a well close to the city. Furthermore, *The Book of the Angel* asserts that certain Holy relics found their way to Armagh - such claims would have been extremely persuasive in an age when relics of this nature would, in the popular mind, have proved the primacy of Armagh beyond doubt.

Scholars, however, dismiss *The Book of the Angel* as mere propaganda for Armagh, and we are left, as for so much of this period, with a lack of factual detail as to precisely where Patrick founded his main church - particularly as the saint gave no indication in his own writings as to the area in question. Typical of many commentators, Walsh and Bradley sift the evidence and state that they cannot "consent unequivocally to the clams of Armagh simply because they have been made so vociferously and for such a long time. Nevertheless, we find it impossible to dissociate Patrick's name from that of Armagh."[11]

Perhaps the best way to summarise the voluminous scholarship on this contentious and important point, is to state that even if there is no concrete evidence to verify that Patrick did found his main church at Armagh, there is equally no firm evidence to suggest that he did not do so. Bishop Hanson, not a scholar to become carried away by myth or legend, states "There is evidence that a cult of Patrick was already well-established in Armagh by the time Tirechan wrote, and the existence of a local cult is good evidence for the historical reality of the saint commemorated there."[12]

What is generally agreed, however, is that Patrick came to Ireland, that his major area of evangelism was in the north, and that his mission was remarkably successful. It is to this that we now turn our attention in the land not only of "saints and scholars" but also of "saints and sinners."

NOTES

1 J.P. Mallory, *Navan Fort, the Ancient Capital of Ulster.*
2 Ibid.
3 Walsh and Bradley Op. Cit. Page 44
4 *The Course of Irish History*, Page 64 edited by TW Moody and FX Martin, and first published by The Mercier Press Cork in 1967, in association with RTE, following a series of 21 television lectures broadcast from 24 January to 13 June, 1966.
5 Gwynn, Op. Cit. Chapter One, Page 1.
7 Hanson Op. Cit. pp 78-79, also Walsh and Bradley Op. Cit. pp 38-41
8 Ibid Page 79
9 *The Problem of Patrick*, Archives of Armagh City and District Council
10 Op. Cit. Page 92
11 Ibid Page 48.
12 Hanson Op. Cit. Page 197

St Patrick trampling on a serpent – an artist's impression from St Patrick's Trian. Some commentators suggest that Patrick's supposed banishment of the serpents from Ireland "may be a vivid and subtle way of recalling how he destroyed pagan devotion".

'... it was most necessary to spread our nets so that a great multitude and throng might be caught for God, and that there be clerics everywhere to baptize and exhort a people in need and want...'

St. Patrick's *Confession*

Though St Patrick is associated in the popular tradition with having brought Christianity to Ireland, this is not strictly true. Scholars agree that the Christian religion was being practised in parts of the island before Patrick arrived to carry out his mission, but they differ about the extent to which pre-Patrician Christianity existed, and where it was practised.

The ancient Irish had strong trading-links with Roman Britain and Gaul, and some with Iberia. Foreign traders brought pottery, metal-work and other goods from Britain and the European continent, while the Irish exported copper and gold, prized wolfhounds, cattle, hides and slaves. It has been noted sagely that "While evangelisation is not the primary motive of the commercial traveller, and while French wine-shippers were doubtless more intent on filling Irish stomachs with liquor than Irish souls with religion, it is possible that foreign merchants used the opportunities afforded by their business contacts to interest some Irish people in Christianity."[1]

There is also a possibility that Christians took refuge in Ireland during the invasion of Gaul by German-speaking invaders in the early fifth century, and there is a tradition - though no conclusive evidence - that a number of Irish saints preceded Patrick. Once again, there is doubt about what really took place, and as Walsh and Bradley note "All we can say with confidence is that British Christians, either directly or indirectly, influenced the spread of the faith to Ireland, and that this influence was probably exerted before 431."[2]

There is also uncertainty, as noted earlier, about the career of Palladius. Prosper of Aquitaine wrote in 431 that Palladius was ordained by Pope Celestine and sent to "the Scotti, who believe in Christ." It is not clear, however, whether this referred to what is now Scotland only. Most scholars agree, however, that Palladius did evangelise in Leinster and the south-east, though for a relatively short period, and there is conjecture that, to some extent, the work of Palladius was confused with that of Patrick, hence the theory in some quarters that there were two "Saint Patricks".

In the absence of any definitive statement from Patrick himself, who is delightfully (some argue maddeningly) vague about such details we are dealing with conjecture. But Bishop Hanson, once again, brings us reassuringly down to earth with his observation on the fifth century church in Britain.

He writes "the British Church in the first half of the century, though we can make little progress in reconstructing its life in detail, and none in tracing a continuous history for it, was clearly a vigorous and successful Church,

A vividly coloured window portraying St Patrick by Beatrice Glenavy, nee Elvery (1881-1970). She was the second daughter of a Dublin businessman whose family had originated in Spain where they were silk merchants. Since 1909 this window was in the Dominican Convent in Eccles Street Dublin. Later it was transferred to the Dominican's new home off Griffith Avenue.

claiming the loyalty of great numbers of people, probably of the majority of the population, pushing its evangelising activity northwards and westwards, patronised and valued by those who were in authority." But he adds "It is reasonable to assume that from about the year 460 onwards, the British Church began to face vicissitudes and dangers which arrested the current of its normal life, precluded it from influences which might have brought it into the larger history of the Western Church as a whole, and prevented its full and natural development."[3]

Hanson claims that Patrick's mission took place in the first half of the fifth century before the decline in the British Church began, and that he enjoyed its broad support. "It was the Church of Britain which had sent Patrick to Ireland, and it was that Church which continued to supply him with funds, even though at times it appears to have suffered from heart-searching as to whether Patrick should ever have been sent."[4]

It is possible, however, that while Patrick was a product of Roman Britain and of the early British Church, his servitude in Ireland from his mid-teens onwards, and his return to the island which, according to Hanson, he deliberately never left again, gave him a particularly Irish affinity. As Thomas Cahill points out "Patrick, operating at the margins of European geography and of human consciousness, has travelled even further from his birthright than we might expect. He is no longer British or Roman, at all. When he cries out in his pain 'Is it a shameful thing ... that we have been born in Ireland?' we know that he has left the old civilisation behind forever and has identified himself completely with the Irish."[5]

It is clear, however, that in blending in as far as possible with the native Irish, Patrick was certainly not the first Christian to set foot on the island.

"The record of the coming of Christianity into Ireland is obscure and even confusing. It cannot be denied, however, that the faith had already taken root in the island before the mission of Saint Patrick, apostle of Ireland. How the new religion established itself in the country is a hazy yet tantalising chapter in our early history. By the time the saint had begun his mission, the ground work had been done and the conditions had been laid for a Celtic Church in Ireland that over the next few centuries would become one of the most vibrant parts of the body of Christ."[6]

The way in which Patrick moulded Christianity within the political and religious structure of fifth century Ireland is impressive in itself, as is his attitude to the pagan practices of the ancient Celtic religion. The druids, who taught that life continued beyond the grave, practised 'magic' and offered sacrifices, sometimes human sacrifices, to their gods. The Celts venerated heads, and their warriors were head-hunters, who regarded severed heads as trophies of war. The Irish worshipped a horned god, evidence of which still survives, as in a carved figure in the chapter-house of the Church of Ireland Cathedral in Armagh, Boa Island, Kells and other places.

Irish society was not only pagan and war-like, it was also promiscuous. Before Patrick's mission "Irish sexual arrangements were relatively improvisational. Trial 'marriages' of one year, multiple partners, and homosexual relations among warriors on campaign were all more or less the order of the day. Despite Patrick's great success in changing the warrior *mores* of the Irish tribes, their sexual *mores* altered little."[7]

Nevertheless, Walsh and Bradley offer an ingenious interpretation of the legend which claims that Patrick drove the snakes out of Ireland. One of the symbols of the horned god was a serpent, widely regarded as a phallic symbol. "It is probably no coincidence that the medieval carving of Saint Patrick from Faughart, Co Louth, now in the National Museum of Ireland, has the saint trampling on a serpent. ... Patrick's supposed banishment of all the serpents from Ireland may be a vivid and subtle way of recalling how he destroyed pagan devotion to the horned god and his attendant serpents."[8]

Patrick had strong views about pagan practices, such as worship of the sun-god. He writes in his Confession

"For this sun which we see rises daily for us because He commands so, but it will never reign, nor will its splendour last; what is more, those wretches who adore it will be miserably punished. Not so we, who believe in, and worship, the true sun - Christ - who will never perish, nor will he who does his will:"

Patrick, though humble and God-fearing, was street-wise. He was a pragmatist, and when necessary, a good political operator. He bought the good-will of kings and of the druids, though he had no truck with their religious practices and beliefs. He was tough-minded, and physically robust in carrying out his mission over rough terrain to a sparse and widely-scattered population. Significantly, he understood the Celtic mind, and its beliefs. Thomas Cahill asks us to assume "that there were characteristic aspects of Irish culture that Patrick had taken to heart and on which he chose to build his new Christianity. These aspects would have included Irish courage, which he admired greatly, but even more would he have been impressed by the natural mysticism of the Irish, which already told them that the world was holy - all the world - not just parts of it."[9]

While not conceding an inch to the paganism of the Celts, Patrick adapted some of their practices for his own purposes. His policy "was one of inculturation: that is, wherever possible he would have attempted to adapt the cherished religious values and practices of the Celts to Christianity."[10]

A model of a weary St Patrick, in the Trian at Armagh. Whenever possible "he would have attempted to adapt the religious values and practices of the Celts to Christianity".

Despite many setbacks, including the capture of his new converts by the soldiers of Coroticus and also the many personal dangers which he faced, Patrick's mission was very successful and - as far as is known - without the death of even one Christian martyr. The success of the mission is well summarised thus; it was "due in part to his own Celtic background, in part to his familiarity with the country since boyhood, in part to the common sense approach he adopted to the task in hand, in part to the magnetism and determination of the man, but above all, as he himself was the first gratefully to acknowledge, to the grace and guidance given to him by Almighty God."[11]

However, while there is general agreement that Patrick's mission was successful, there is uncertainty as to where that mission was carried out. No places are mentioned in his *Confession*, where Patrick states simply that "we are witnesses that the Gospel has been preached unto those parts beyond which there lives nobody".

In the writing of Muirchu and Tirechan, as was noted earlier, there was no undue hesitation in setting out the geographical details of Patrick's mission. Muirchu confines his ministry broadly to the north-east of the island, but Tirechan claims that he ordained 350 bishops and that he in fact toured round the island, as a wonder-working but also practically-minded saint.

However, in a much later book - *Historical Memoirs of the City of Armagh*, printed in 1819 by Alexander Wilkinson of Newry - the author, James Stuart, has no inhibitions about the dates and details of Patrick's career. (Incidentally, Stuart wrote a long and laborious introduction "In which the arguments adduced by Edward Ledwich LLD to prove that Saint Patrick never existed, are examined and refuted.")

Having established to his own satisfaction, and hopefully to that of the reader, that the saint had indeed existed, Stuart states, inter alia that Patrick, with 34 "attendants" landed in Wicklow in 432 at the age of 60, "yet time had not abated his energies nor diminished his fortitude."[12] According to Stuart, Patrick moved to Dublin, then to Dundrum, where he founded a church nearby, and later carried out his mission in various parts of Ireland, including Meath and Louth, Tara, Co Mayo, Donegal, "Dunboo" in "the barony of Coleraine and the county of Derry", then Armagh where in 445 he "built a cathedral and some other religious edifices", then in 447 he allegedly went to Britain and the Isle of Man, came back to Meath again and Leinster "When by his indefatigable zeal, our Irish Apostle had established Christianity in Dublin", then to Cashel, and later Ardagh, before relinquishing "the Bishoprick of Armagh" in 455, and visiting Rome six years later.

Patrick according to Stuart, spent the rest of his life "partly in devising and establishing rules in synodical councils for the regulation of the church, and partly in retirement and contemplation. After having established three hundred and sixty-five churches, ordained a like number of bishops, and three thousand presbyters, he died n the abbey of Saul on the seventeenth of March 493, at the patriarchal age of one hundred and twenty years."[13]

Though Stuart's colourful account contained shades of Muirchu and Tirechan, it was a former Roman Catholic Archbishop of Armagh, Cardinal Tomas O'Fiaich, who provided a more measured judgement of the likely geographical territory of Patrick's mission: "It is probable that most of his missionary work took place north of a line running from Galway to Wexford. Most of the churches which claimed St. Patrick in person as their founder are situated in this half of the country. Of the twenty churchmen whose obits are entered in the annals in the generation after St Patrick's death, almost all are associated with the same area."[14]

Given that Patrick most probably laboured in that territory north from Galway and Wexford, and that he focused on the north-east of the island, what did his mission achieve? In the short-term it made thousands of Christian converts, many of them well-connected to the secular power-brokers, and firmly established an ecclesiastical network of synods and monasteries which, in the longer-term, led to the great flowering of Irish education and European missionary work and created for Ireland the deserved reputation as "the island of saints and scholars."

Patrick introduced a form of Episcopal government, with bishoprics and sees, then prevalent in the Britain and Europe of his day, and he also established a monastic system which increased in influence, particularly after his death. As Cardinal O'Fiaich notes "Within a century new monasteries had ousted many of the older Patrician foundations as the important centres of religion and learning; and ultimately Ireland became unique in western Christendom in having its most important churches ruled by a monastic hierarchy, many of whom were not bishops."[15]

Patrick's immediate successors were bishops, but by the end of the fifth century Cormac, who ruled in Armagh, was called its "first abbot." Increasingly the leading cleric at Armagh was a bishop and an abbot, until the eighth century when the abbot at Armagh had a subordinate who was called a bishop. Eventually the dioceses were replaced by groups of monasteries, where many of the abbots were chosen from the same family as their founder - a somewhat inbred process which opened the way for the large ruling families to assume power in the monasteries themselves.

Monastic life was hard. Discipline was strict, with a daily round of worship, study, mortification, and manual labour on the farm, or in fishing, as appropriate. Despite the hardships, converts flocked to monastic life, with medieval sources claiming that there were some 3,000 monks at Clonard and Bangor, which included their satellite houses. It was not uncommon, however, to find more than 100 monks in some of the larger houses.[16]

The main study was the Scriptures, particularly the Psalms, which were

Celtic warrior 500AD - a figure in St Patrick's Trian, Armagh.

Mullabrack Mass stone.

often committed to memory. The copying of manuscripts was of vital importance, not least in the *Book of Armagh* and the *Book of Kells*.

However before the Viking hordes terrorised the Irish in the ninth and tenth centuries, Ireland had enjoyed many years of relative peace, (relative, certainly, to what came later) as well as blossoming education and prosperity, as Kathleen Hughes points out; "In the seventh and eighth centuries the old Celtic and the new Christian-Latin ways of looking at things joined together. Because that happened we can today study the Old-Irish law tracts and enjoy the Old-Irish tales; because of that, Irish artists gained a new vision, and yet interpreted the Christian message in their own individual style. So we have what is often called the Irish Golden Age. No doubt there was hardship - we know very little of what simple people thought - but on the whole Irish society must have been comparatively prosperous and there was much of beauty to be seen."[17]

Irish ecclesiastical schools taught Latin and the Scriptures, but there were also secular schools of poets and lawyers which for a long period remained separate from the Church. With time, however, the distinctions between the two became less pronounced and, as Kathleen Hughes notes, "Laymen and clerics came together. Latin and Irish learning met and mingled."[18] The early Irish, like their successors in modern times, were good Europeans. Monasteries welcomed new books from the continent; Irish missionaries blazed a trail across Europe; and none more so than Columbanus, whose great missionary journeying to France, Switzerland, Austria, and to Italy where he founded his last monastery at Bobbio in 613, is reminiscent of the travels of St. Paul himself. Even a cursory glance at a map reveals the extensive influence of Irish Christianity in the British Isles and Europe from the sixth to the eighth centuries - Lindisfarne, Whitby, Glastonbury, Liege, Cologne, Trier, Wurzburg, Regensburg, Salzburg, Vienna, Lucca, Fiesole and other centres of religion.[19]

The contribution of the Irish to the Europe of this period is well-summarised thus;

"So the Irishman's love of learning, fostered by centuries of pagan tradition, combined itself with the art of writing and the Latin books brought by Christians to Ireland. Irish artists learned to decorate the manuscripts they wrote with old patterns and new designs. Irish smiths turned their ancient skills to glorify the Christian church. Irishmen went out in pilgrimage, 'seeking salvation and solitude', but they also evangelised pagan peoples; they built up libraries on the continent, wrote works of scholarship and helped to make ready for the flowering

St Patrick at his death. This carving in the Chapter Room of St Patrick's Church of Ireland Cathedral, Armagh is believed to be the most accurate representation of the Saint, who reputedly died on 17 March - a tradition which dates back to at least the seventh century. According to tradition St Patrick lived to be 120.

of learning which was to follow in ninth century Gaul."[20]

Against this broad background of developments in Ireland and Europe, the church at Armagh continued to be a centre of influence. Stuart tells us that Patrick had founded at Armagh "a school, or college which, in process of time, became famous through all Europe" and that "About the same period, he built an abbey in that city, which he dedicated to Saint Peter and Saint Paul." Stuart continues "Here, during many centuries, a convent of regular canons of the order of Saint Augustin, continued to flourish"[21]

Stuart refers to a long line of St Patrick's successors, starting with Benignus in 455 and followed by Jarlath, Cormac, Dubtach, and from 513 Ailild "a married man", down to Torbac Mac Gorman who died only a year after his succession in 807. Stuart also gives us insights about the numerous setbacks which the population faced. He notes from the *Ulster Annals* "that in the years 664 and 665 the nation was visited with a dreadful pestilence. These annals state that there was an eclipse of the sun, on the ninth hour of the kalends of May, AD 664. In the course of the summer, the sky seemed to be on fire, and, in August, an awful mortality swept off multitudes of the people. Two thirds of the inhabitants of Ireland are said to have perished in the pestilence."[22]

Stuart also notes that Armagh had its own troubles and that it was "twice consumed by accidental fire", in 670 and 687, but such setbacks, considerable as they were, paled into insignificance compared to the almost routine destruction in the city at the hands of the Vikings, referred to by Stuart as "The piratical tribes by which Ireland was so dreadfully infested in the ninth century."[23]

The first raids took place on the Christian settlement in Iona, and also at Lambay off the Dublin coast in the year 795. The jewelled shrines and ornaments of the monasteries were obvious targets and in the first attack on the Iona community, the buildings were ransacked and burned. The Norsemen returned in 801, and again in 806 when 68 monks were tortured and killed. Following these catastrophes, the abbot returned to Ireland with precious relics and the *Book of Kells*, where he founded a new monastery.

For the next 40 years or so, waves of Vikings attacked many sites along the Irish coast, including remote monastic settlements such as Skellig Michael, built on an outcrop in the Atlantic, off Kerry. They brought with them accomplished horsemen who made long overland journeys to the heart of the Irish countryside. Armagh, given its strategic and ecclesiastical importance, was a prime target, and Stuart claims that the city was taken over by "the Danes and Norwegians" for the period of one month in 830. He writes "During this period, the inhabitants suffered every species of indignity, and endured every kind of misery, which victorious barbarians, inured to blood and unrestrained by moral feeling or religious principle, delight to inflict on the vanquished. At last the invaders were driven back to their ships by the irritated people. In their retreat, they robbed the inhabitants and set fire to the city itself."[24]

This contrasts, however, with the account in the *Annals of Ulster* which records "832 -the first plundering of Armagh by the heathens three times in one month." Stuart may have been somewhat premature in his account of the

first Viking attack on the city, but his colourful prose conveys the panic, suffering and mayhem generated by such barbarities. The sense of fear, particularly on the part of the inhabitants of the monasteries which were such prime targets is well-conveyed by the plaintive cry of an Irish monk listening to the wind on a stormy night:

> *The wind is rough tonight*
> *tossing the white-combed ocean*
> *I need not dread fierce Vikings*
> *crossing the Irish Sea.*[25]

From late in the third decade of the ninth century, these maurauders from the valleys and fjords of western Scandinavia started to arrive in fleets of ships, rather than in a few raiding vessels, and began to establish permanent bases in Ireland. By 841 the Viking foundations were being established for what became the city of Dublin, while the monasteries all over Ireland were systematically plundered. In that year the Abbot of Armagh was driven out by a Viking leader named Turgesius.

"Turgesius, whom his victorious army had proclaimed king of Ireland, marched against the city of Armagh, which probably weakened by intestine division and not yet recovered from the effects of its late capture, was altogether unable to resist his progress.

"As he advanced, the Danish sovereign waged an unrelenting war against Christianity and its meek teachers. He levelled the churches to the earth, and treated the clergy with wanton insult and inhuman barbarity. When, therefore, this merciless Pagan had seized upon Armagh, he expelled its bishop Faranan, with all the students of the college, and the whole body of religious devotees from the city.

"The bishop and such of the clergy as escaped his rage, fled to Cashel. Here, however, they were pursued by the emissaries of the inexorable Turgesius, and compelled with the clergy of that place to lurk for years in obscure woods, bogs and subterraneous caves."[26]

In the face of such a sustained onslaught, the Irish initially did little to combat the invaders. There were some 200 tribal chieftains in territories ruled over by a handful of provincial kings, and each was concerned with extending his own dominion. Some of the Irish destroyed and looted churches for their own ends, and from the middle of the ninth century there are accounts of strategic, and often temporary, alliances between some of the Irish and the invaders, and even of in-fighting among the Norse themselves, often at sea.

The fierce battles for supremacy among the Irish chieftains reached a climax, and in the second half of the century the power of the Kings of Tara began to increase, culminating in a battle in 908 when the King-Bishop of Cashel was defeated. There was a diminution in Viking activity as the century drew to a close, but within a short time there were yet more invaders. In the year 914 a large fleet sailed into Waterford, and the Vikings plundered large parts of the country and established yet more settlements, including the foundations of what was to become the city of Limerick.

The Norsemen began to encounter stiffening resistance in the north of

Opposite: Round Tower at Glendalough. Round Towers provided a refuge for monastic settlements terrorized by the Vikings.

The burial procession of Brian Boru, reproduced in St Patrick's Trian.

Ireland, and the doughty leader Muircertach "beat the invaders at sea on Strangford Lough in 926, burned Dublin in 939, ravaged Norse settlements in the Scottish Isles with an Ulster fleet in 941 and died in combat in 943."[27] Meanwhile, the history of Armagh during these years is one disaster after another. Stuart records that Armagh was attacked and plundered many times. In 850 he states that "the Normans (Norsemen) marched against Armagh which they stormed and despoiled on the Sunday after Easter." Two years later "Armagh was again stormed, pillaged and set on fire by the victorious Ostmen. One thousand of the native troops and citizens were slain on the spot, or left miserably wounded, to perish in the flames."[28]

As if the trouble from the Norsemen was not bad enough, the Archbishop of Armagh had to deal in 889 with a "tumult and sedition" in the city, caused by two warring chieftains and their followers. Archbishop Moel-Brigid quelled this "factious contest", but "deemed it necessary to punish the rioters for the marked irreverence which they had manifested towards the church of God, and their open disrespect of Saint Patrick." Accordingly he imposed a fine on both parties of 200 oxen, exacted hostages as to the chieftains' future good conduct, and "caused six of the most active ringleaders to be executed on a gallows."[29] Those were the days when the "clout of an Archbishop's staff" really did have some meaning!

Throughout the tenth century, Armagh continued to suffer in misery from the ravages of the Norsemen. Stuart records that Armagh was "seized again" in 913: sacked in 919, though the churches, the sick and the infirm were spared; two years later "a Presbyter of Armagh was put to death; the 'Normans' again sacked the city in 941, and in 989 Armagh was 'reduced to a most deplorable situation.' In 995 "the city with its churches and other edifices, was again destroyed by fire generated by lightning." In 1011 "A pestilence raged in Armagh, from the Feast of All-Souls, till the commencement of May. Many pious and learned men and many members of the academy fell the victims of this deadly disease."[30]

The visit to the city by Brian Boru in 1004 (some scholars claim that it was in 1005) was a turning point. He came to Armagh and his action in placing 20 ounces of gold on the high altar of St Patrick's church was no mere act of piety. He was not only recognising the ecclesiastical supremacy of Armagh in Ireland, but also possibly offering a bribe to secure the support from the church for his attempt to win the overlordship of the entire island. It was no coincidence that during this visit, he ordered a reference to himself as "Emperor of the Irish" to be inserted in *The Book of Armagh*.

Brian Boru, by all accounts was a remarkable warrior-chieftain and visionary. Stuart, writing circa 1819, had no doubts about his prowess. "Brian was one of the most extraordinary men of the age in which he lived... Sagacious, humane, pious, munificent and valiant; he overcame his enemies as much by the splendour of his character and the glory resulting from his philantrophic acts, as by military achievement and force of arms."[31]

A modern writer broadly confirms this view.

A nineteenth century impression of Brian Boru being slain by Brodar, King of Man, after the Battle of Clontarf, 1014.

"Brian Boru was a gifted military strategist, but also a pragmatist who chose his battles carefully. He only fought when he was certain he could win. Otherwise he was not above bluffing the enemy. Some of his victories were bloodless, the result of his opponent having been fooled into thinking he was outnumbered and leaving the field. Horses had long been used by the Irish nobility for riding and transport, but Brian was the first to establish a cavalry. He also created a personal navy. At one time over three hundred boats and Viking-style longships were anchored in the Shannon below Kincora. Brian Boru was a man born centuries ahead of his time"[32]

Having established himself as High King of Ireland at Tara in 1002, Brian Boru set out to subdue those Irish kings who were still dissident and to impose his rule on an island which had, among its population, many Viking settlers. For more than a decade he looked like succeeding in bringing peace and order to replace what had been constant turbulence, but the King of Leinster allied himself to the Dublin Norse and other Vikings from overseas. In 1014 yet another invasion force set sail from Scandinavia, and they were met by Brian Boru, then over 70, and his troops on Irish soil. On 23 April, incidentally Good Friday, a fierce battle raged at Clontarf, with many casualties, and the invaders were routed. Tragically Brian Boru and his eldest son and grandson were killed, but the High King had won for his people a resounding victory. There were occasional Viking raids after his death, but Brian Boru had rid Ireland for ever of the curse of the Norsemen.

He was buried in Armagh. Stuart records:

"His mortal remains, pursuant to his wish, rest in Armagh. It is recorded that Maelmurry Mac Eoch, primate of Armagh, and many of the elders of the church proceeded with the sacred relics to the monastery of Saint Columba, at Surdense, (Swords), and from thence they removed the bodies of Brian Boroimhe and Murchard his son, which had been deposited there in state.

"These, with the heads of Conaing his nephew, and Methlin prince of the Deisies were conveyed to Armagh, where the remains of the warriors lay in great funeral state, attended by the clergy, during 12 successive nights. Psalms, hymns and prayers were chanted for their souls. Brian was inhumed on the north side of the great church, in a stone (or hewn marble) coffin, placed by itself. Murchard, the heads of Conaing etc were interred on the south side. Brian's surviving son Doncha returned to Kilmainham, and from thence sent jewels and other treasures, as pious offerings to Saint Patrick's successor and his subordinate clergy"[33]

Although the island had been rid of the spectre of further Viking attacks, the dynastic wars in Ireland were to lead to further internecine conflict. Despite the chaos of the preceding years and the warfare to come, one point was clear as Ireland moved steadily into the second Millennium. The great High King of Ireland, Brian Boru, had paid ample tribute to Armagh, during his life and also by choosing the city as his last resting-place. More than 500 years after Patrick's death, his beloved Armagh was still the undisputed ecclesiastical power in the land.

NOTES

1   Walsh and Bradley Op. Cit. Page 3
2   Ibid. Page 5
3   Hanson Op. Cit. pp.69–70
4   Ibid. Page 139
5   Cahill Op. Cit. Page 113
6   Walsh and Bradley Op. Cit. pp.8–9
7   Cahill Op. Cit. pp.134–135
8   Walsh and Bradley Op. Cit. Page 32
9   Cahill Op. Cit. Page 135
10 Walsh and Bradley Op. Cit. Page 37
11 Ibid. Page 37
12 Stuart Op. Cit. Page 79
13 Op. Cit. pp.79–85
14 O Fiaich Op. Cit. Page 62
15 Op. Cit. Page 65
16 The Course of Irish History, Page 72
17 Ibid. Page 88
18 Ibid. Page 81
19 Ibid. Page 73
20 Kathleen Hughes Op. Cit. Page 90

21 Stuart Op. Cit. Page 86
22 Ibid. Page 90–96
23 Ibid. Page 98
24 Ibid. Page 100
25 St. Gall Priscian, Stokes and Strachan
    (ed.), *Thesaurus palaeohibernicus*, (ii)
    (1903), page 290, translated by Liam de Paor
26 Stuart Op. Cit. Page 101
27 Jonathan Bardon *A Shorter Illustrated History
    of Ulster*, page 23. Published by
    The Blackstaff Press, Belfast 1996
28 Stuart Op. Cit. Page 112
29 Ibid. Page 113
30 Ibid. pp.113–119
31 Ibid. Page 120
32 Morgan Llywelyn, the historical novelist,
    writing in *Ireland of the Welcomes*, Volume
    49 No. 2. Page 52
33 Stuart Op. Cit. Page 123

*'Ravening wolves have devoured the flock of the
Lord, which in Ireland was indeed growing
splendidly with the greatest care ...'*

St. Patrick's *"Letter to Coroticus"*

When Brian Boru became High King of Ireland in 1002 it seemed as if the country was moving at last towards a strong central monarchy, despite the local dissidents who were still inclined to accept no power but their own and to extend their influence by every means possible. Boru imposed his authority in no uncertain way. For example, on his expeditions to the north - including his visit to Armagh in 1004 - he took hostages to demonstrate and underpin his control.

The very wording of the entry in the *Book of Armagh* informed the world in general and Cashel in particular, that he was supreme. "I, Mael Suthain, have written this in the presence of Brian, emperor of the Irish, and what I have written he has determined for all the kings of Cashel." His death at the Battle of Clontarf and that of his son and his leading henchmen meant that there was no family figure powerful enough to succeed him, and the High-Kingship passed back to its erstwhile incumbent Mael Sechnaill of Tara, who had been High King from 980, until his death in 1022.

During the next one hundred and fifty years or so, until the arrival of the Normans, the situation in Ireland was violent and confused as various chieftains and their followers vied for power, with bloody conflicts and often with resultant mutilation and blinding of the vanquished. It was not all bad news, however, and cultural and artistic activity experienced a revival after the Viking years of turmoil. The church, largely monastic in organisation, was still flourishing and was self-sufficient, in the sense that while it was in communion with Rome, it remained largely self-governing.

Despite this, there was a need for church reform. The Viking upheavals had left their mark, and there was a spiritual and moral laxity in a society where few priests were engaged in pastoral work, largely because the church was monastic rather than diocesan. "Deeds of violence were frequent, even against priests and nuns and against church property. The sacraments were neglected, there was a reluctance to pay tithes, and the marriage laws of the church were disregarded."[1] However, reform of the church, in which Armagh played a leading role, began to take place from the early part of the twelfth century.

The story of Armagh, in the decades following the death of Brian Boru, reflects the turbulence of the times in Ireland generally. Stuart tells of many fires, incursions and associated disasters, including that of 1016 when "the Normans of Dublin, under Sitric the son of Amelanus, marched into Ulster and burned Armagh." Four years later, when the city was scarcely rebuilt, "a

Opposite: Cashel - the seat of Brian Boru's powerful enemies. His addition to the *Book of Armagh* underlined his supremacy over " all the Kings of Cashel"

43

great portion of it was consumed by fire". Archbishop Maelmurry MacEoch, who had officiated at the burial of Brian Boru, "mourned incessantly over his ruined capital and the miseries of his people, and fell the victim of anguish on the third of June 1021." He was succeeded by Amalgaid, who himself died in 1050 and was succeeded by Dubdalethy III, the son of Maelmurry MacEoch.[2]

There were yet more fires in 1074, when Armagh was "wasted", and further fires in 1091 and 1092. In 1103 it was besieged for a fortnight by "an army of Meathans and Conatians" who "injured the city extremely." However, there was more to the city's life than fires and attacks from its enemies, and between the lines of Stuart's narrative, a picture emerges of the lasting influence of Armagh and its senior clergy. For example, in 1022 "Malachy MacDomnald King of Ireland was buried in Armagh with splendid ceremonies", just as Brian Boru had been, and it was through the influence of the Archbishop of Armagh, Donald Mac Amalgaid in 1101 that peace was made between two warring chieftains. The King of Aileach liberated the King of Ulidia "from captivity and chains", and "Peace was made betwixt the contending parties and ratified, in the Cathedral, by solemn oaths, sworn on the staff of Jesus."[3] It was clear that the Archbishop of Armagh had real "clout".

Cellach, a figure of authority, was consecrated as Archbishop in 1106, and "he made a visitorial circuit through Ulster, and according to an established mode of taxation, received from each district containing what was denominated a senary of persons, one ox and from each ternary, a heifer, with other gifts and oblations, offered in the simple, submissive spirit of the times. He also this year visited Munster, and from each cantred or district of a hundred villages or hamlets, he obtained seven oxen, seven sheep and half an ounce of silver, with many other gifts."[4] The vow of clerical poverty obviously did not apply to Armagh.

Cellach, also known as Celsus, was the seventh member of an influential family who held the position of Archbishop of Armagh without having taken Holy Orders. Indeed several were married men. Cellach was consecrated Bishop as "heir of Patrick", and recognised as Primate.[5] Stuart asserts that Cellach was a married man and that he belonged "to the regal family which claimed an hereditary title to the primacy." He also states that Cellach was only 27 when he became Primate "and was probably the youngest Archbishop who had attained that dignity in the see of Armagh."[6]

Cellach, like his predecessors, did not have to seek his troubles. In the year 1112, he was "compelled to witness the destruction of a great portion of his capital", again through fire. In 1125 he organised the tiling of the Cathedral roof which had only been partly repaired after another fire some one hundred and thirty years previously, and a year later he consecrated the rebuilt church of St Peter and St Paul. However, a prelate in those days had more than church buildings on his mind. For the next eighteen months he was absent from Armagh trying to build bridges among the warring Irish chieftains, as Stuart relates:

"... he was greatly occupied in allaying the feuds and animosities by which the princes and chieftains of the country were then agitated. ... He succeeded in

1128, in making a truce or peace for a year, betwixt the people of Munster and Connaught".[7]

Significantly, however, in such a busy primacy he also had time to undertake important reforms in the structure and administration of the church. In the year 1111 Cellach chaired a Synod near Cashel in the presence of the High-King Moriertach O'Brien, who supported the various reform movements in other parts of Ireland, including those centred in the Waterford and Limerick areas. It was attended by "Moelmurry O Dunan, senior clerk of Ireland, fifty bishops, three hundred priests and three thousand other ecclesiastics"[8] – a figure which gives some indication of the size of the church in Ireland in the early twelfth century. It was obviously an important and fruitful Synod which resulted in the division of Ireland into twenty four sees, thus effectively replacing the old monastic system, though it took forty years to implement this new organisation fully.[9]

One of Cellach's most important acts was to consecrate the young Mael Maedoc, better known later on as Saint Malachy, as a presbyter in 1120, and four years later as Bishop of Connor. Stuart claims that Saint Bernard of Clairvaux believed that Malachy, a close friend, accepted this promotion with reluctance as "The people of his diocese were rude and barbarous, Christians in name, Pagans in act." He writes that "Malachy discharged his pastoral duty with amazing patience, assiduity and zeal, and wrought such a reformation in the morals of his people, as greatly endeared him to the meek and pious Celsus (Cellach) primate of Armagh. On his deathbed therefore, this learned divine not only nominated him his successor, but sent him his staff, in token of his appointment to this high office."[10]

The best-laid plans of prelates, as well as of plain people, do not always work out as expected, and Malachy did not exercise his primatial rights during his first year of office because in 1129 a Maurice Mac Donald, the son and grandson of previous Primates of Armagh, had usurped the see. The situation was so bad that Malachy, despite starting to exercise his rights at the behest of the people at the end of his first year, was too frightened to enter Armagh for a further two years "lest sudden and destructive tumults might have been excited by the powerful sept which supported their kinsman Maurice."[11]

After holding "a kind of disputed possession of the primacy" for two more years, Maurice "was finally evicted, repented of his crime, and died full of remorse, on the seventeenth of September 1134."[12] However, the battle was not over, and a relation of Maurice, a certain Nigel MacAid, put forward his claims to the Primacy, assisted by a family faction, "and by exhibiting the Staff of Jesus and other relics of which he had robbed the church, obtained considerable support from the people". He was evicted finally "by the princes, the prelates and the nobility", and died in 1139. However, he was given a bad press by Saint Bernard in his life of St. Malachy, who "verbally consigned him and his whole sept to the endless pains of hell".[13] Most modern clerical scandals seem tame by comparison!

Despite the not inconsiderable difficulty in his own back-yard, Malachy was concerned with the wider picture, and in 1139 he went to Italy to consult with Pope Innocent about the requirements to bring the Irish church

Stained glass window commemorating St Malachy in St Patrick's Roman Catholic Cathedral, Armagh.

more in line with Rome. The Pope received him warmly, and advised him to convene an Irish Council to further process the requests for the pallia which were necessary to establish Archbishoprics in Ireland. "He then placed his mitre on Malachy's head, presented him with the stole and maniple which he used in the celebration of divine service, and dismissed him with the apostolic benediction and the kiss of peace."[14]

During his travels in Europe, Malachy stayed with Saint Bernard of Clairvaux and was so impressed that he introduced the Cistercian Order to Ireland. The first settlement was begun in 1142 at Mellifont. The Abbey was completed fifteen years later and consecrated in the presence of many Bishops and Kings. In effect, the advent of the Cistercian Order brought to an end the era of the old Irish monasteries.[15] Back home, St. Malachy worked hard to bring the Irish church more into line with Rome, and he was strongly opposed to matrimony among the clergy "which was deemed both by him and his friend Saint Bernard, a crime of great turpitude in that sacred order."

St Malachy set out for Rome again in 1148, but died at Clairvaux "in the arms of his friend Saint Bernard, who plaintively laments his death". However, his lifetime's work bore further fruit, and in 1152 a Synod at Kells divided Ireland into 36 sees, with the Papal Legate Cardinal Paparo distributing the pallia to Armagh, Cashel, Dublin and Tuam.[16] Stuart sums up "Malachy was a pious, learned, unassuming and benevolent man", and he concludes that "This indefatigable prelate partly succeeded in his efforts to reduce the church of Ireland to a conformity with that of Rome."[17]

Within Ireland, Armagh continued to consolidate its authority. In 1157, Primate Gelasius, who succeeded Malachy in 1137, convened a Synod in Mellifont, which was attended by the Papal Legate and seventeen other bishops, as well as Murtouch O Lochlin, High King of Ireland and other Royal princes. At this Synod the King of Meath, Dunchad O Melachlin, was excommunicated and deposed, and his lands were given to his brother Dermot because of a remarkable ecclesiastical and political misjudgement. "He appears to have been deemed an atheist, for insulting the Primate and treating Jesus' staff and the clergy with disrespect."[18] It was also in 1157, as has been noted earlier, that the bishops and kings attended the consecration of Mellifont Abbey, in some style, and possibly around the same time as the Synod which punished the King of Meath. Such time -

efficiency might be described today as "business with pleasure".

Armagh also continued to underline its authority in terms of scholarship. A Professorship of Divinity was established in the city by Turlough the Great, and in 1162 a Synod of 26 Bishops, meeting in the diocese of Kildare, decreed that no person should be admitted as a public reader of divinity who had not been an alumnus of the school, or university, of Armagh "lest impostors or illiterate persons might undertake to lecture on theological subjects "[19]

However, theological niceties such as this, while important, should be

seen against the prevailing background of communal savagery. In 1165 Eochod, the King of Ulidia, invaded the territory of Maurice O Lochlin, the King of Ireland and killed "many of his subjects." Maurice retaliated, marched into Ulster "wasting the country with fire and sword", expelled Eochod, took hostages and made for Armagh. Here Eochod asked for mercy, and with the intercession of the Archbishop, peace broke out. The two monarchs swore on the staff of Jesus to keep the peace, but a year later "Maurice surprised Eochod and put out his eyes." Then an ally of Eochod raised an army of nine thousand veterans and killed Maurice at the battle of Letter-Lunn. Not surprisingly "These barbarous proceedings grieved the gentle spirit of the meek and peaceable Gelasius."

In 1170 Gelasius convened another Synod, this time in Armagh itself, shortly after the beginning of the Norman invasions. The clergy reflected upon the turbulent events, which were taken by some to be a Divine retribution on the Irish for their sins. "At this synod, the point was gravely

St Malachy's Church, Irish Street, Armagh. By the twentieth century St Malachy's Church in Chapel Lane had become too small for the city congregation and in 1935 a fine new church in the Romanesque style on a basilica plan in Navan limestone commenced to be built in Irish Street.
It was completed in 1938 and the old chapel was replaced by St Malachy's Primary School in 1956.

Top left: The statue of St Malachy, outside St Patrick's Roman Catholic Cathedral, Armagh.

and earnestly debated and it was concluded that God had chastised the people for their sins, especially for the inhuman practice of purchasing Englishmen from pirates and selling them as slaves. On this account the offended deity had, they conceived, selected the Britons, as the instruments of his vengeance. It was therefore decreed that every English bondsman should now be immediately manumitted."[20]

No doubt, St Patrick himself would have had strong views on this subject if he had been alive, but the release of English slaves as a penance to a "wrathful" God did not halt the Norman invasion which changed the face of Ireland radically and which brought to an end the old Gaelic hegemony. The Bishops continued to concern themselves with church order and social morality. For example, the Council of Cashel in 1172 dealt with such matters as marriage within prohibited degrees, child baptism at the font, the distribution of "dying mens properties" and other matters - but the steady invasion of the country by the Normans would give them much else to worry about, and not least in Armagh which, once again, bore the mark of the invaders, as it had done in Viking times.

Ironically the Norman invasion was triggered by a bitter quarrel between the Irish chieftains, including Dermott MacMurrough the King of Leinster, and Tiernan O'Rourke the one-eyed King of Breifne whose wife Dervorgilla had been abducted (for a period) by MacMurrough - though some would say that the lady had put him up to it. However, hell hath no fury like the husband of a wife abducted by his enemy, and O'Rourke was determined to get even. After a complex series of developments and alliances involving a major struggle for political supremacy between the most powerful kings in the North and Connaught, MacMurrough was forced to flee. Instead of going quietly and seeking exile somewhere on the continent of Europe he took his case to Henry II in 1166, in order to try to regain his kingdom in Leinster.

Henry was very much a European monarch who had many other things on his mind, but a decade earlier he had considered the possibility of an invasion of Ireland. It was important, however, to cover such naked territorial ambitions with the cloak of ecclesiastical respectability. Pope Adrain IV, an Englishman, is said to have duly obliged by granting Henry permission to invade Ireland and, insultingly, "to proclaim the truths of the Christian religion to a rude and ignorant people".[21]

Ten years later Henry II was too pre-occupied with events in the rest of his empire to lead an invasion himself, but he recognised a good opportunity when it presented itself, and he exhorted his subjects to help the exiled Irish king. The offer was taken up in Wales by the Earl of Pembroke, better known as Strongbow, and in May 1169, an invading force landed in Ireland. The rest, as they say, is history. Within a short time Waterford and Dublin, both Viking cities, had been captured, Meath and Leinster were taken, and with the sudden death of MacMurrough, Strongbow reigned supreme in Leinster.

Henry could not allow this success on the part of one of his Norman subjects to continue unabated, and in October 1171 he landed at Waterford with a large army to make the point that he was ultimately in charge. To keep Strongbow in check in Leinster, the territory of Meath was given to Hugh de Lacy. Several years later John De Courcy marched north from Dublin with a small army to take Ulster, which he eventually did - despite spirited resistance from the locals whose courage was no match for the superior armour and strategy of the invaders. The Ulster resistance was broken in the mid-summer of 1177, and de Courcy ruled Ulster for 27 years, establishing Norman centres at Carrickfergus, Downpatrick, Dromore, Coleraine, and several other places.

Norman rule was to bring many benefits, including a centralised administration, the extension of internal and external trade, the construction of cathedrals in Dublin, Limerick and Kilkenny, the establishment of coinage and other developments, but these were not without a price. Gelasius, the Archbishop of Armagh, made an Episcopal tour of Connaught in 1172, at the ripe age of 85, and was said by English sources to have paid homage to Henry II in Dublin - though Stuart claims that the Ulster clergy, unlike those in the rest of Ireland, apart from Connaught, kept their independence. Incidentally, according to Stuart, Gelasius' only food on the journey was the milk from a white cow which was "driven before him".[22] Gelasius died two years later, in March 1174, "a man of meek and Christian spirit, learned, active, humane and pious", but whether he had paid homage to Henry II or not, his beloved Armagh was again badly damaged at the hands of the King's noble subjects.

In 1178, according to Stuart, de Courcy was so strong "that we find him sufficiently powerful to seize upon and plunder Armagh, where Thomas O Corcoran, archdeacon of the abbey, was murdered...and..the city with its churches et. cetera were burned."[23] To add extreme insult to conspicuous injury, a certain William Fitz-Aldelm stole the staff of Jesus from the city and took it to Dublin where it was "presented to the cathedral of the blessed Trinity." He carried out further 'dreadful barbarities' in Connaught , but later "was seized with a species of horrible convulsions, in which his features were violently distorted and his whole frame agitated by the most excruciating pain. He died in agony, and his body was denied the rites of Christian sepulture. The corpse of this unhappy man was borne, by his enemies, to a ruined village in Connaught, whose inhabitants he had destroyed, and was there ignominiously cast into a pit from which it has never been removed."[24]

The progress of the invaders "was ruinous to the churches and monasteries of the country. ...The churches and abbeys soon became theatres of sanguinary warfare, and many of them were ruined by the contending parties." To add to the troubles, a Papal bull in 1182 ordained "that no archbishop or bishop should hold any assembly or hear any ecclesiastical causes in the diocese of Dublin, without the consent of the archbishop of Dublin, unless authorised to do so by the papal see or its legate. "This led to a long controversy between Dublin and Armagh which "endured for centuries and was at last decided in favour of the see of Armagh."[25]

In 1184 there was more trouble in Armagh. Philip of Worcester, then Lord Justice of Ireland, subjected the city "during six successive days, to the lawless pillage of his ferocious soldiers. He spent the season of mid-Lent in riotous and indecent feasting, and then proceeded to levy the most severe pecuniary extractions from the clergy, who by law were exempt from all such imposts."[26] Five years later De Courcy again "marched against Armagh, the headquarters

The Franciscans arrived in Armagh in 1264 and the remains of their friary - the longest in Ireland - still survive within the Palace Demesne.

The Vikings in Ulster - an aerial view of Portaferry and Strangford at the mouth of Strangford Lough. The Lough was a centre for Viking raids throughout east and mid-Ulster.

of his enemies, which he assailed, stormed, pillaged and burned."[27]

Later, however, de Courcy fell from favour, and Hugh de Lacy, the younger son of the first Lord of Meath, was authorised by the Crown to march against him. After a five-year struggle, de Courcy was ousted, and in 1205 King John appointed de Lacy as Earl of Ulster. Sadly, there was no respite for Armagh. Stuart records that "Armagh, of course, constituted a part of the territory assigned to this new favourite of the British king; but it appears to have derived no benefit from the change. In the year 1206, the city was pillaged by Hugh de Lacy the younger, who continued his depredations during ten successive days. ... Armagh was again pillaged by the troops of De Lacy, on the vigil of Saint Brigid, in the year 1208."[28]

It is worth noting, however, that despite such repeated setbacks under Norman rule, the invasion did bring benefits to the church at large. Apart from the construction of cathedrals, as mentioned earlier, the abbeys - including that of the Benedictines in the north - benefited greatly. The Normans also welcomed Dominicans, Franciscans, Augustinians and Carmelites to Ireland. "These were the new religious orders, men dedicated to preaching, to popular religion, beloved of the people. Wherever the Normans went, clusters of friars followed: their churches and friaries sprang up throughout the Norman territories; they even penetrated ahead of the Normans into Gaelic territory where they were also welcomed."[29]

Even Armagh benefited, and in 1236 a castle was built on a prime site granted to King Henry III by the Archbishop. In 1261 Mael Patraic O Scannail, a Dominican friar and Bishop of Raphoe, who became the new Archbishop, restored the ancient cathedral - thus giving it the medieval plan which was typical of European monasteries of that time. In 1263 the Pope was reported to have issued a bull addressed to the Archbishop, confirming the primacy of all-Ireland to Armagh, though Stuart records that later writers differed as to its authenticity.[30] In 1264 the Franciscans arrived in Armagh, and the remains of their friary - the longest church in Ireland - still survive today within The Palace Demesne.

With time, the native Irish began to show sterner resistance to the invaders. By the middle of the century the Norman impetus began to lose momentum, and a half century or so later the tide was beginning to turn against them. Ulster remained turbulent, but the de Burgos, father and son, ruled firmly from mid-century and were able to exploit the ever-present local rivalries in the north. However, shortly after the start of the new century, yet another invader sailed over the horizon. This time it was Edward Bruce, who landed with a large Scottish army near Larne in May 1315, with resultant fierce fighting across the land. The Earl of Ulster, Richard De Burgo, desperately tried to repel the invader but was defeated at the Battle of Connor, and his broken troops sought refuge at Carrickfergus Castle, which surrendered in 1316 after a year's siege.

Meanwhile, Edward Bruce "miserably wasted the see of Armagh and reduced its Archbishop Roland De Jorsey to a state of extreme poverty by the reiterated incursions of his troops."[31] He was joined in Ireland by his brother King Robert of Scotland, with reinforcements, but their victories in battle as far south as Limerick were offset by a devastating famine; and a shortage of food and supplies forced them back to Ulster. In a final attempt the Bruce dynasty tried to maintain their power-base but were defeated at a pitched battle near Dundalk, where Edward Bruce perished. De Jorsey, who had succeeded his brother Walter "a man of exquisite learning and great gravity" as Archbishop in 1311, was reported to have taken a most active part in the battle near Dundalk.

He "moved from rank to rank, bestowing benedictions on the soldiers, stimulating them to deeds of valour, and pronouncing a plenary absolution of sins to all who should die combating in so honourable a cause. Doubtless such zealous and animated conduct must have had a powerful effect on the minds of the soldiery, who probably deemed that the powers of heaven would be thus engaged on their behalf, and that, if they survived the battle, victory and triumph would be their glorious reward; but if they fell in the field of fight, immortal happiness awaited them in paradise."[32]

It all seemed such a far cry from Saint Patrick, but Archbishop Jorsey was not the first, and by no means the last, cleric in Ulster to believe in the heat of conflict and violence that God was on his side.

Carrickfergus Castle which
surrendered in 1316 to Edward
Bruce after a year's siege.

NOTES

1   Brian O Cuiv in *The Course of Irish History*, Op. Cit. p.117
2   Stuart, Op. Cit. p.124
3   Ibid. pp.124–126
4   Ibid. pp.126–127
5   O Cuiv Op. Cit. Page 118–119
6   Stuart Op. Cit. pp.128–129
7   Ibid. pp.127–128
8   Ibid. p.127
9   O Cuiv. Op. Cit. p.120
10 Stuart. Op. Cit. pp.131–132
11 Ibid. pp.129–132
12 Ibid. pp.129–130
13 Ibid. p.132
14 Ibid. p.133
15 O Cuiv Op. Cit. p.120
16 Ibid. p.120

17 Stuart, Op. Cit. p.134
18 Ibid. p.139
19 Ibid. p.140
20 Ibid. p.141
21 O Cuiv Op. Cit. p.108
22 Stuart. Op. Cit. p.142
23 Ibid. p.160
24 Ibid. p.160
25 Ibid. p.161
26 Ibid. p.162
27 Ibid. p.163
28 Ibid. pp.168–169
29 FX Martin Op. Cit. p.141
30 Stuart Op. Cit. p.176
31 Ibid. p.179
32 Ibid. pp.179–180

'We have now...arrived at that particular point of time when the church of Ireland began to be separated, by the law of the land, from the see of Rome. Two distinct ecclesiastical hierarchies, shortly after this period, coexisted in Ireland; the one presiding over the religion of the state, the other over that long adopted and steadily adhered to by the great majority of the people.'

James Stuart
Historical Memoirs of the City of Armagh 1819

The defeat of Edward the Bruce marked the end of a concerted attempt to drive out the invaders and to create a united Ireland under the banner of this newly-crowned, and unlikely, High-King of Ireland. Nevertheless, there was a significant resurgence in Gaelic Ireland, with the recovery of lost territories and a new flowering of local institutions and culture. The beleaguered English colony around Dublin continued to be a financial drain on the Royal purse, at a time when the war with France was also a heavy burden.

However, at the end of the fourteenth century King Richard II, having made peace with France and a truce with Scotland, saw his opportunity to intervene in Irish affairs. He did so, apparently decisively, when he came to Ireland in 1394 and after a successful war in Leinster, received the submissions of the major Gaelic chieftains. However, the Irish remained unruly, some might say ungovernable, and when Richard's heir Roger Mortimer was killed, the King returned in fury in 1399.

Subsequent events proved that this was not necessarily a wise move, because by that stage the political landscape in England was changing radically. While Richard busied himself with errant Gaelic chieftains in Ireland, his enemy, Henry of Lancaster, seized the English throne. However, the Lancastrians themselves, beset by their own considerable problems, had neither the resources nor the time nor the inclination to subdue Ireland, which was largely left to its own devices. The Gaelic and the Anglo-Irish had to learn to live with one another, while the English colony shrank back into the Pale around Dublin where it withstood, with difficulty, the attacks from the local Gaelic chieftains.

By the middle of the fifteenth century, England herself was seriously weakened by the Wars of the Roses. Ireland had been drawn into the wider political picture by contributing to the downfall of one English King-Richard II - in 1399, and later by allowing itself to become enmeshed in the struggles between the Lancastrians and Yorkists - in this case by espousing

PACATA   HIBERNIA

Elizabeth I eventually moved with ruthlessness against the native Irish with the intention of complete conquest.

the causes of the Yorkist pretenders Lambert Simnel and Perkin Warbeck.

As the 16th century progressed, it became clear the Tudor monarchs were determined to subjugate all of the country, partly from motives of self-defence in a situation where they believed, not without justification, that Ireland was an inviting "back-door" for their enemies. To add to the complexity, the Reformation and Henry VIII's break with Rome introduced a new element of religion to politics, and created that potent mixture which continues even today to create havoc in Northern Ireland, and further afield. Anyone who reads Irish history with a fresh eye can only conclude that the more things seem to change, the more they remain the same - in the north of Ireland at least.

In the midst of such continual upheaval, Armagh - the city of St Patrick - survived as best it could. It suffered not only from repeated plagues, storms and other set-backs, but also from an endless series of fires, sackings, occupations and what might be called 'man-made' disasters. The story of Armagh during these years is a far-cry from the order, prosperity and Christian charity which its patron saint would have wished for it, no doubt, but it is also a story of life at the sharp-end of events in a small local community during a period when the political map of the British Isles, and indeed of Europe, was being re-written radically and decisively.

Fleeting references to Armagh are made in a number of broad-brush histories of the period, but the most intimate guide to life in the city and surrounding districts is given by Stuart in his seminal study. As well as recording the political and ecclesiastical development of the times, he had an unerring eye for natural disasters. He records, for example, that in 1330 'whirlwinds and tempests swept the land, rivers burst their usual boundaries and deluged the champaign country. In particular the Boyne, swollen to an irresistible torrent, hurried away in its course, houses, bridges, mills and abbeys. Incessant rains ensued; so that much of the standing corn could not be reaped before the feast of St Michael. Famine was the natural result.'[1]

Eight years later, "an intense frost prevailed over the whole island. 'Games at football, as well as dancings, racings and other amusements of a similar nature, were held on the Avon-Liffie. Fires were kindled and fish dressed on the ice'."[2]

As well as such natural phenomena, the Black Death which swept through Europe in the winter of 1348-49, wreaked havoc in Ireland. The then Archbishop of Armagh, Richard FitzRalph, a noted scholar who preached before the Pope at Avignon, spoke to his people in Drogheda at the height of the Black Death in 1349 and exhorted them "to put their trust in Mary who will deliver them from their present distress."[3]

According to Stuart, there was another calamity in 1361, when "a pestilence raged in England and Ireland, which swept off multitudes of men, but few women. It commenced about Easter, and without doubt, its deleterious effects were as severely felt in Armagh, as in other portions of the country. This pestilence was followed, in the year 1370, by another still more calamitous and deadly in which ...died many noblemen and gentlemen, citizens also and children innumerable."[4]

The Church in general went though a difficult period during the turbulent years of the fifteenth century. Stuart again noted, in a curious paragraph, that John Foxalls, a Franciscan, was consecrated Archbishop of Armagh in 1475 and that, in the same year the King "appointed him an umpire betwixt John, Earl of Ormond, and the Earl of Kildare, whose animosities, at that time, distracted Ireland. Before the bishop could effect this reconciliation, Ormond went on a pilgrimage to the Holy Land, and Kildare died. Primate Foxalls himself died in 1476, having never visited his diocess".[5]

Inevitably, the Archbishops of Armagh found themselves drawn in to political developments. When Lambert Simnel, the Yorkist pretender, came to Ireland in 1487, to much rejoicing from the Irish nobility, the Archbishop of Armagh Octavian De Palatio stood firm in his allegiance to King Henry "In the midst of this almost general defection" Octavian, who had been appointed to the see in 1480 by Pope Sixtus IV and remained in office for more than 33 years, clearly had a mind of his own. Octavian wrote to Pope Innocent as follows:

> "The clergy and seculars are all distracted at the present, with a king and no king, some saying he is the son of Edward, Earl of Warwick: others asserting he is an impostor: but our brother of Canterbury hath satisfied me of the truth, how his majesty hath shewed the right son of the said Earl to the publick view of all the city of London, which convinces me that it is an error willingly made to breed dissension."

However, the Archbishop's warnings were ignored, and Lambert Simnel was crowned "Edward VI of England" in Christ Church, Dublin, with the Bishop of Meath preaching the sermon to a congregation including the Lord-Deputy and other senior officers of state. Octavianus, however, remained aloof, and according to Stuart

> "The archbishop of Armagh not only remonstrated with the Lord-Deputy and endeavoured to dissuade him from this rash measure, but when he found all his efforts to prevent the coronation unavailing, refused to be present during the absurd pageantry, and finally withdrew altogether from the earl and those councils, where his warning voice had been so totally disregarded."

Octavianus was proved right. Lambert Simnel and his supporters were roundly defeated at Stoke three months later, and the impostor - somewhat fortunately in those desperate days - was spared, and made to serve in a lowly position in the King's kitchens. The people of Dublin threw themselves on the mercy of King Henry and craved

"your highness's clemency towards your poor subjects of Dublin, metropolis of your highness's realm of Ireland etc." However, Stuart pointed out tartly "Into this gross error they could not have fallen if they had followed the prudent counsel given to them by their Primate, the Archbishop of Armagh."[6] In other words " I told you so."

Nevertheless, only four years later the Irish welcomed yet another Pretender - Perkin Warbeck - who was greeted in Cork as "Prince Richard," with the backing of the Earls of Desmond and Kildare. Although this proved abortive, King Henry VII could not continue to ignore the direct threat from Ireland. Sir Edward Poynings, a trusted and capable soldier and administrator was despatched to Dublin to restore order, and to prevent Yorkist Pretenders from using Ireland as a potential springboard for the English throne.

The Parliament summoned to Drogheda in 1494 enacted what came to be known as Poyning's Law and stipulated that the Parliament could meet in Ireland, only after Royal permission had been granted. "Though variously interpreted in the three centuries that followed, its main purpose at the time was to prevent an Irish parliament giving official recognition to a Pretender to the English throne such as Lambert Simnel, as had happened in 1487."[7]

By the time of Archbishop Octavianus' death in 1513, the Primatial City "had been reduced, by various causes, from its former splendour to the state of extreme wretchedness and insignificance, sarcastically described in Latin rhymes viz 'The City of Armagh, a vain city, devoid of good morals; where the women go naked, flesh is eaten raw, and poverty resides in their dwellings'. "[8]

One of the difficulties facing the Church in Ireland was the division in secular society, which stretched far back into history. "One indication of just how disorganised the native Irish church had become by the eleventh century is the fact that the first bishops of the now Christian Norse settlements based in the emerging cities, although Irish-born, chose to acknowledge the supremacy of Canterbury rather than that of Armagh. This was in order to avoid the system of hereditary abbacies and bishoprics which was endemic in the Irish church. Thus already, long before the sixteenth-century Reformation, there is evidence of a split within the Irish church, with the old stock of the rural areas giving their allegiance to Armagh, and the urban newcomers preferring to defer to Canterbury"[9]

The divisions continued down the years. Commenting on the period during the early sixteenth century, one historian notes "The Archdiocese of Armagh itself was split between the Pale residents of the south and the Gaelic Irish of the north; and the Archbishop was able to exercise little jurisdiction over his flock 'among the Gaelic Irish', as he commonly lived not at Armagh but in his castle at Termonfeckin, County Louth. During the fifteenth century, English bishops appointed to dioceses in the Gaelic Irish area found themselves unable to understand either the language or traditions of their flocks, and often deserted to England to act as assistant bishops in English sees."[10]

The parlous state of religion in Ireland was underlined by one observer in 1515 :

"For there is no archbishop, no bishop, abbot nor prior, parson nor vicar, nor any other person of the Church, high or low, great or small, English or Irish, that is accustomed to preach the word of God, save the poor friars beggars."[11]

However, it was the "poor friars beggars" - the Franciscans, Domnicans and Augustinians - who literally "kept the faith" and provided a traditional spiritual bedrock amid the rigours of the Reformation.

> "It was these men, who through constant preaching and administration of the sacraments, kept religion alive in Ireland during this period and stiffened Irish resistance to the religious innovations of Henry VIII when he broke with Rome after his marriage to Anne Boleyn in 1533."[12]

The accession of Henry VIII to the throne marked the beginning of a more determined and aggressive policy towards Ireland, which by the end of the reign of Elizabeth I, had resulted in the conquest of the entire island. Henry, not content with the title of his predecessors "Lord of Ireland", was declared "King of Ireland" by the Irish Parliament in 1541. Henry proceeded not only firmly but cunningly against the old Gaelic 'establishment' and by the end of his reign, with many of the major Gaelic lords having agreed to accept Henry's jurisdiction and to adapt English uniformity in language and dress, the decline of the old Gaelic world was underway, despite the violent struggles that marked the final part of the conquest under Elizabeth.

Henry, having assumed the title of supreme head of the English Church, and having thus usurped the Pope's authority, set about the dissolution of the monasteries. The smack of firm Tudor government also decreed that, if only in the interests of uniformity, the Reformation should also be imposed, as far as possible, upon Ireland as well. The religious houses were dissolved in the Pale, but the old religion proved difficult - indeed impossible - to eradicate. During the reigns of Edward VI, Mary and Elizabeth, changes and counter-changes were tried, with Mary attempting to restore the old religion and Elizabeth swiftly counter-manding this in her drive to impose a Protestant uniformity.

The developments which led to the perpetuation of a permanent division within Christianity in Ireland have been well-summarised thus;

> "The Irish Parliament of 1560 - which, like all the Parliaments of the century, represented only the more anglicised parts of the country - tried to make Ireland Protestant by religion: but the religious conservatism of the people, the fact that the reformed religion was associated with an alien Government, and the missionary efforts of the agents of the counter-reformation - the Jesuits and other priests who came to Ireland from the continent - all combined to entrench Catholicism. The old religion, professed by Anglo-Irish and Gaelic Irish alike, soon disclosed itself as a force making for Irish unity, and for resistance to England. As time went on, it became increasingly clear that the established church was the church of the new English colony and of the official class."[13]

One cannot help but wonder what St. Patrick would have made of all this.

A key figure in these turbulent times was George Cromer, an English cleric who was consecrated Archbishop of Armagh in 1522 and became Lord-Chancellor of Ireland shortly afterwards. Described as 'a learned, grave and courteous man'[14], he stoutly resisted attempts by Archbishop Browne of Dublin to implement the King's measures. Cromer was so incensed that he pronounced a curse on those who would recognise the ecclesiastical supremacy of the King, and he despatched two messengers to Rome to warn

the Pope about what was happening in Ireland.

In an attempt to preserve the old religion, the Ulster chieftain Con O'Nial took up arms against "heresy and the Pope's enemies" and began to muster troops for an invasion of the Pale. The English Lord-Deputy made a pre-emptive strike, marching north and occupying Armagh for two days. Though the surrounding countryside was pillaged, Armagh was unscathed - a development which, according to Stuart, might lead one to conclude that the people of the city had not made common cause with their Primate or O'Nial.

Though Henry and Archbishop Browne did not enjoy unanimous backing in the Pale, it appears that Cromer was eventually worn down. According to Stuart "It is probable that even Primate Cromer himself, at last submitted to the authority of the king, and ceased to give any opposition to his measures."[15]

Cromer, who was in effect the last, undisputed Archbishop of Armagh in the old church, died in 1542, and was succeeded by Archbishop Dowdall, who was consecrated a year later. Dowdall was appointed by Henry VIII, against the wishes of the Pope, who appointed his own nominee - Robert Waucop - to what he regarded as a vacant see. At this point in his narrative Stuart notes clearly a significant parting of the ways in the old Irish church. He states:

"We have now, in these historical sketches, arrived at that particular point of time when the church of Ireland began to be separated, by the law of the land, from the see of Rome. Two distinct ecclesiastical hierarchies, shortly after this period, coexisted in Ireland; the one presiding over the religion of the state, the other over that long adopted and steadily adhered to by the great majority of the people. Waucop ought, of course, to be classed, as the first titular Primate of all Ireland, in right of his appointment

A nineteenth-century impression of Shane O'Neill.

by the Pope, or in other words, as the first Roman Catholic Archbishop of Armagh, nominated in this country, after the commencement of the Reformation, by the Papal see."[16]

Henry VIII died in 1547 and was succeeded by Edward VI who ordered that the liturgy of the English church should be imposed on the Irish church, and read in English. Archbishop Dowdall, despite pressure from the King and the Viceroy in Ireland, stoutly resisted this measure, even though the Pope had appointed another incumbent to the Armagh see which he already held. Dowdall's firmness "met with the approbation of the great majority of the people, and he was generally regarded as the leader of the Roman Catholics of Ireland."[17]

The King's men were not to be outdone, and by Royal order he was deprived of the primacy which was then vested in Archbishop Browne in Dublin. Dowdall recognised wisely that he was not going to win this argument and decided to move to a safe haven. "At the very moment when his popularity had risen to the highest pitch, and when it might have been dangerous for King Edward to have proceeded one step further against him, he deserted his dignified station and fled in alarm to the continent."[18]

Edward replaced him with Hugh Goodacre, described by Stuart as "the first Protestant prelate who presided over the see", and this topsy-turvy world of political and ecclesiastical intrigue took on another twist when Edward died in 1553 and was succeeded by Mary. She immediately set out to restore the old Catholic religion and recalled Dowdall from the continent-Goodacre having conveniently died a few months earlier. Dowdall was reinstated to the see of Armagh in 1554 and restored as "Primate of all Ireland".

Not surprisingly, Archbishop Browne and two of his senior clerical supporters were expelled from their sees, partly on the grounds of being "married and impenitent", which was possibly the easiest excuse for a new Royal regime which was making a clean sweep of its perceived enemies. In 1558 Archbishop Dowdall died, some ten months after the Lord-Lieutenant had marched into Ulster to quell yet another insurrection, and in the process set fire to Armagh, sparing only the Cathedral.

Queen Mary died in November 1558, and was succeeded by Elizabeth I who wasted no time in dismantling the political and ecclesiastical structure which had been put into place by her predecessor. Elizabeth appointed Adam Loftus, a Yorkshire man to the see of Armagh in 1562 and five years later to the see of Dublin "which was then more productive with respect to pecuniary emolument than the primacy: for the city of Armagh, with the cathedral itself, had been destroyed by Shane O'Nial, and the whole province impoverished and wasted by his conflicts with the British Army." [19]

O'Nial (O'Neill) was, by all accounts, a remarkable figure. "He was munificent, social and hospitable, but frequently intemperate at table, addicted to venery, and, if his enemies may be credited, a persevering votary of Bacchus. His cellar is said to have usually contained at least two hundred tons of wine, of which, as well as of Usquebaugh (whiskey), he was in the habit of drinking to excess. When, by copious libations to the jolly god, he became intoxicated, his attendants placed him chin-deep in a pit, and then cast earth around him. In this clay-bath he remained, inhumed as it were

Hugh O'Neill, Earl of Tyrone – a
seventeenth-century Italian
portrait.

alive, until the velocity of his blood had abated and his body had
attained a cooler temperament."[20] All of which might have
been an early Irish prototype for the sauna in reverse.

The incessant uprisings, feudings and general
mayhem took its toll on the Church as well as the
general population. "In the year 1576, inquiry was
made into the ecclesiastical state of the country,
and scarcely any churches or officiating curates
could be found. The people had not adopted the
Protestant religion, and the Roman Catholic
clergy had either fled, or had been expelled from
their parishes. Many of the laity had never been
baptised and knew nothing of religion. A
commission was therefore appointed to rectify
this deplorable state of affairs."[21] Obviously the
prevailing wisdom was, then as now, if in doubt
form a committee.

In 1585 Richard Creagh, who had been appointed
some twenty years earlier by the Pope as Archbishop, died
in the Tower of London. He was an important figure in the
early Irish Counter-Reformation. He had been imprisoned in 1565
and was released after five weeks, but later reincarcerated "after the lapse of
many years". According to Stuart "His zeal for the advancement of the
Roman Catholic religion, and probably some political considerations
rendered him obnoxious to Queen Elizabeth, by whose spies he was seized
in Ireland, and transmitted to London where he was closely imprisoned ...
he was fettered, and various efforts were made both by means of threats and
of proffered rewards, to induce him to change his religion, but he remained
steadfast in his original faith. ... The Archbishop was falsely accused of having
forcibly attempted to deflower the daughter of his gaoler. His accuser, a
beautiful and elegant girl, came forward to give evidence against him. But
when she looked steadily on the countenance of this injured and innocent
man, a sudden pang of remorse seized her soul. She became conscience-
stricken and unable to bear the false evidence against him, which she had
previously meditated. ... The Archbishop, thus honourably acquitted, was
brought back a prisoner to the tower, where, in a few days, he expired AD
1585."[22]

The Archbishop, according to Colm Lennon , writing in the Autumn
2000 edition of *History Ireland*, was "above all a champion of the rights of the
Roman Catholic Church in Ireland against all obtruders, whether in the
form of Crown officials, ill-disciplined clergy or intrusive Irish magnates
such as Shane O'Neill. It was not surprising therefore that he was reckoned
to be 'a dangerous man to be among the Irish.'"

Archbishop Creagh was succeeded by Edward MacGauvran "who, in the
beginning of the year 1594 was appointed by the Pope as his envoy to the
Irish, for the purpose of animating the Roman Catholics to take up arms in
defence of their religion. He was charged also with a commission from
Philip II of Spain, to the Irish chieftains, to whom that monarch promised

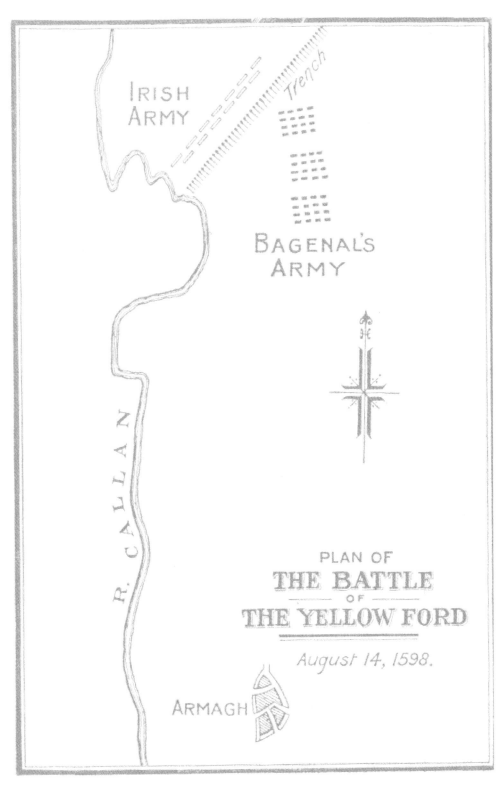

IRISH ARMY

Trench

BAGENAL'S ARMY

R. CALLAN

PLAN OF
THE BATTLE
OF
THE YELLOW FORD

August 14, 1598.

ARMAGH

The Battle of the Yellow Ford, 14 August 1598 where the English suffered a disastrous defeat.

effectual aid."[23] MacGauvran took his commission so seriously that he accompanied a force of Irish troops into battle against the English and "was transfixed by a horseman's spear". He was succeeded as Archbishop of Armagh by Peter Lombard who so impressed Pope Clement VIII that he made him his domestic prelate and assistant.

Perhaps there was more to this appointment than met the eye.

"It is probable that, at this period, the Roman Catholic primates of Ireland could have derived but little, if any, emoluments from their sees; and Lombard's promotion, in Rome, may have been of essential service to him in pecuniary matters, independent of the honour he received from his confidential intimacy with the Pope. It was, in fact, at that period, and for a considerable time prior to it, difficult or impossible for any titular archbishop to fulfil the function of his office in Ireland, such were the jealousy of the state and the intolerant spirit of the times."[24]

Meanwhile, on the political and military front, the young Queen Elizabeth, having survived the murderous intrigue of her family, including the execution of her mother by her father and also imprisonment by her sister, showed she had the ruthlessness and steel to move against the rebellious Irish once and for all. She pursued with success a firm policy of the Anglicisation of Ireland, but Ulster remained a law unto itself and until it was defeated the Tudor conquest could not be complete. Hugh O'Neill, himself a formidable leader in the vanguard of the struggle in Ulster, knew that he needed the help not only of England's enemy Spain but also the support of Irish allies to take on the might of Elizabeth's forces.

This led to a fierce struggle from which the city of Armagh, given its strategic, ecclesiastical and symbolic importance, could not possibly escape. Time and again a beleaguered English garrison in Armagh had to be relieved by the Queen's forces, and in 1598 Field Marshall Sir Henry Bagnall was despatched to quell yet another Ulster insurrection. He marched from Newry and relieved the garrison at Armagh, and then prepared his large forces to relieve the garrison at Blackwater. He had some 4,000 infantry and 300 cavalry, facing a similar force on the Irish side.

Bagnall left Armagh before sunrise, but he and his troops marched into a trap that had been prepared carefully by O'Neill and his allies. The English were routed at the Battle of the Yellow Ford, in which Bagnall lost his life. More than 800 of his officers and men had perished, 400 others were wounded, and around 300 deserted to the Irish lines. According to one recent history "Many regard the Yellow Ford as the most disastrous defeat the English ever suffered at the hands of the Irish."[25] The survivors fled to Armagh "and took refuge in the churches of that city."[26] During the night, however, they moved out, and both the garrisons at Armagh and Blackwater surrendered.

This significant victory at the Yellow Ford underlined how formidable the Irish could be, but so, too, was Charles Blount, alias Lord Mountjoy, the new Lord Deputy who landed at Howth in 1600. Mountjoy was "prudent in counsel, prompt in act, cautious and secret in maturing his plans, but bold and decisive in their execution."[27] He was to prove more than a match for the Irish, and when O'Neill unexpectedly retreated from the Moyry Pass, this allowed Mountjoy's troops to move through, and the resistance of the

Irish was worn down systematically. When a Spanish force landed at Kinsale in 1601, O'Neill and his allies moved south to join up with them. However, at the Battle of Kinsale on Christmas Eve 1601 they were outmanoeuvred by Mountjoy and his troops, and roundly defeated. The Spanish surrendered Kinsale, and it was only a matter of time before the whole island, including troublesome Ulster, would be placed under the control of Mountjoy and the English throne.

Kinsale - the site of a decisive battle on Christmas Eve, 1601.

After the Battle of Kinsale, the Irish leaders returned North, and the final struggle for supremacy was again centred in Ulster. The next year, Mountjoy brought the English army into Armagh to subdue O'Neill's own country in Tyrone. Finding the accustomed ford over the Blackwater at Blackwatertown strongly defended, he led a troop on a scouting mission and thus located an unguarded ford some two miles down stream.

Having brought his army thus into Tyrone, a defensive position was created to guard the crossing where a bridge had been built across the river. He named it Charlemont Fort by combining parts of his own name Charles and Mount. Captain Caulfeild was left to hold the fort, and in 1603 he was made Governor, and knighted as Sir Toby Caulfeild.[28]

It had been a turbulent period since the previous attempt under Edward the Bruce nearly three centuries earlier to drive out the invaders and unite Ireland under a new High-King, who was an outsider himself. The Tudor

BATTLE OF KINSALE
DECEMBER 1601

ENGLISH CAMP

A FORCE OF 4000 SPANIARDS
OCCUPIED KINSALE, WHICH WAS THEN
BESIEGED BY AN ENGLISH ARMY OF
6600 FOOT AND 650 HORSE, UNDER
MOUNTJOY.

THE MAIN ENGLISH CAMP WAS IN THIS
VICINITY, AND LAY ASTRIDE THE OLD
HIGHWAY TO CORK.

THE IRISH ARMY, UNDER O'NEILL, WAS
ENCAMPED ABOUT 3 MILES NORTH.

conquest of Ireland was virtually complete by the time Elizabeth died in 1603, and the "Flight of the Earls" in 1607 confirmed the end of the old Gaelic world. A new order was under way, and a new word - Plantation - was in vogue. This would transform the face of Ulster and also pave the way in the longer-term for a new Armagh. It would retain the tradition of its patron saint but even Patrick himself would hardly recognise the changes that would take place in the city that had been so close to his heart.

NOTES

1 Stuart Op. Cit. p.184
2 Ibid. p.185
3 JF Lydon *The Course of Irish History* p.150
4 Stuart Op. Cit. p.188
5 Ibid. p.202
6 Ibid. pp.202-208
7 Dr Art Cosgrove, *The Course of Irish History* p.170
8 Stuart. Op. Cit. p.214
9 Alannah Hopkin, *The Living Legend of St Patrick* p.72, published by Grafton Books, 1989
10 Dr Art Cosgrove, Op. Cit. p.172
11 Ibid. p.172. Also State Papers, Henry VIII, Ireland, ii 15
12 Cosgrove Op. Cit. p.172
13 Dr GA Hayes-McCoy, *The Course of Irish History*, p.181
14 Stuart. Op. Cit. p.217
15 Ibid. p.234
16 Ibid. p.236
17 Ibid. p.239
18 Ibid. p.241
19 Ibid. p.247
20 Ibid. p.252
21 Ibid. p.266
22 Ibid. pp.249-250
23 Ibid. pp.269-270
24 Ibid. pp.269-271
25 Bardon. Op. Cit. p.60
26 Stuart. Op. Cit. p.288
27 Ibid. p.291
28 JJ Marshall *Charlemont Fort*, Belfast 1924

'Armagh hath lost all its ancient beauty and grandeur and nothing remaineth but a few wattled cottages with the ruinous walls of the monasterie, priorie and Primat's pallace'.

From a Map by R. Bartlett circa 1600

"The flight of the Earls", and nearly a hundred of their followers, provided a golden opportunity for the English to settle the chronic Ulster problem on their terms, once and for all. With most of the leaders of the Irish resistance to the Crown now fled to the European mainland, the Government set about Plantation, a systematic recolonisation which confiscated the land from their perceived enemies - the native Irish - and gave it to their perceived supporters-the new settlers from England and Scotland.

The strategy was simple and stark. On paper it appeared a neat solution to what had been an intractable problem. If the native Irish were not going to be loyal to the Crown and accept English culture and religion, namely Protestantism, then they would be replaced by those whose loyalty to the Crown and the Protestant cause was unquestioned.

However, like most "neat" solutions, it did not work out as planned. The native Irish, not surprisingly, bitterly resented the loss of their lands and basic rights, including the right to worship freely, and it was only a matter of time before they would seize their opportunity to fight back. The original idea to separate completely the Irish and the newcomers also failed to work, partly because there were not enough settlers to take full advantage of the new opportunities. Many of the Irish were allowed to stay as worker-tenants and some as landowners.

The way of life in Ulster changed radically. The settlers brought their own culture and customs which differed from those of the native Irish, and there soon developed a "them and us" mentality. This became the Province of the "haves" and the "have nots", of the oppressor and the oppressed, of a sense of injustice and a feeling of triumphalism which cast its long shadow down the savage and turbulent seventeenth century.

It was only after the Williamite Wars and the final victory for Protestantism in the British Isles that Ireland enjoyed a long period of peace. This led to the foundation of a new order in Ulster, with an improved economy and the development of new towns, of which Armagh became one of the finest. However, this new prosperity and apparent peace had its own price. The seeds of wrath which had been sown by the Plantation and subsequent wars, fought over territory and religion, left a dark legacy which continued to poison relationships between Roman Catholics and Protestants in Ulster, even to the present day.

The spectacle of marchers, bands, flag-waving and confrontation which so pollutes the Ulster calendar each year is a continual astonishment to the

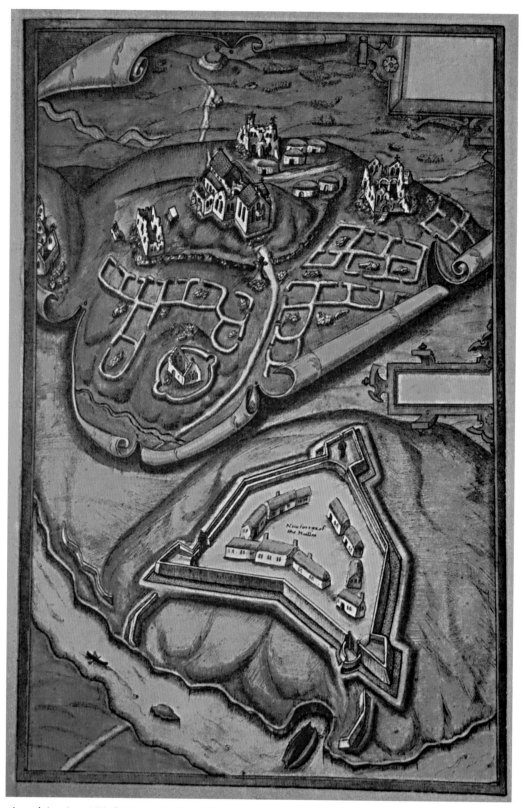

Armagh in ruins c.1600, from a map by Richard Bartlett.

outside world which has moved on from such seventeenth century sectarianism. Part of the tragedy of Northern Ireland lies in the fact that the exploits of those ancient heroes and anti-heroes, and the battles won and lost which are now part of the undergrowth of history, are still as fresh in the Ulster psyche as each new morning.

The seventeenth century politicians, civil servants and soldiers who thought that they had a "neat" solution to the Irish problem by imposing the Plantation, in effect devised a radical but deeply-flawed plan which not only failed to end the agony of the Province but ensured that the same "Irish" problem would still be unsolved as the world moved into the third Millennium. Anyone who attempts to understand the recent annual confrontations between Orangemen attending worship at Drumcree Church and the Roman Catholic residents of the Garvaghy Road area of Portadown cannot begin to do so without reading widely and carefully the history of seventeenth century Ulster and Ireland.

After the "flight of the Earls", much of the counties of Armagh, Cavan, Donegal, Derry, Fermanagh and Tyrone was confiscated and portioned out to the settlers on easily affordable rents. Severe measures were promulgated against the native Irish, and the Roman Catholic clergy "were ordered to depart from the Kingdom unless they consented to conform to the laws of the land, relative to religion."[1] The Augustinian friars, who had been supported by Hugh O'Neill from his own resources, withdrew from Armagh, following the seizure of their lands.

Repression, however, only served to deepen the faith. The Counter-Reformation led to a greater strengthening of the organisation of the Roman Catholic Church in Ireland, while strong links were maintained with Catholicism in Europe. As one historian has noted, in Ulster, "the uncompromising spirit of the Counter-Reformation faced the inflexible determination of the Puritan settlers. Hostility, suspicion and uncertainty created a dangerously unstable atmosphere in the Province."[2]

The troubles which beset Charles I, in deep conflict with his Parliament, encouraged the native Irish leaders, who were chafing under such discriminatory rule, to foment rebellion in 1641. Though the plot was discovered through careless talk in Dublin before the uprising had properly started, Sir Phelim O'Neill had taken the initiative in Ulster and and his followers were soon in control of large parts of the Province, including Armagh and further afield. This led to the slaughter of many settlers, including the murder of some eighty men, women and children at Portadown, where they were forced into the River Bann by the rebel Manus O'Cahan and his followers, and perished - a massacre which is still kept alive in the folk-memory, and depicted on Orange banners even today.

However, there was untold savagery on both sides as the Government

Owen Roe O'Neill, nephew of the great Hugh O'Neill, led his forces to a famous victory at the Battle of Benburb in 1646, but failed to follow it up.

forces fought back and, according to Stuart,

"It is totally impractical to give in this historic narrative, a detailed account of the horrible acts perpetrated by the contending parties, in the progress of the insurrection."

Early in May 1642, Sir Phelim O'Neill, again according to Stuart, retreated from Armagh in face of an advancing force of Anglo-Scots and "Actuated by a spirit of revenge, he set fire to the cathedral and city, and slew a considerable number of the Protestant inhabitants".[3] This followed the murder of seventy-eight civilians in Newry by Government troops under the command of Major-General Robert Munro.

Later that year Owen Roe O'Neill, nephew of the great Hugh O'Neill, landed in Donegal to help the Irish cause. With the outbreak of the English Civil War in August 1642, Irish affairs became even more complex than usual, with various alliances and factions in Ireland becoming allied or opposed to the Royalist cause. Hostilities dragged on, and the situation was further complicated by the arrival in Ireland of the Papal Nuncio Rinuccini in 1645, with supplies for the Irish rebels - the war having been sanctioned by a Catholic Confederacy, including the clergy, at Kilkenny.

The timely help from Rinuccini fortified the Irish resistance, and in 1646 Owen Roe O'Neill and his army had a major victory when they famously defeated Major-General Monro and the Crown forces at the Battle of Benburb (see page 77). Unaccountably, O'Neill failed to press home his victory in the North, and instead turned his attention south to assist Rinuccini and the Catholic Confederacy of Kilkenny. Later on, events took a decisive turn with the execution of Charles I in January 1649, and the arrival of Oliver Cromwell in Ireland.

The main motives of Cromwell's Irish campaign, well-chronicled elsewhere, were revenge and reconquest. The savagery of his massacres and his measures against the Irish created another folk-memory of English brutality which is still not forgotten today. Anglo-Irish history remains a fertile seed-bed for any faction which chooses some of the excesses of the past to justify their current behaviour. Cromwell, having overcome all Irish resistance, exacted a bitter retribution, including execution,

Top: Oliver Cromwell carried out a savage Irish campaign of re-conquest.

Bottom: Sir Phelim O'Neill, leader of the 1641 Rebellion. He was executed in Dublin in 1652.

Sr Phillom O Cheife Traytor Neale of all Irelan

exile, transportation and the confiscation of large areas of land. This, in turn, had significant implications.

As one historian notes "The Cromwellian settlement was not so much a plantation, as a transference of the sources of wealth and power from Catholics to Protestants. What it created was not a Protestant community, but a Protestant upper class."[4] In Ulster the new order was clear, as Jonathan Bardon points out "The Gaelic aristocracy, already shattered by the Ulster plantation, was all but wiped out and the foundations of the Protestant Ascendancy had been firmly laid."[5]

Meanwhile, Armagh had received its Charter in 1613, but as Roger Weatherup points out in an essay titled "God's Own City", this was not its first charter. "An entry in the Archiepiscopal Registers refers to the regrant of a patent in 1467, and there is an attestation of the document again noted in 1558."

With or without its Charter, Armagh - as it had done throughout the centuries - survived as best it could in the upheavals and political changes which had swept across the face of the land. Standing on one of the cross-roads of history, it was subjected to occupation by one or other of the protagonist in the wars, with their resultant pillage and burning. A map by Richard Bartlett dating from approximately 1600 shows Armagh in ruins, with the comment "Armagh hath lost all its ancient beauty and grandeur and nothing remaineth but a few wattled cottages with the ruinous walls of the monasterie, priorie and Primat's pallace."

Apart from the unwelcome attention of men at arms, the city as the ecclesiastical capital of the island also had to adjust itself to the new post-Reformation reality of being the seat not just of one but of two Archbishops from the now differing traditions of the one faith.

Two of the most impressive incumbents in the 17th century were Dr James Ussher, who was appointed Church of Ireland Archbishop of Armagh in 1624, and his Roman Catholic counterpart Dr Oliver Plunkett who held office from 1669 until his execution in 1681. Each was decidedly different in his own way, but both made a mark on the history of the city, the province and the people they were called to serve. (See pages 70, 71)

Meanwhile, on the broad political front, the accession of Charles II to the throne had brought about a period of comparative peace and economic improvement. However in the topsy-turvy world of seventeenth century religion and politics, the accession of James II to the throne in 1685 again tilted the balance towards Roman Catholicism, with the resultant settling of old scores.

Stuart, who chronicled Armagh's early history in such detail but also with an eye to broadbrush developments, had no doubt about his new monarch. He stated icily "James the 2nd was better qualified, by nature and by habit, to manage the ecclesiastical affairs of a friary, than to govern a spirited, turbulent and divided people, or to direct the councils of a mighty empire. His steadiest and most intelligent friends perceived the deficiency of his understanding, and foreboded the ruin of his affairs, from his absolute subserviency to the priesthood."[6]

The worst fears of the Protestant ascendancy were realised when Richard

Dr James Ussher, Church of Ireland Archbishop of Armagh 1625-1656, who claimed that the universe was created in exactly 4004 BC - a date widely accepted in the Western world until the nineteenth century.

 James Ussher

Dr James Ussher, who was appointed Church of Ireland Archbishop of Armagh in 1625, was one of the most learned and influential incumbents of that office. His career reflected the tumultous political and ecclesiastical upheavals of his time. Because of his friendship with King Charles I he was forced to seek refuge, on occasion, in the homes and estates of his friends in England and Wales, and yet he had the respect of Oliver Cromwell who took charge of the details of his funeral and paid for it at his own expense.

Ussher, the son of a Dublin lawyer, was ordained in 1601 and was Professor of Divinity and former Vice-Chancellor of Trinity College Dublin, where his library was placed, on the orders of Charles II after his death. In his early years Ussher so impressed King James I that he appointed him Bishop of Meath, and later as Archbishop of Armagh.

For some fifteen years he was based in the Armagh diocese, but in 1640 he crossed to England with his wife and family, never to return. In the 1641 rebellion all his property in Ireland, apart from his library and the furniture of his house in Drogheda, was destroyed. He was briefly Bishop of Carlisle before moving to Oxford. He was invited to join the Westminster Assembly of Divines but declined, and preached against its legality, which greatly displeased the ecclesiastical and political Establishment.

He sought refuge in Cardiff and later at the castle of a friend in Glamorganshire, but was ambushed on the way by local highwaymen who, much to his distress, stole priceless books and manuscripts then in his possession. However, within three months these were recovered, with the exception of a few volumes.

From 1647 to 1654 he was preacher at Lincoln's Inn, and during this period he was able to visit the unfortunate Charles I, of whom he was a strong supporter. He witnessed the King's execution and, according to Stuart, "His eyes were suffused with tears, involuntary sighs burst forth, and he stood with uplifted hands, as if silently addressing the merciful Creator, in behalf of his unhappy King". But when the executioners began to address themselves to the Royal victim, "a deadly paleness" began to pass over Ussher's countenance, "his heart seemed bursting with unutterable sorrow, and his attendants were obliged to bear him, almost lifeless, from the dismal and tremendous scene."[1]

Ussher wrote widely on Christian themes, was highly regarded by other scholars, and was an expert in Patristic literature and ancient Irish history. His chronology was the standard accepted in editions of the English Bible, and he claimed that the Universe was created in exactly 4004 BC – a date widely accepted in the Western world until the 19th century.[2]

Though Stuart described him as having attained "the first rank amongst the literati of Europe,"[3] he noted that he had two faults – he was intolerant of Roman Catholics in Ireland, and he lacked the perseverance and energy to reform the ecclesiastical courts.[4] Ussher died in 1656, and was buried after a service in Westminster Abbey which was attended by a large congregation of leading clergy, politicians and public representatives.

Saint Oliver Plunkett

Saint Oliver Plunkett was a classic example of a religious man who was in the wrong place at the wrong time. He was born in 1629 in County Meath, and educated and ordained in Rome. He entered the Irish College and represented the Irish Bishops at the Holy See. He was Professor of Theology from 1657 until his nomination as Roman Catholic Archbishop of Armagh in 1669.

He set about restoring discipline and order in the diocese, and kept on good terms with both the English and the Protestant Establishment until 1673 when, during a period of renewed repression of Catholicism he went into hiding. In a climate of panic and terror surrounding the Popish Plot by which Catholics were alleged to have been planning the murder of the King. Plunkett was betrayed, arrested and incarcerated in Dublin Castle.

He faced trumped-up charges to have conspired with the French and to join an invading force at Carlingford. This was thrown out by a Protestant jury in Dundalk but, notwithstanding, Plunkett was taken to London where, after farcical proceedings, he was sentenced to death.

Among his accusers was the layman from Armagh Florence MacMoyre who was also the Steward of the *Book of Armagh* and pledged it for £5 to help pay his fare to London for the trial, as has been noted earlier.

Archbishop Plunkett, protesting his innocence to the end, was hanged, drawn and quartered before a large crowd at Tyburn in 1681. His head is preserved in Drogheda and his body was taken to Downside Abbey, near Bath. He was the last man to suffer martyrdom for the Roman Catholic faith in England, and he was Beatified by Pope Benedict XV in 1920, and Canonised in 1975 by Pope Paul VI.

He was described thus by James Stuart as "a most learned and pious man" who "laboured assiduously to amend the morals of the people committed to his ecclesiastical jurisdiction, and to diffuse a spirit of Christian love through the community."[5]

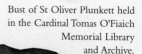

Bust of St Oliver Plunkett held in the Cardinal Tomas O'Fiaich Memorial Library and Archive.

NOTES

1 Op. Cit. page 331
2 *Concise Dictionary of Biography,* Oxford University Press
3 Op. Cit. page 335
4 Ibid. pages 337–38
5 Op. Cit. Page 358

King William of Orange and Queen Mary. William landed at Carrickfergus in 1690 to carry the battle to his father-in-law, King James II. Both portraits hang in the Armstrong Room of the Palace, Armagh.

Talbot, the Earl of Tyrconnell, arrived as Lord Deputy in Ireland and began promoting Roman Catholics, while at the same time demoting Protestants. In England there was equal alarm about the intentions of James II, and when the Protestant establishment turned to William of Orange for help, the Dutch monarch, embroiled in defensive alliances against the powerful Louis XIV of France, was only too eager to accept their invitation.

King William landed at Brixham in Devon in 1688. James, his father-in-law, showed little stomach for initial confrontation, and removed himself to France. The accession of William to the throne seemed like a deliverance to the Protestant ascendancy but when James landed in Kinsale with French support, it was clear that Ireland would be the theatre of war in which the Protestant cause would be won or lost. Not for the first time Ireland, which more than once had suffered directly from the consequences of a change of English monarch, would play a pivotal role in the destiny of the Crown.

The breaking of the Siege of Derry, and the remarkable resistence of its inhabitants, helped to turn the Jacobite tide and placed them on the defensive. The Duke of Schomberg and the Williamite forces moved south but failed to take the advantage to press further forward, and were unable to overcome the Jacobites at Dundalk. William decided that his presence in Ireland was necessary, and accordingly he landed at Carrickfergus with a large Army in June 1690 to carry the battle to James.

Armagh, as in previous confrontations between opposing armies, was drawn into the conflict. King James's garrison was based at Charlemont, and on his way north to Derry the King stayed for a few days in Armagh. He described the city as "pillaged by the enemy and very inconvenient, as well for himself as his train."[7]

James returned to Armagh, following the major setback at Derry, and it

The Duke of Schomberg whose troops took possession of Armagh. The veteran soldier took pity on the starving Irish garrison and gave each man a loaf from his army's stores.

This portrait hangs in the Palace, Armagh.

is believed that he stayed at an inn in Abbey Street, and later at Market Street. His troops had a store-house in a lane to the south of Scotch Street, and "in a garden contiguous to this old building, many of his coins have been dug up, from time to time."[8]

In 1690 Schomberg's troops took possession of Armagh, following the capitulation of the soldiers in the Irish garrison, as well as women and children. Schomberg said, when he saw so many women and children coming out, "Love, rather than policy, prevailed in Irish garrisons." But the veteran soldier took pity on the starving troops, and gave each of them a loaf of bread from his own Army's stores.[9]

The Protestant cause was secured by William's decisive victory at the Boyne, followed by the defeat of the Jacobites at Aughrim over a year later, with great loss of life. The success of William's Irish campaign had repercussions far beyond Ireland. It strengthened his position against Louis XIV in greater Europe, and James gave up the struggle on Irish soil to regain the English throne. The Protestant Establishment consolidated its position, with the further confiscation of land and the imposition of Penal Laws which promulgated severe measures against Catholics to deprive them not only of territory but also of economic and political influence.

Systematic discrimination was not unknown elsewhere in Europe, where majorities persecuted minorities, but Ireland was different in that the minority set out to persecute the majority. The wholesale attempt to restrict Catholic worship became largely unworkable in practice, and though many members of religious orders and leading clergy were exiled, registered priests were allowed to take Mass. However, the sheer vindictiveness of some of the measures taken by certain individuals against Catholics is illustrated by the fate of the Dean of Armagh, who, though old, bedridden and poverty stricken, was arrested and put in prison, where he died before his trial. The individual who had been instrumental in his arrest, the cousin of a leading Government official, stated that "not withstanding this mischance, he may not be deprived of the reward of £50 which he would have been entitled to, on the Dean's conviction."[10]

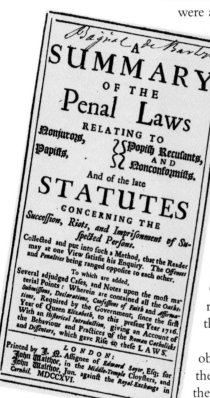

The Penal Laws promulgated severe measures against Roman Catholics.

In 1681 Dr Dominic Maguire was appointed Archbishop of Armagh by Pope Innocent XI on the death of Oliver Plunkett, but he went into exile in France where he died in 1707. His successor Dr Hugh MacMahon stoutly defended the Primacy of the Armagh See against claims from the Archbishop of Dublin Peter Talbot, and stressed that he was the genuine successor to St. Patrick. As Stuart points out, it may seem strange that Roman Catholic prelates should have been so tenacious of their ecclesiastical rights "apparently nominal" when the law of the land had transferred the power and privileges to the Protestants.

However, in a telling observation, he points out that voluntary obedience and support was still given to them by their flock. "They, therefore, possess a real, operative authority, not indeed derived from the law of the land, but founded on the powerful basis of public opinion, and on the respect and reverence which members of their own communion think justly due to the acknowledged pastors of what they deem a divinely-established church."[11]

According to Stuart, "little or no traces are to be found" about the details of Dr MacMahon's successors, and he relies on a list of eighteenth century prelates supplied by the Roman Catholic Bishop of Dromore Dr Edmund Derry, including Archbishops Bernard and Ross MacMahon, Micheal O'Reilly and Anthony Blake, who died on 11 November, 1787. His successor, Archbishop Richard O'Reilly, by all accounts brought order and harmony to what had became a diocese "disorganised by confessed anarchy".

"It was the glory of Primate O'Reilly, and the first blessing of his auspicious entry, to have tranquilized this most ancient diocess. At his presence the demon of discord, with his horrid train of attendants, disappeared." Dr O'Reilly "worn out by a combination of diseases, and full of merit, gave up his precious spirit to God, January 31st, 1818."[12]

Stuart, however, is on surer ground when he lists the Church of Ireland Archbishops, from the Restoration onwards. Dr John Bramhall, who succeeded to the Archbishopric in 1660 was an influential Yorkshireman who sold his English estate and settled in the Omagh area. However, he fell foul of Parliament, as did his patron the Earl of Strafford, and was imprisoned, but later released following a petition to the King on his behalf by Primate Ussher. After a long exile in Continental Europe he found favour with Charles II and was appointed to Armagh where he "governed his diocess with great firmness and wisdom. His conduct to non-conformists was prudent, liberal and conciliating."[13] Bramhall died in 1663 and in his will he stipulated that seventy black gowns, the number equalling his age, should be made up specially and given to poverty-stricken men.

Some of the details in Stuart's faithful narrative of the Archbishops are particularly illuminating. He reveals, for instance, that Archbishop Boyle, who became Primate in 1678 carried out many good works and was responsible for a number of important development projects, including the establishment of Blessington. He died on 11 December, 1702 at the age of 93, and "was buried, at midnight, without any pomp, in St Patrick's Church, under the altar."[14]

Narcissus Marsh, his successor, was one of a series of eighteenth century Archbishops cast in the same mould-English, well-connected, scholarly, and with a flair for development projects. He built a library in Dublin, and rebuilt a dwelling-house in Armagh for the Archbishop and his successors, as well as an establishment in Drogheda "for the reception and maintenance of twelve widows of decayed clergymen, who had been curates in the diocese of Armagh", or to others in need, as appropriate. He was liberal towards dissenters, but not so his successor Thomas Lindsay. He was generous to his own church, providing funds for an enlarged choir and for improvements to the Cathedral, but exacted heavy penalties from local Presbyterians and forced them to abandon their meeting-house on Church of Ireland land, and build anew on freehold property.

Dr Hugh Boulter, who succeeded Lindsay on his death in 1724, was a considerable figure in his day. He came from an influential English family, was educated at Oxford and was chaplain to King George I and preceptor to his grandson. The King was so pleased with Boulter's service that he appointed him to the See of Bristol and the Deanery of Christ Church, Oxford in 1719. Five years later he was offered Armagh. Boulter's initial reaction was to decline, but the King's insistence stiffened his resolve, and he accepted.

He made up for his early reluctance by pursuing a dynamic career in Ireland where he took an active part in the Privy Council, supported the new linen industry as well as the development of the Newry canal, built houses in Drogheda, contributed to the education of impoverished clergymen's children and gained a considerable reputation as a generous benefactor. He died at his London home in 1742 and was buried in Westminster Abbey.

Though Stuart observes that while "in the management of Irish affairs, he entertained too great a partiality for England and for Englishmen," he was

Dr Hugh Boulter, Archbishop of Armagh 1724-1742. A considerable figure in his day, he was Chaplain to King George I who offered him the post at Armagh. He initially declined but the King's insistence changed his mind.

also "liberal-humane-munificent. Of serene and placid temper, he was calm in deliberation -prompt in decision - alert and resolute in act."[15]

The Primate for the next four years was another Englishman, Dr John Hoadley who maintained the "English interest" in the manner of his predecessor. He was, among other things, a noted agriculturist "who delighted in practical farming and was beloved by his tenentry."[16] It was during his time that the Privy Council issued a proclamation, which he signed, for the strict enforcement of the Penal Laws by which chapels were closed, and as a result some priests sought out places where they could celebrate Mass secretly. One priest did so in a partially ruined building in Dublin which collapsed at the end of the service, killing ten people-including the priest himself, and injuring many others. As a result, the Lord-Lieutenant relaxed the severity of the enforcement of the Penal Laws, and the chapels were opened again on St Patrick's Day, 1745.[17]

Dr George Stone, who succeeded Hoadly in 1746, was "more of a politician than of a divine-and paid more minute attention to the management of the State, than to the due regulation of the church affairs." However, he was a courageous campaigner on behalf of the Catholic majority and was more willing to unite the people than his immediate predecessors, who had supported the "English interest" at the expense of the locals. Stone, despite his political preoccupations, also made significant improvements to Armagh, including the development of a new road which greatly improved communications to and from the city.

According to Stuart, "The opening of this new line of road has been of more essential service to Armagh than any other improvement which has been effected during the 18th century, by a private individual."[18]

However it was the next Archbishop of Armagh, Dr Richard Robinson, succeeding Dr Stone in 1765, who really put the city on the map. At a time of comparative peace and increasing prosperity he made Armagh arguably the finest settlement in Ulster and laid the foundations of the city which today bears the fruits of his vision and industry. After centuries of war, upheaval, and the unwelcome attention of invading and retreating armies, the city of St Patrick was about to blossom with elegance and style.

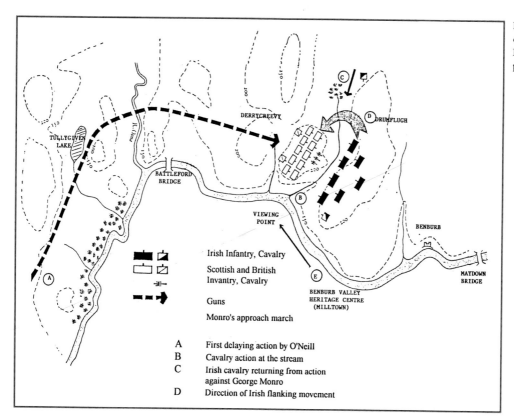

Disposition of opposing forces at the Battle of Benburb (see page 68).

Irish Infantry, Cavalry

Scottish and British Invantry, Cavalry

Guns

Monro's approach march

A First delaying action by O'Neill
B Cavalry action at the stream
C Irish cavalry returning from action against George Monro
D Direction of Irish flanking movement

NOTES

1 Stuart. Op. Cit. p.342
2 Bardon. Op. Cit. p.74
3 Stuart. Op. Cit. pp.370-71
4 Aidan Clarke, *The Course of Irish History* p.203
5 Bardon. Op. Cit. p.80
6 Stuart. Op. Cit. p.411
7 Ibid. p.416
8 Ibid. p. 417
9 Ibid. p. 420
10 New edition of Stuart's *Historical Memoirs of the City of Armagh*, revised by the Reverend Ambrose Coleman. p.273
11 Stuart. Op. Cit. pp.404-5
12 Ibid. pp.408-10
13 Ibid. pp.378-384
14 Ibid. p.390
15 Ibid. pp.423-433
16 Ibid. p.434-435
17 Ibid. p.435
18 Ibid. p.437-444

There was a strong oral tradition, from the time of the Penal Laws, that Dr Patrick O'Donnelly (or Donnelly), 1649-1716, was also the "Felim Brady" and "The Bard of Armagh" in the famous ballad of that name. It is believed that Dr O'Donnelly, a gifted musician, lived in hiding in South Armagh and also moved around the province carrying out his priestly duties under the disguise of an itinerant musician.

A figure depicting the Bard of Armagh, in the Cardinal Tomas O'Fiaich Memorial Library and archive.

THE BALLAD : "THE BARD OF ARMAGH"

"Oh list to the strains of the poor Irish harper,
And scorn not the strings from his poor withered hand,
But remember his fingers did often move faster
To raise up the memory of his dear native land.

At fair or at wake I would twist my shillelagh
Or dance the fine jig with my brogues bound with straw,
And all pretty colleens in village and valley
Loved the bold Felim Brady, the Bard of Armagh.

And when Sergeant Death in his cold arms shall embrace me,
Oh lull me to sleep with sweet Erin go bragh,
By the side of my Kathleen my young wife Oh place me,
Then forget Felim Brady, the Bard of Armagh."

MACES AND CHARTER

Armagh was incorporated by James I in 1613 and had a Sovereign, twelve Burgesses and Commons, who returned two members to Parliament. They were empowered to have a seat and to appoint Serjeants-At-Mace. In the year 1799, John Hill, Mace-Bearer, received £1 10s per annum for the discharge of his office.

When the corporation was suppressed under the Municipal Corporation Act in 1832, the two maces fell into the custody of Mr William Paton, survivor of the old Sovereigns. At his death they were presented by his daughter, in 1887, for preservation to the Public Library Armagh, where they are exhibited.

The maces of the Sovereign and Burgesses of the Corporation of Armagh were made by Nicholas Seward, Goldsmith, Dublin in 1656. They are of silver with plain stems, a central plain knop, and a base, round the bottom which is engraved.

THE SOVEREIGN'S MACE:
Length 20.5". Diameter Top 3 1/2 Bottom Knop inscribed: Made for the Burough of Ardmagh.

The new charter for Armagh which was handed over by the Queen in 1995 in the Primate's Chapel together with the City Mace and Her Majesty's signature. These are on display at the Council offices in the Palace Demesne.

Archbishop Richard Robinson, Baron Rokeby, whose appointment was a turning point in the history of Armagh. He helped to turn it into a city of exceptional architectural merit, the finest in Ulster. He was described as "a man of tall stature, robust, yet dignified form, penetrating eye and commanding aspect". (Portrait by Sir Joshua Reynolds).

'During the period occupied in erecting and establishing these public buildings, Armagh was rapidly improving. Its commerce revived, the spirit of the inhabitants increased with their wealth, and the city which had been reduced to a state of the most melancholy degradation, began to assume its long lost respectability and beauty'.

James Stuart *Historical Memoirs of the City of Armagh 1819*

A major turning-point in the history of St Patrick's city was the consecration in 1765 of Dr Richard Robinson, later Lord Rokeby, as Archbishop of Armagh and Primate of All-Ireland. Using a large portion of his personal wealth, he employed some of the outstanding architects and most gifted craftsmen of his day to give substance to his vision of Armagh as a city of exceptional architectural merit which would be worthy of the undisputed spiritual capital of the country.

In doing so he created a city of Georgian splendour in the classical style to rival that of Dublin, the secular capital, and formed the basis of much of the Armagh of today. He spent between £30,000 and £40,000 on building up the city, a fortune in the currency of his time. He also provided steady employment for many workers engaged on such a vast and continuing enterprise, and he gave the local community a palpable pride in their resplendent new city. The resurgence of Armagh as a centre of outstanding beauty and of learning under the visionary leadership of Archbishop Robinson was a far cry from the observations of Bartlett more than a century and a half earlier.

Richard Robinson was born in 1709 at Rokeby in the North Riding of Yorkshire. The fifth son of William Robinson and one of seven brothers, his family were wealthy and highly-respected landowners and members of the Church of England. He was educated at Westminster School and at Christ Church, Oxford, graduating in 1730 with a primary degree, and with an MA three years later.

He was not only well-connected but also able, and in 1751 he came to Ireland as one of the Chaplains to the Duke of Dorset, the Lord-Lieutenant. He soon found preferment and was quickly promoted to the See of Killala and Achonry. Eight years later he was appointed Bishop of Ferns and Leighlin in County Wexford, and in 1761 he became Bishop of Kildare, and Dean of Christchurch, Dublin. In 1765 he was consecrated Archbishop of Armagh, having secured the position through the influence of a close friend the Duke of Northumberland, the then Lord-Lieutenant. It is said that Robinson was offered the Armagh See after two other English Bishops had turned it down, and that the then Prime Minister George Granville was not entirely in favour of his appointment. One can only speculate about the subsequent history of Armagh if Robinson had not been drawn to the city for which he did so much.

Undoubtedly an outstandingly gifted personality, opinions differed about him as a man. Horace Walpole dismissed him as a "proud but superficial man without talents for political intrigue." He was said to be "publicly ambitious of great deeds and privately capable of good ones." His sermons were said to be "excellent in style and doctrine", though his low voice made his words hard to hear.

An interesting insight on Robinson was provided by the playwright Richard Cumberland, son of the Bishop of Kilmore. Cumberland often visited Robinson, and described his experience when accompanying the Archbishop to the Cathedral for Sunday service. His coach was pulled by six horses, and attended by three footmen. The Archbishop, an imposing figure, entered the Cathedral with dignity and ceremony behind a procession of other clergymen. Following the service, the clergy came to the Palace but Cumberland noted that none were invited to dinner. He also believed that the Archbishop did not treat his farm workers as well as his father did on the Kilmore farm.

An engaging pen-portrait of Robinson is provided by the indefatigable Stuart in his *Historical Memoirs of the City of Armagh*:

"Lord Rokeby was a man of tall stature, robust, yet dignified form, penetrating eye, and commanding aspect. To his friends, and to those whom he esteemed, he was affable, mild, attentive and polite. The unworthy and the obtrusive he repelled with a frown.

"Quick in discernment, and acquainted with the inmost recesses of the human heart, he was inaccessible to flatterers, or when assailed by their adulation, silenced them at once by the mixed sternness and indignation which his expressive countenance assumed. On such occasions his reserve was mistaken for pride-and the peculiar dignity of his character for needless and repulsive austerity."[1]

Despite Robinson's vision for the continuation of Armagh as a centre of learning, his legacy to posterity was more practical than academic.

"His fame is of a less durable and extensive kind than that of Ussher, who has erected for himself the imperishable monuments of the mind. None, however, of his (Robinson's) predecessors resided so constantly in his diocese, nor so punctually fulfilled its duties. None of them gave so powerful a stimulus to the industry of the people, or effected such permanently-useful improvements in the country."[2]

However, if stones could speak, the story of Robinson's achievements would tell a powerful tale. Today his main creations are lasting monuments to his vision and insight. Nevertheless this master-builder approached his major project with caution. When he was appointed to Armagh, the City was in a bad state, and only three houses had slated roofs. The Archbishop's dwelling, largely unused by previous Primates, was situated near the junction

of English Street and Russell Street, but was in poor repair.

Significantly, Archbishop Robinson had decided to live in the city, unlike many of his predecessors who had preferred the relative comfort and safety of County Louth, or in Dublin where their duties frequently obliged them to attend the Irish Parliament. For two years, Robinson lived in the village of Richhill - at that time in a better state of repair than Armagh - while the old Primatial residence was being repaired, but even when this had been completed he was not satisfied with the house.

With characteristic vigour, he decided to build an entirely new Primatial Palace, and when he was unable to obtain land at Lisanally, near the city, around 300 acres of the land owned by the Church of Ireland was set aside for the Archbishop by Parliament. On this green rolling countryside he built a splendid new Palace, mainly with local limestone which was plentiful. He commissioned Thomas Cooley, a young English architect who had risen to prominence in Dublin, and whose work on this and other buildings brought "an unexampled classical sophistication to Armagh."[3]

Arthur Young, the agriculturist and writer who visited Archbishop Robinson at Armagh in 1776 praised the design of the new Palace and noted that its appearance was helped "because there were no wings on the building." He also mentioned nearby out-houses, which were probably the stables built around the same time with a limestone and sandstone conglomerate, and which had a pinkish appearance. Young also mentioned a large lawn which had been created around the Palace.

Archbishop Robinson displayed a number of Royal portraits in the Palace, including those of King George III and Queen Charlotte by the

Portraits of King George III and Queen Charlotte which were completed in 1762, one year after the Royal marriage. Both portraits were painted by the celebrated artist Allan Ramsay, and it is believed that a number of portraits were presented by Royalty to the Archbishop. These two are displayed in the hallway of the Palace, now the office of Armagh City and District Council.

celebrated portraitist Allan Ramsay. Completed in 1762, one year after the Royal marriage, both portraits are displayed at the entrance hall of the former Palace, which was taken over by Armagh City and District Council for its offices in the mid-Seventies. It is believed that some of these portraits were personal gifts from Royalty to the Archbishop. Robinson also placed all the portraits of the Church of Ireland Archbishops from Reformation times in the Palace, and these are now in Church House beside the Cathedral.

In 1781, Archbishop Robinson began the building of a private Primate's Chapel, which stands to the west of the Palace, and which is considered to be one of the best examples of Georgian neo-classical architecture in Ireland. Completed in 1786, it was originally the work of Thomas Cooley but following his death in 1784 it was finished by Francis Johnston, an Armagh man and a pupil of Cooley, who became one of Ireland's most celebrated architects. It is important to note also the work of other outstanding architects, including Johnston's nephew William Murray, who made their mark on the city.

The outside of the Chapel was built with dressed ashlar limestone, similar to that of the Palace, and the facade of the Ionic-style portico contains intricate carved stone detail. The roof was constructed of sheet copper. The elaborate oak craftsmanship of the interior of the Chapel has been described as one of the finest examples of carved joinery in Ireland, while the stained glass depicting Biblical scenes, and the coffered ceiling with its ornamental

frieze and rosettes add greatly to the beauty of the building. In 1985 the Chapel underwent major refurbishment which restored it to its former glory. It was in this building that Her Majesty the Queen handed over a new Charter in 1995 to formalise Armagh's ancient status as a city.

One of the distinctive and most beautiful features of Armagh is The Mall, which in 1760 was known as "The Common" with a surrounding race-course. In 1773, Robinson had the race-course removed, and The Common was leased to the Sovereign and Burgesses to provide a public park, which was later developed over a long period to become a most elegant area surrounded by some of Armagh's best classical architecture, including the Court House, and the former Gaol. On a summer afternoon, with the whites of cricketing attire blending with the green trees and foliage, and the spires of the churches etched against the blue sky, this could be a scene from rural England.

In 1783, Archbishop Robinson masterminded the building of a monument in the Demesne to his benefactor, the Duke of Northumberland. The limestone obelisk built of locally-quarried limestone is 114 feet in height, and is now a feature of the local County Armagh golf course.

Robinson turned his attention to the construction of other notable buildings, particularly in the field of education, and the development of the Public Library, the Royal School and the Observatory which will be described later on. However there were other significant developments, including the provision of a hospital.

In 1766 Robinson started a fund for the construction of a County Infirmary, later the City Hospital, which closed in 1992, but which became the campus for the new Queen's University of Armagh in 1995. The Archbishop gave more than £113 as a donation to the fund, and many other

In 1766 Archbishop Robinson started a fund for the construction of a county infirmary, later the City Hospital. It closed in 1992 but three years later the building became the campus for the new Queen's University at Armagh. The original fourteen bed hospital was completed in 1774, with eight beds for men, four for women, and two for emergencies.

wealthy people contributed–including his brother Sir William Robinson who gave £105. The 14-bed hospital was completed in 1774. Such provision would be described as "sexist" today, with eight beds for men and only 4 four for women, and the other two for emergencies.

In 1773 Robinson built a new military barracks, and seven years later he erected a new gaol to replace a former prison in Market Street. Robinson had several houses built on Vicar's Hill, near four other dwellings which had been created by Archbishop Boulter in 1724 for the widows of Church of Ireland clergy. He also built the Shambles market area with slated sheds where butchers sold meat, though no cattle were slaughtered there.

The Archbishop was conscious that he alone could not give the city the character he wished it to adopt, and in an early example of environmentally-friendly leadership, he refused to renew the leases of tenants who would not take steps to improve their houses. He also encouraged the sinking of wells, the flagging and paving of streets, and the provision of sewers. It is recorded that in 1770 some sixty of the local workers described themselves as labourers, and there were many tradesmen with a wide variety of skills, including masons, stone-cutters, nailers, carpenters and brick-layers.

Not surprisingly, Archbishop Robinson turned much of his attention to improving the Cathedral on the site of St Patrick's main church which had been damaged many times by fire and by the deliberate incursion by men of violence as the tides of turbulent history moved back and forward through the city. As has been noted earlier, the Cathedral was struck by lightning in 995 and remained roofless for more than a century until Archbishop Celsus re-roofed it with shingles in 1125. Following more fires, it was virtually re-built by Archbishop O'Scanlan in 1261, and it is from this time that the history of the existing buildings can be said to have begun.

Roughly a century later, in 1365, Archbishop Milo Sweetman rebuilt the Nave and aisles, excepting the old west wall. After yet another fire, this time accidental, Primate Swayne restored the Cathedral in 1428.

The Cathedral suffered considerable damage in the 16th century, and in 1566 it was burned by Shane O'Neill after it had been turned into a fortress by the Lord Deputy during the seemingly never-ending conflicts between the English and the native Irish. In 1605 it was in ruins, but following repairs by Archbishop Hampton in 1613 at considerable cost, it was burned yet again, this time by Sir Phelim O'Neill in 1642.

Following the Restoration, refurbishment started under Archbishop Bramhall, who organised, among many other things, the construction of a beautifully-carved oak chair to denote the return of the Monarchy and the old Episcopal order under King Charles II. This chair retains an honoured place in the Sanctuary where it is still used at the Consecration of Bishops, the ordering of priests and deacons, and during confirmation. Bramhall's successor, Archbishop James Margetson, who was consecrated in 1663, continued the work of restoration and conserved the ruins of the old Cathedral which became the nucleus of the present church.

Opposite and above: The Primate's Chapel, considered to be one of the best examples of Georgian neo-classical architecture in Ireland.

The next noteworthy attempt at further restoration took place in the time of Archbishop Robinson. When he first came to Armagh, Robinson slated part of the roof and refurbished the interior. In 1782, he set out to build a taller tower and spire, the latter to reach 101 feet above the roof and to be an imitation of the Magdalen Tower at Oxford.

The work was entrusted to Thomas Cooley and continued until 1783, when the tower had reached some 70 feet above the roof. According to Edward Rogers in his *Memoir of the Armagh Cathedral* (1881) a number of parishioners, including "some old ladies", expressed fears about their safety when the arches beneath the tower began to crack, and Robinson very sensibly had it removed.

In a letter dated 2 January, 1823 the architect Francis Johnston looked back upon upon the architectural problem which had caused the Archbishop such worry;

"Having spent I may say some years in and out of the old Fabrick, I am almost acquainted with every stone of it, and am very sorry to add that it is a dangerous subject to attempt any considerable improvement upon. The Lord Primate Robinson fitted up the west aisle for the morning service about fifty years ago and made other repairs and improvements to the Church, and no alteration, no, not even a brush of paint has, I believe, been used (at least on the west aisle) since that time, even the hangings of the Throne were the same when I saw it about three years ago.

The Bramhall Chair, dating from 1661, belonged to John Bramhall, who was Archbishop of Armagh from 1661-1663. This important symbol of the Restoration of Charles II is still used in the Church of Ireland Cathedral, Armagh at the consecration of Bishops, the ordering of Priests and Deacons, and confirmation.

"A very superb steeple was designed by Mr Cooley from that of Magdalen College, Oxford and was carried up under by superintendence about seventy feet above the roof of the Church, when the piers and arches supporting it were perceived to be giving way, and the Primate immediately ordered it to be taken down. His Grace's intention at that time was to have had the tower and steeple erected at the west end of the Church, but Mr Cooley's death and other circumstances occurred to prevent His Grace's intention from being carried out."[4]

It would be the task of others to add to the work of Robinson in making further improvements to Armagh, but when the bachelor Primate died at Clifton, near Bristol, in 1794, he had left an indelible mark on the city to which he had given so much time, energy, wealth and vision. In his will he stipulated "I desire my remains may be deposited in the Cathedral Church of Armagh, as that City has been the principal place of my residence, since my advancement to the Primacy, and the inhabitants have been witnesses to the regular exertion of my mind for a succession of years, in promoting a variety of public works for the future benefit and improvement of that ancient city in which the Christian Religion was first preached in Ireland."[5]

Given the controversial background to the introduction of Christianity in Ireland, Archbishop Robinson may be allowed some literary licence in claiming that Christianity was first preached in Ireland at Armagh, but there is no doubt that St Patrick would have been proud of the work of his distinguished successor in helping to make Armagh one of the most beautiful cities in Ireland and in continuing to emphasise its tradition of scholarship.

James Stuart, writing only a quarter of a century after Robinson's death, was rich in his praise for the work carried out in the Archbishop's lifetime. "During the period occupied in erecting and establishing these public buildings, Armagh was rapidly improving. Its commerce revived, the spirit of the inhabitants increased with their wealth, and the city which had been reduced to a state of the most melancholy degradation, began to assume its long lost respectability and beauty."[6]

He continued, further on:

"...Armagh is boldly situated on the far-famed hill of Druimsailech. The country through which we approach the city is, in almost every direction, exquisitely beautiful ... The ancient cathedral which crowns the summit of Druimsailech-hill, is at once the most central point, and the most conspicuous object, in the city of Armagh. Towards this venerable church, some of the streets seem to converge, like radii, to a common centre-others ascend, in more oblique directions, from the base of the hill, and are intersected by those of greater magnitude, which encircle the town.

"The citizens' houses are neatly built with calcareous stone, and generally slated. Numerous public edifices, erected with hewn limestone of a very vivid colour, and finished in a chaste style of architecture, unite beauty with utility, and give peculiar interest to the city.

"The sites of these edifices have been so judiciously selected, that the buildings are not concealed from view by contiguous dwelling-houses, nor degraded by the neighbourhood of any uncouth or despicable objects. They are each possessed of unity and elegance, and being distinctly visible, in various directions, are at once ornamental to the town itself, and to the surrounding country."[7]

This countryside itself, and the profitable linen trade in County Armagh, were also described in lyrical terms.

"The linen weavers of Ulster, unlike the mere manufacturers of Great Britain, are free agents, whose employments are diversified and rational. They are sometimes engaged in the labours of the loom, and sometimes in the cultivation of their farms, and in this voluntary alternation of business, they find health and recreation.

"Lawns, streams, pure springs, and the open atmosphere, are necessary for perfecting the process of bleaching. Hence our eminent bleachers, and all their subordinate assistants, reside in the country. It cannot, therefore, be a matter of wonder, that in the county of Armagh, the towns are of small extent, and that every hill and vale should abound with rural habitations.

"Notwithstanding the minute subdivision of land, which is the natural result of these peculiar circumstances, the farmers of this district are more than competent to supply its population with vegetable, though not with animal, food and some of the less productive and less crowded parts of Ulster receive a considerable supply of oats, barley and flour, from the county of Armagh."[8]

In essence, the most succinct summary of Armagh at the beginning of the nineteenth century was given by Stuart at the start of his epic memoir of the city: "Armagh, situated on the sloping sides of a gently-ascending hill, and adorned with many public edifices built in a simple but correct and striking style of architecture, is probably the most beautiful inland town in Ireland."[9]

This fulsome word-picture of Armagh and its surrounding countryside at the beginning of the 19th century was a re-assuring confirmation of the relative peace and prosperity of those decades which helped to make possible to significant development of St Patrick's city. Many more developments were to come in building upon the considerable legacy of Archbishop Robinson.

Archbishop Richard Robinson is commemorated in Armagh Cathedral in an impressive memorial by the sculptor Nollekens, but - as was said of Sir Christopher Wren in the context of St. Paul's Cathedral in London - "If you seek a monument, look around." Robinson's legacy is to be seen throughout Armagh, though his immediate successors did comparatively little to add to it.

Another 28 years were to elapse before Archbishop Lord John George de la Poer Beresford, an Irishman, followed the pioneering trail of Robinson in making the city of St Patrick a particularly beautiful spiritual headquarters for the country. Beresford was Primate from 1822-62, but this period in Armagh's history also witnessed another significant milestone, namely the laying of the Foundation Stone of St Patrick's Roman Catholic Cathedral, and the steady development of the building itself.

Archbishop Newcome, who succeeded Richard Robinson and who was Primate for only five years compared to his predecessor's 30-year incumbency, "was a man of mild, pleasing and unaffected manners - a pious, humane and deeply-learned divine."[10] However he was no master-builder, and he was essentially a scholar who wrote extensively on theological subjects and became embroiled, for example, in a controversy as to whether Christ's earthly ministry lasted more than three years or, as his main opponent claimed, for only one year.

Despite living in Armagh and attending to his religious duties punctiliously, he could not have been a greater contrast to Robinson. Stuart tactfully concluded that Newcome's life had "terminated before he had an opportunity of conferring any very essential benefits on the city; but his gentleness, urbanity and benevolence, secured him the respect and the affections of the people; and his literary works will transmit his name with honour to posterity."[11]

It is worth noting that Stuart, at this period of history, was writing about his contemporaries or near contemporaries, and that he was without the benefit of the historical perspective that succeeding decades and centuries undoubtedly bring. Today it is obvious that Newcome and his writings left almost no mark on the city or its history, compared to Robinson.

James Stuart was in even greater difficulty when writing about Newcome's successor Archbishop William Stuart, who held office from 1800-1822, at precisely the time as his namesake was researching, writing and producing his book. James Stuart decided not to write a detailed biography of the then current Archbishop of Armagh, but paid tribute to his industry and vigilance. He noted "... it would be impossible to raise him higher in the estimation of those who have witnessed the whole tenor of his life, and have made his worth the measure of their approbation."[12]

Archbishop Stuart was said to have been a lineal descendent of Robert

II, King of Scotland, and his wife was a descendant of William Penn, founder of Pennsylvania. Stuart is commemorated in the Cathedral as a kneeling figure in marble, created by the sculptor Sir Francis Chantrey. As a dutiful Prelate he tried to make improvements to the building, but with limited success, as modern commentators have pointed out.

According to the Official Guide to the Cathedral, the works carried out in Stuart's time "tended more than any previous ones to obliterate the history and alter the fabric of the building." The historian Dr Peter Galloway stated bluntly that "a very poor restoration took place in 1802 at the beginning of the archiepiscopate of William Stuart" and it was left to Archbishop Beresford to take the place in hand. By 1834 the Cathedral was reported to be in such a state of decay as to be "unworthy of any considerable expenditure towards its improvement."

The original intention of building a new Cathedral was opposed by the Archdeacon of Armagh Edward Stopford, and others. Instead, Archbishop Beresford supervised the restoration between 1834-37 at a cost of £34,000, of which he supplied the then very considerable sum of £24,000 from his own pocket.[13]

Beresford, the younger son of the second Earl and First Marquis of Waterford, came from a wealthy background and like some Archbishops before him he had the means, and the inclination and vision, to be a generous benefactor to Armagh and its people. Again, like his predecessors from well-connected and privileged backgrounds, he had access to the most prestigious educational establishments of his day, including Eton and Christ Church, Oxford, where he graduated with a BA in 1793, obtaining his MA three years later. He received his DD in 1805.

He was ordained in 1797, and was appointed Rector of Clonegan and Newtown Lennan in the Diocese of Lismore, Waterford. He steadily made his mark in church circles, holding various appointments including successively the Bishoprics of Cork and Ross, Raphoe, and Clogher, before becoming Archbishop of Dublin for a brief period, and then Primate at Armagh.

Though improvements to the Cathedral were by no means the first undertaking which consumed the energies and attention of the new Archbishop, they were of crucial importance. He commissioned a young English architect Lewis Cottingham to carry out the work. The entire building, except for the tower, was faced with sandstone. The restoration included changes to the great west door, which ruined some of the fine old architecture. The spire was removed and the tower left as it is today. A stone screen was erected between the nave and the choir, but this was removed during further work carried out from 1887-88. The screen now stands in the south transept between the Regimental Chapel of the Royal Irish Fusiliers and the choir vestry.

There is no doubt, according to one observer, that Cottingham's restoration was

> "thorough and effective and saved the building from demolition. But his work involved the virtual rebuilding of the cathedral and the obliteration of what remained above ground of Archbishop O Scannail's cathedral".[14]

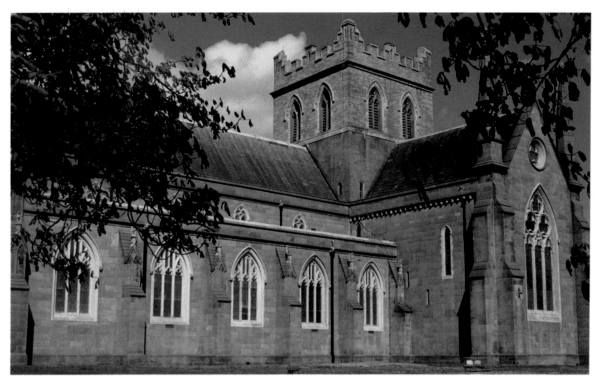

St Patrick's Church of Ireland Cathedral, Armagh, which was visited by W.M Thackeray in the 1840's. He noted "The Church is small, but extremely neat, fresh and handsome - almost too handsome". He was impressed that the sermon lasted only twenty minutes, and asked "Can this be Ireland?"

The resplendent lectern in the Church of Ireland Cathedral.

Despite the restoration and the alterations, the cathedral in the opinion of some contemporary observers, lacked a certain antiquity - given the long history of church buildings on this site, and the lack of direct and discernible continuity with the past, as evidenced in the 19th century building. This feeling was well-summarised by W M Thackeray, who visited the Cathedral in the early 1840's.

He noted

"The church is small, but extremely neat, fresh and handsome - almost too handsome - covered with spick and span gilding and carved work in the style of the 13th century".

He was also impressed that the sermon at Morning Service lasted only twenty minutes, and exclaimed "Can this be Ireland!"

His overall view of the Cathedral only a few years after the Beresford-Cottingham restoration was perceptive, and to the point;

"The Cathedral is quite too complete. It is of the twelfth century, but not the least venerable. It is neat and trim like a lady's drawing-room. It wants a hundred years at least to cool the raw colour of the stones, and to dull the brightness of the gilding; all which benefits, no doubt, time will bring to pass, and future Cocknies setting off from London-bridge after breakfast in an aerial machine, may come to hear the morning service here, and not remark the faults which have struck a too susceptible tourist of the nineteenth century."[15]

Apart from Thackeray's prophetic observation about Londoners travelling by air after breakfast and arriving in time for morning service in Armagh (even more convenient if one has breakfast on the plane), the present generation has the benefit of some 150 years hindsight to see whether his comments about the sandstone colour of the Cathedral improving with age were borne out, or not.

Galloway, however, notes that while Cottingham's work regrettably masked much of the ancient fabric, and even if it was alien to Armagh, it

Lord John George Beresford, Archbishop of Armagh 1822-1862 who followed the pioneering trail of Archbishop Robinson and further enhanced the city of Armagh.

remains antiquarian in inspiration. "He bridges the gap between Strawberry Hill Gothick and the romantic revival. He was on the list of architects condemned by The Ecclesiologist, but his restoration represents an old-fashioned pre-Tractarian High Church tradition that has an integrity of its own."[16]

Whatever the merits, or otherwise, of the Cathedral's architecture in Beresford's time, he had many other matters to occupy his mind. Shortly after he was appointed to Armagh, there was an outbreak of typhus in the area, and as a consequence he erected a Fever Hospital on Caledon Road, now Cathedral Road. It was described thus in Lewis's *Topographical Dictionary*, written in 1841;

> "The Fever Hospital was erected ... at an entire cost, including the purchase and laying out of grounds, of about £3,500, defrayed by the present Primate ... by whose munificence it is solely supported. It is a chaste and handsome building of hewn limestone ... with a projection rearward containing on the ground floor a physician's room, a warm bath and washing room and on the other floors, male and female nurses' rooms and slop rooms in the latter of which there are shower baths.
>
> "On the ground floor of the front building are the entrance hall, the matron's sitting and sleeping rooms and a kitchen and pantry; the first and second floors are respectively appropriated to the use of male and female patients, each floor containing two wards - a fever and a recovery ward - the former having ten beds, the latter five, making in all thirty beds.
>
> "The subordinate buildings and offices are well calculated to promote the object of the institution; there is a good garden with walks open to convalescents; and in regard to cleanliness, economy and suitable accommodation for its suffering inmates, the hospital is entitled to rank among the finest in the Province."

In 1851 the hospital became the Macan Asylum for the Blind, and was named after Arthur Jacob Macan who was Sovereign of the City, (Council leader) from 1795-97. In the 1970's this building, then in disrepair, was demolished and replaced by modern housing.

Archbishop Beresford not only masterminded new projects, but he also updated a number of significant developments which had been initiated by Archbishop Robinson. These included, in 1825, the addition of an entire storey to the Palace itself as well as important changes to farm buildings

MARY,
MANY YEARS THE WIFE,
AND 13 YEARS THE RELICT OF
JAMES STUART, ESQ., LL.D.
DIED ON THE 15TH DAY OF NOV. 1853, AGED 75.
THE WIFE AND WIDOW OF ONE
SO GIFTED AND SO USEFUL IN HIS GENERATION.
HERSELF WORTHY, CLAIMS REMEMBRANCE.

"THE GRAVE HISTORIAN PENS THE DEEDS OF OLD,
HIMSELF TO VANISH AS A TALE WHEN TOLD;
THE BOLD POLEMIC WIELDS ITHURIEL'S SPEAR,
THEN STANDS WHERE CROWNS, AND HARPS AND PALMS APPEAR
AND LOVE TO CHEER HIS EARTHLY TOIL IS GIVEN,
WHOSE NIGHT ON EARTH IS ENDLESS DAY IN HEAVEN."

JAMES AND MARY STUART
A plaque to the memory of
James Stuart and his wife, which
was formerly in Christ Church,
Belfast, and is now in the Armagh
Public Library.

within the estate. The farm was a going concern and was well-managed. A copy of one of the bills for the "Outgoings" in 1854 shows that a mare cost the equivalent of £20.50 in today's money, a harness £13.75 and horse-shoeing £7.68, while a steward's salary was £80.00. It is also worth noting that there was a payment of £5.87 for "Income Tax under schedule D", thus proving that the only two certainties of life, then as now, were "death and taxes!"

In 1827 the Archbishop had a new Corn Market built at the Shambles, partly with money from a Toll Committee which received tolls from people selling goods at different markets in the town. In the 1820's, and later, Beresford made substantial financial contributions to the Observatory, in 1845 he extended the Public Library, and in 1849 he donated funds for the enlargement of the Royal School.

Beresford was noted for his philantrophy and it was estimated that "his Grace's expenditure on objects of benevolence and for the advancement of religion and literature exceeded £280,600"[17] This included not only his donations towards buildings and improvements in Armagh but also gifts to poor clergy and other people falling on hard times. He was also a considerable benefactor to Trinity College Dublin, where he became Vice-Chancellor in 1829, and Chancellor in 1851. As has been noted earlier, he was instrumental in helping to preserve the Book of Armagh. As well as paying £300 to help secure it for the Library at Trinity, he also gave his Chaplain Dr Reeves £500 to have it printed.

Beresford, like Robinson, was unmarried, but he had a favourite sister Lady Anne who often stayed at the Palace, and also in a cottage near the present entrance to the Demesne. There was a walk from Lady Anne's cottage towards St Bridget's Well, which was then part of the Demesne but is now in the grounds of Armagh Rugby Club. St Bridget's Well was said to have been visited by the Saint in the 6th century and the waters were reputed to cure diseases, particularly those of the eye. Lady Anne is reported to have sent some of this water to Queen Victoria when the Primate visited the Queen in 1837.

On 18 July 1862, Archbishop Beresford died at Woburn Abbey, near Donaghadee in the home of George Dunbar who had married one of his nieces. The Primate, then in his 89th year, had been ill for some months and had gone to the coast in the vain hope that the sea air might lead to a recovery. His body was brought back to Armagh and he lay in state in the private Chapel until his funeral on 30 July. An un-named writer described of the events of that day;

"Following a brief service in the Primate's Chapel, the procession was formed with all the care and accuracy of detail that Sir Bernard Burke, the Ulster King of Arms, was capable of. The high crimson velveteen sarcophagus with its arms, mitre, the jewel of the Prelate of the Order of St Patrick and other decorations, was escorted down the main drive and through the narrow streets of the City, where it passed in stately dignity.

"The bells tolled on Macha's Hill. The four horses and his carriage - the harness decorated with silver mitres, the carriage with the arms of the See of Armagh and the bearings of the Beresfords - with its coachmen and footmen was empty.

"The town commissioners in mourning cloaks and black staves led. After them came the Palace servants, then the clergy in gowns, followed by the Ulster King of Arms in heraldic attire. Next the Lord Lieutenant, followed by Marquesses, Earls, Viscounts, Barons and Baronets, rank upon rank. Behind them the relatives, the Bishops, the Privy Councillors, the Judges and Members of Parliament, all in due array according to their degree.

"At the Cathedral gates, white-robed choristers chanted Purcell and Croft on the way into the church and again proceeding to the crypt where the burial took place, and so ended the pomp of the last of the great heraldically arranged funerals so dear to earlier generations." It was also reported that at the Archbishop's funeral and Roman Catholic Primate, Dr. Dixon, and the Presbyterian Moderator, Dr. Cooke, walked side by side.[18]

Archbishop Beresford was succeeded by his relative Marcus Gervais Beresford, the second son of George Beresford, Bishop of Kilmore and Ardagh, and the last Archbishop to be appointed by the Crown. Within seven years the long-threatened legislation to dis-establish the Church of Ireland was given Royal assent, and for the rest of the Archbishop's term of office, until his death in 1885, he was deeply involved in the onerous task of providing for the future organisation and well-being of the Church .

This meant that he had little time to improve upon the elaborate building programme of his predecessor and namesake Primate Lord John George Beresford, and that of Primate Richard Robinson earlier. The magnificent work carried out by these two men in the period from the mid-18th to the mid-19th centuries was unsurpassed, but the period between the mid-19th and early-20th centuries also witnessed another important development which changed the face of the landscape in St Patrick's city. This was the establishment of the magnificent St Patrick's Roman Catholic Cathedral which sits on a hill looking across at the Church of Ireland Cathedral, both of them representing the twin pillars of Irish Christendom.

NOTES

1 Stuart. Op. Cit. p.453
2 Ibid. p.454
3 Hugh Dixon. p.9
   The Buildings of Armagh,
   published by the Ulster Architectural
   Heritage Society, 1992
4 Op. Cit. GO Simms. p.3
5 Stuart. Op. Cit. p.455
6 Ibid. pp.450-451
7 Ibid. pp.468-472
8 Ibid. p.467
9 Ibid. p.74
10 Ibid. p.459
11 Ibid. p.461
12 Ibid. p.463
13 P.15, The Cathedrals of Ireland, published by the Institute of Irish Studies of The Queen's University of Belfast, 1992, and also p.6, Fallow, Cathedral Churches of Ireland
14 Galloway, Op. Cit. p.15
15 The Irish Sketch-book, 1843, pp.216-217
16 Galloway, Op. Cit. pp.16-17
17 Coleman, Op. Cit. p.415
18 Archives of Armagh City and District Council

James Stuart

James Stuart, whose seminal work *Historical Memoirs of the City of Armagh for a Period of 1373 Years* has been quoted widely in this volume, gave a unique portrait of St Patrick's city from the earliest Patrician times up to 1819, when the book was published.

Nearly a century later, a new edition was published at the instigation of Cardinal Logue. This was in connection with the Great Bazaar of 1900 which raised a large sum for the final stages of building St Patrick's Roman Catholic Cathedral. The new edition was "revised, corrected and largely re-written" by the Reverend Father Ambrose Coleman, a Member of the Royal Irish Academy. He adopted a new arrangement of chapters, made necessary corrections in accordance with the historical scholarship and sources available after Stuart's time, and produced a system of more standardised spelling.

However the narrative remains remarkably faithful to that of Stuart, to whom Father Coleman pays gracious tribute in his Introduction:

"When it is borne in mind that Stuart lived in a time of religious rancour, it will appear remarkable how free his history is from bigotry. The narrative is as accurate as the authorities warranted; controversy and controverted questions are avoided; the same treatment is accorded to Catholics as to Protestants."

Coleman points out that certain omissions are to be expected "from a Protestant historian" such as Stuart, and refers to the "dreadful persecution which the Catholics were subjected to for centuries". To be fair, quite a number of these were mentioned by Stuart, but perhaps not sufficiently so to satisfy Father Coleman, who was writing nearly a century later.

However Coleman's regard for Stuart's text and his sensitive comments bear witness to his understanding of the duty of the historian who is obliged to take a dispassionate and clearly objective view of the facts at his disposal, though – as he points out himself – a total lack of bias is almost humanly impossible. Coleman expresses the hope that he himself, where he applies criticism or brings out "adverse" facts, "has done so without bias" to Protestants and Catholics alike.

"The historian, it is a truism to say, must not colour facts in the interests of any party, but place them on record as they really happened; yet, such is the power of personal bias and religious rancour, that an unprejudiced narrative is very rarely to be found."

Coleman also provides an intriguing biography of Stuart, who was born in Armagh in 1764 and educated at the Royal School. He graduated with a BA degree from Trinity College Dublin in 1789, at the age of 25, and was called to the Irish Bar, but never practised. Instead, he turned to journalism and became the first editor of the *Newry Telegraph*, from 1815 to 1819, as well as editor of *The Newry Magazine*.

During this period he worked on his *Historical Memoirs of the City of Armagh*, which the Newry Telegraph printed and published in 1819, under his direct supervision. Father Coleman notes generously "Considering the difficulties under which he laboured, the pressure of his journalistic duties, his imperfect access to authorities, and the generally deficient state of Irish historical studies at the time he wrote, the book is a monument of patient industry and of devotion to learning."

Stuart later moved to Belfast and became editor of *The Belfast News-Letter*. He published some theological letters in book form, under the title *The Protestant Layman*, and in 1827 founded a publication called *The Guardian and Constitutional Advocate*, but he had to give this up due to ill-health.

He died, without issue, in Belfast in 1840 at the age of 76, and was buried in the Belfast Cemetery on the Antrim Road. He was commemorated by a plaque, according to Coleman, "in the north-east aisle of Christ Church, Belfast". Almost a century after the publication of his *Historical Memoirs of the City of Armagh* it is a fitting tribute that his book is still regarded as a collector's item, and is widely-used and quoted by a large variety of authors writing about the city of Armagh and its surrounding area.

Professor Leslie Clarkson of Queen's University, Belfast notes that although Stuart's history "is laden with apparently irrelevant detail and prefaced by a seemingly even more irrelevant introduction" about the existence of St Patrick, in fact neither is irrelevant. "The detail adds much to our knowledge of the eighteenth-century city."[1]

Clarkson further points out that Stuart's description of Armagh and the neighbouring countryside "was not mere community loyalty – although it was that- but acute observation."[2] He continues: "It is easy to sentimentalise the state of Armagh from Stuart's devoted – almost devotional – history. The city was disturbed by sectarian rioting in 1717 – although to judge from the accounts, the trouble was fuelled more by alcohol than by faith – and it was touched by clashes between Peep-o'Day Boys and Defenders at the end of the century.

"The racecourse where the Mall now is, was the focus for debauchery, drunkeness and riot. The city suffered badly from hunger and disease during the 1750's. And until Archbishop Robinson set about rebuilding, the place was a slum."[3] However, there was an economic boom during the 18th century, especially from about 1730, and based to a considerable extent on the export of yarn and cloth.

"Armagh was ideally situated in the linen triangle to reap the economic benefits and it was located, too, in the fertile northern part of the county. The city was, additionally, an ecclesiastical, educational and legal centre. It was governed by people who fitted Adam Smith's stereotype of economic man driven by self-interest, but in the process maximising the utility of all. The handsome face of Armagh that so pleased Stuart reflected a solid and well-founded prosperity."[4]

The revised version of Stuart's memoirs by the Reverend Father Ambrose Coleman, published in 1900. The picture is of Cardinal Logue, who suggested the project.

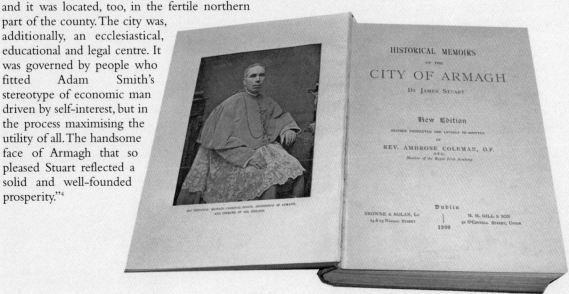

NOTES

1 "The City of Armagh in the Eighteenth Century, Page 1, in a book "Armagh: History and Society", edited by Dr AJ Hughes and Professor W. Nolan and published by Geography Publications, Dublin 2001
2 Ibid. Page 2
3 Ibid. Page 21
4 Ibid. Page 21

Hanged for Cow-Stealing

The harshness of life in 18th century Ulster is illustrated by the story of the execution of a man called Mackin for stealing a cow. He was found guilty at the Armagh Assizes in 1704.

"The day before his execution, he gave public notice that it would be worth people's while to come ten miles to see him at the gallows, and hear what he had to say. Upon mounting the ladder and viewing the gallows, he said 'Hah! am I come to you at last?' and then, turning to the people 'Pray, gentlemen, do not crowd together. The farthest off shall hear me as plain as the nearest.' Then he began 'Gentlemen, I have been guilty of every crime except murder'."

An extraordinary banter between the condemned man and the crowd ensued. A bystander shouted out "Pray Mr Mackin, do you know anything of my heifer?" "Yes" said he. "Pray, then what is become of her?" "I took her to Middleton" said Mackin – "I knocked her on the head – I sold the skin – the beef was very good – I sold it at a good rate – and I put the money in my pocket. After this, gentlemen, as little as you think, I stole half a dozen of wethers near this town, and drove them through the midst of it." One asked whether any of the Bishop of Kilmore's sheep were among them? "Yes," said he "and they were the best mutton I ever handled".

Tiring of such banter, Mackin turned his gallows humour onto the sheriff. He asked, "Will you give me leave to step down?" "No," said he "I cannot now grant you that favour." "Well," said Mackin "I am sure of going to heaven, for the priest gave me absolution yesterday." Upon which, he was turned off, bidding the sheriff farewell.

The criminal's mother, above seventy years old, was present when her son was cut down. She went to Dr Sheridan's house to beg towards a winding sheet for her son. Some persons there contributed on the occasion. It was delivered to the old woman by a young gentleman. She was so elated, after her success, that after giving her thanks and blessing, she said, "My Johnny always had good luck!"[1]

As an assize town, with a steady stream of people literally going to and coming from the law, Armagh generated good business for its inn-keepers. One particular favourite was a Mrs Peggy Stringer, whose death in 1747 inspired the following lines:

> "Here lies Peggy Stringer who lov'd in her soul
> A toast – and a lawyer – a bout – and a bowl;
> And because in a grave there's no drink to be had,
> For abelly-ful living, had drunk herself dead."[2]

NOTES

1 Stuart. Op. Cit. pp.530-531
2 Clarkson. Op. Cit. p.12

'The zeal of great Primates had inspired the work … of building St. Patrick's Cathedral …. but it would never have been done without the loyalty of priests and people. Priests had gone all over the world to collect money, and at home the people had answered every appeal, particularly in the historic parish of Armagh.'

Official Guide to St. Patrick's Cathedral

Prior to the decision to build a new cathedral, the Roman Catholic population in Armagh had worshipped at the local Chapel in a side street, which was built shortly after 1750. Despite enlargements and improvements to the building, it proved inadequate for the needs of a growing congregation. Writing some seventy years later, Stuart noted that

> "Dr Byrne preaches to a very large, and very respectable, congregation. His chapel, though capable of containing a multitude of people, is excessively crowded on Sundays; and it frequently happens that numbers of his hearers are unable to gain admission, and are obliged to worship in the open air."

> "The Roman Catholic inhabitants of the parish of Armagh, unlike those of Killeavy etc. can all speak the English language fluently. They are remarkably fond of their spiritual pastors, on whose superintending care they place the utmost reliance; and are in general a peaceable, well-conducted, and devout body of people."[1]

Though this " Old Chapel " was still used until 1935, it was obvious even more than a century earlier that a much larger church was needed, but the impetus to build a Cathedral was not just the result of a need for better premises. It was also part of the resurgence of Roman Catholicism in the wake of a successful campaign for Catholic Emancipation.

In the late eighteenth century, Catholics formed the largest group in Armagh but they were the worst off. In 1770, thirty-two per cent of the households were Anglican, twenty-seven were Presbyterian and forty-one per cent Roman Catholic. One third of the Presbyterian householders were employed in manufacturing, transport and trade, compared with only seventeen per cent of Catholic householders and twenty-two per cent of Anglicans.

In contrast, fewer than four per cent of Presbyterians were labourers, whereas thirty per cent of Catholics were labourers. "For Anglicans the figure was under three per cent. But only eight per cent of Presbyterians held positions in government or the professions, whereas among Anglicans the figure was twenty percent. Only three point five per cent of Roman Catholics could be classed as professionals."[2]

Daniel O'Connell, who dominated politics in Ireland during the first half of the nineteenth century. His successful campaign for Catholic Emancipation led to the return of the Roman Catholic Archbishops to live in Armagh after some three centuries of absence.

Roman Catholics occupied the lowest strata of society.
"Although they could be admitted to the freedom of the city, they could not become burgesses or sovereigns unless...they renounced their faith. " Sixty-one of the 70 labourers in 1770 were Catholics. They were well represented in trades dealing in food, particularly butchers. There was some geographical segregation of Catholics and Protestants. In 1770 the former were concentrated in three streets-Callen, Irish and Castle-then almost the suburbs of this tightly-knit city, whereas the Protestants lived in the commercial heart formed by Market, English and Scotch streets."[3]

However, it is important not to exaggerate the social cleavage between Protestants and Catholics.
"The city was small and Callen, Irish and Castle streets soon ran into Market, English and Scotch streets. Anglican, Presbyterian and Catholic clergy associated freely- Primate Lindsay was an exception - and all denominations rubbed shoulders in the market place."[4]

There were differences in the composition of households.
"Church of Ireland households were eight per cent bigger than Roman Catholic households, and six per cent larger than those of Presbyterians. The difference was explained mainly by the presence of servants in Anglican households, but who were almost totally absent in Catholic establishments."[5]

However, there was another important difference.
"The Catholic households were much more likely to be composed of conjugal family units-parents and children- than Protestant households. Among the Church of Ireland community in particular, seventeen per cent of all households consisted of only one person. The houses built for clergy widows provide part of the explanation. But Anglicans could afford to live apart from their relatives to a much greater extent than could Catholics. So Anglican households embraced both large groups composed of families and servants and lonely widows or spinsters, the ageing survivors of once large families."[6]

When the Act of Union was passed in 1800 most of the old penal laws enacted between 1695 and 1728 had been repealed. Catholics could now maintain schools, vote in elections and join the professions, but they could not sit in Parliament, or hold high office in the civil service, the legal profession, or the armed forces. In the first two decades of the nineteenth century, the struggle for Catholic emancipation was carried on by an uneasy alliance of landlords, merchants and professional men. However, the campaign began in earnest from 1823, with the formation of the Catholic Association by Daniel O'Connell. Significantly, he was able to harness the considerable backing of the Catholic clergy. Added impetus was given by the inauguration of a Catholic Rent of one penny a month, which even the poorest could afford. This was a master-stroke because it involved thousands of ordinary Catholics who felt that they had a direct stake in the campaign.
"To pay a subscription to a movement increases one's interest in it, and now many thousands of Catholics, in all walks of life, were identified with the Catholic Association. Contemporary observers noticed the improved morale and corporate spirit of the Catholic body. As a Church of Ireland Bishop, Dr. Jebb of Limerick, noted:'There is what we of this generation have never before witnessed, a complete union of the Roman Catholic body...In truth, an Irish revolution has, in great measure, been effected.'"[7]

Opposite: Archbishop William Crolly, whose vision and drive led to the establishment of St Patrick's Roman Catholic Cathedral, Armagh - outside which his statue now stands.

The statue of Archbishop Daniel McGettigan who finished the structure of St Patrick's Roman Catholic Cathedral, Armagh.

On 13 April, 1829 the Catholic Emancipation Act became law and all the major remaining restrictions on Catholics were removed. It was an outstanding victory for O'Connell and the Catholic Association, and even though Catholics were still barred from becoming Lord-Lieutenant or Lord-Chancellor, they could become MP's, judges, generals and admirals.

"And even if the number of Catholics who could aspire to any of these positions was very small, the whole body gained in morale from the removal of the taint of inequality."[8]

One of the most visible signs of the new freedom was the return of the Roman Catholic Archbishops to live in Armagh after some three centuries of absence, and "everywhere a miracle of church building began which never lost momentum for the next fifty years"[9]

By January 1846 it was reported that seventeen new churches had been consecrated in the previous decade, that five more were nearly ready for consecration, and that the archdiocese would then have one hundred and two churches. Those completed and consecrated included Mountjoy, Coalisland, Eglish, Portadown, Moneymore, Ardboe, Dundalk, Magherafelt, Ballinderry, Newtownhamilton and Donaghmore.[10]

However the *piece de resistance* was undoubtedly the Cathedral itself, the establishment of which owed much to the vision and drive of Dr William Crolly, Archbishop of Armagh from 1835-49. He was born in Ballykilbeg, near Downpatrick, in June 1780 and educated at a local preparatory school, which had Catholic staff and also some Protestant pupils. At fourteen he went to a school in Downpatrick where he was given a classical education by the local Presbyterian Minister, Dr James Neilson, whose Assistant was a local Catholic named Doran. When Mr. Doran later set up his own school, it was attended by the young Crolly.

During the 1798 rebellion Doran was arrested for his allegedly seditious political views and he was incarcerated in Downpatrick gaol. However, the prison Governor allowed him to continue giving lessons, and the future Archbishop of Armagh "was among the pupils who pursued his secondary studies in this unlikely and uncongenial environment."[11]

Having read a life of St. Patrick, and having been inspired by this volume and by the Patrician associations with the Downpatrick area, the young William Crolly decided to become a priest. At twenty one he entered the then newly-established Maynooth seminary, and he was one of the first students to be appointed to its staff, and later one of its first graduates to become a Bishop. For thirteen years he was a parish priest in Belfast, and for ten years Bishop of Down and Connor. During his time in Belfast he built up a considerable reputation for pastoral service, academic ability and administrative competence, as well as enjoying good relationships with the

Protestant clergy and laity in the predominantly Presbyterian city.

"Catholics were not alone in wishing the Primate well in his new mission. The Northern Whig paid him a kind tribute:'It is almost superfluous to say, that he deservedly carries with him from Belfast the respect and esteem of all denominations...we can only express our general opinion when we say, that as a citizen of Belfast, his conduct for a long series of years, was eminently calculated to command admiration and regard.' " [12]

On his appointment as Archbishop of Armagh, he made the important decision to reside in the city, just as Archbishop Robinson had done in his time, though he reportedly also resided for part of the year in Drogheda, in "Paradise Row." Perhaps it was no coincidence that both men showed that they had a stake in the city by living in it and by instituting, in their different ways, important building programmes which would underline the special role of St Patrick's city in the religious and spiritual life of the country.

Baron George Minne, the distinguished Belgian musician and organist of St Patrick's Roman Catholic Cathedral, Armagh, since 1959.

As Archbishop of Armagh from 1835-49, Archbishop William Crolly played a key role in the ecclesiastical and religious affairs of Ireland at a time of serious controversies affecting the Roman Catholic Church, but this did not deter him from his pastoral and religious role within the city and diocese of Armagh. His first task was to build a seminary, St Patrick's College, to cater for vocations to the priesthood, (this is mentioned in a later chapter) and he then turned his attention to the development of a National Cathedral of Saint Patrick.

He negotiated for suitable land with the Earl of Dartrey, who offered a splendid hilly site which afforded commanding views over the city and countryside, and which would be a most appropriate setting for the new show-piece Cathedral. According to tradition, as has been noted earlier, this is the hill where St. Patrick himself carried the fawn on his shoulders to a "safe place", with the doe following.

From the start, the Catholic Cathedral would differ from the Protestant building on St Patrick's hill. The Church of Ireland Cathedral had evolved through many centuries, and its development had been seriously damaged, and sometimes virtually halted, by acts of nature and the violence and incursions of man, and at times by the " improvements" of well-intentioned but misguided benefactors.

Much of the development of the Protestant Cathedral, particularly from the seventeenth century onwards, had been financed by those Archbishops who had the vision and to funds to carry out refurbishments. The Roman Catholic Cathedral, on the other hill, enjoyed the advantage of starting literally from the ground up, with no historical baggage. But it also meant that the building work did not have the patronage of wealthy Archbishops,

"St Patrick and the Fawn", a sculpture by John Behan (O'Fiaich Memorial Library and Archive).

and much of the finance had to be raised through public subscription. To this end Archbishop Crolly formed a local committee of laymen, and they in turn, with the clergy, organised house-to-house collections, first in the parish of Armagh, and later throughout the diocese.

The architect appointed was Thomas J. Duff of Newry, and his plan envisaged a cathedral in Perpendicular Gothic, in a style which he had used in the cathedral he had designed for Newry. It was to be built of Armagh limestone, and Dungannon freestone.

The foundation stone was laid on St Patrick's Day 1840, in the midst of a great gathering of people.

"The first stone was laid, with impressive ceremonies, amid a vast assemblage of clergy and laity. St Patrick's plant 'the dear, immortal shamrock' decorating every breast on that day, bore a more than ordinary significance to the eyes of those who came to witness the laying of the foundation-stone of the new cathedral"[13]

The money continued to come in, and the building-work went on until 1847, when the Great Famine was at its height, and collections were diverted to provide funds for famine relief. The causes, ravages, and social and political implications of the famine have been well-chronicled elsewhere, but Ambrose Macaulay in his life of William Crolly, summarises its effect, particularly on the clergy, many of whom became victims themselves.

"When the famine eventually ended it had claimed about one million lives and well over a million had emigrated. It was the greatest natural catastrophe in Europe in the nineteenth century, and given the constraining principles within which British economic thought operated, it would have required intervention of a kind that the government was not prepared to make.

"Clergy of all denominations were overwhelmed by the sheer magnitude and duration of the catastrophe. All they could do was to organise and sponsor relief measures within the means at their disposal and co-operate at local level with the official schemes approved by the government. And as the toll of victims among them indicates, they did their best in very trying circumstances."[14]

With Cathedral funds diverted to famine relief, work on the building came to a halt, when the walls were at a height of only thirty-four feet. (The so-called " Famine Line" can be seen in the Cathedral's interior structure even today.) Nevertheless in 1848 Dr Crolly was negotiating for the timber which was to form the roof of the Cathedral,[15] but his death due to Asiatic cholera in 1849 put an end to any more work on the building for a further five years.

Archbishop Crolly's funeral was well-attended. "Lord John Beresford, Archbishop of Armagh, clergy of the established and Presbyterian Churches, and gentry of the county joined Catholic bishops, clergy and laity in one of the largest funeral processions ever seen in the north of Ireland."[16] Archbishop Crolly was buried, as he had stipulated, under the sanctuary of his unfinished Cathedral, and today his statue is displayed, most appropriately, outside the completed building.

Dr Paul Cullen, Archbishop of Armagh from 1849-52, made his mark as a leading prelate. He "stamped the trademarks of discipline, devotion and docility on the Irish Catholic Church in the 1850's "[17]. Though he brought to Armagh the teaching communities of the Sacred Heart and the Irish Christian Brothers, (this is recorded in a later chapter) he was- according to the Official Guide to the Cathedral- " indifferent to this particular project," that is, the completion of the building.

Archbishop Cullen, who was appointed Archbishop of Dublin in 1852 and became Ireland's first Cardinal in June 1866, was not only conservative in doctine but also resolutely opposed to armed nationalism. However, there was another side to him. "If he made enemies among the revolutionary groups of the time, Paul Cullen remained a life-long friend of the poor....At Eccles Street, he led a simple, rather frugal work-filled existence. In the afternoons he often liked to walk in the grounds of his beloved Clonliffe College, which he founded in 1859 to train priests for the diocese.

" Even there, his nephew and chaplain, Fr. William Cullen recalled, he kept his pockets full of small coins for the numerous beggars who were only to ready to relieve him of them on his stroll through the grounds."[18]

The development of St. Patrick's Cathedral was left to Cardinal Cullen's successor Dr Joseph Dixon, Primate from 1852-66. He determined that the building-work should continue, and Easter Monday 1854 was declared Resumption Monday, with a pontifical High Mass being held in the still roofless Cathedral.

"The weather was most unpropitious. A dreadful storm raged during the Mass and sermon, and showers of pitiless hail came down on the bare heads of the congregation, in places where the covering above had been rent by the force of the wind. Just after the Elevation, a gust of wind swept through the whole Cathedral and extinguished the candles on the altar. But the violence of the storm did not damp the ardour of the people: a large collection made was the augury of still better things for the future.[19]

The original architect Thomas Duff had died, and his successor James Joseph McCarthy, an outstanding neo-Gothic Irish architect, was known as ' the Irish Pugin." He designed other Roman Catholic Cathedrals in Ireland including those in Monaghan, Derry and Thurles, and at Armagh he changed the Perpendicular Gothic style of Duff to that of the Decorated Gothic of the 14th century.

To fund these developments a huge week-long Armagh Bazaar was held in 1865, and prizes were donated by the Pope, and the Emperors of Austria and France. Incidentally a grandfather clock which is still in the Vestry was a prize which remains unclaimed! The appeal for support was answered generously and the then large sum of £7,000 was raised from home and abroad.

Dr Dixon died in 1866 and his successor Dr Kieran, a sick and ageing man, was unable to maintain the momentum of the building project. In 1870, however, the year of the first Vatican Council, Dr Daniel McGettigan, a Donegal man, became Archbishop, and he was determined to finish the structure. In August 1873 the Cathedral was dedicated in the presence of a large congregation of 20,000 people including many who had come from

Standing the test of time - this Dublin made clock which is still in the vestry of St Patrick's Roman Catholic Cathedral, is an unclaimed prize in an 1865 Bazaar to raise funds for the building. Prizes were donated by his Holiness the Pope and the Emperors of Austria and France. Some £7000 - a large sum in those days - was raised from home and abroad.

Erected by a few Irish patriots to the memory of Hugh Carberry of Armagh, a volunteer of the Transvaal Irish Brigade who fell at the battle of Modder Spruit, 23 October 1899, aged 32 years, "bravely fighting for the Boers against the unjust aggression of England".

Cardinal Michael Logue, Archbishop of Armagh 1887–1924. He was created a Cardinal in 1893. Under his guidance the interior of the Cathedral was completed, the freehold of the lease was secured for less than £1000, and the building consecrated in 1904.

Britain, Australia and America.

A statue of Archbishop McGettigan, who finished the building, stands outside the Cathedral, not far from that of Archbishop Crolly, who started it off. During Dr McGettigan's time also, the Archbishop's House "Ara Coeli" was completed, as well as the Sexton's lodge and the broad sweep of the steps up to the Cathedral.

When Dr – later Cardinal – Michael Logue was Archbishop, the final stages of refurbishment were completed beautifully, under his direction.. " In 1899 he took stock of the situation. The cathedral foundation stone was as old as himself, having been laid in 1840, the year of his birth. A new century was about to begin and still the cathedral remained unfinished due to lack of funds. Action was needed."[20] In 1898 the freehold of the lease for the Cathedral grounds was secured from the Earl of Dartrey for less than £1,000.

106

In 1900 a second Great Bazaar was held, and the then huge sum of £30,000 was raised. However there was more disappointment when it was discovered that major repairs had to be carried out on the roof and spires. Nevertheless in 1904 the consecration of the Cathedral marked the final stage of a long process to complete a most beautiful building which has been rightly described thus:

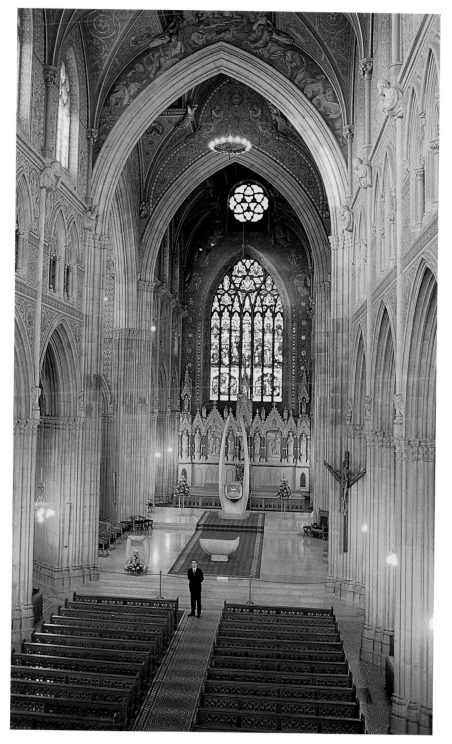

An interior view of St Patrick's Roman Catholic Cathedral, Armagh, with the new Sanctuary.

1.

2.

3.

4.

1. Cardinal O'Donnell,
Primate 1924-1927.

2. Cardinal MacCrory,
Primate 1928-1945.

3. Cardinal D'Alton,
Primate 1946-1963.

4. Cardinal Conway,
Primate 1963-1977.

" Entering it for the first time is a breathtaking experience. The great
height, the exquisite pefection of architectural detail, and the caring decoration
of every surface of the walls, which is neither garish nor overdone, uplifts the
heart and mind. The unstained clerestory windows give a wonderful high-level
brightness, and although the building has a soaring loftiness, there is not a trace
of gloom. This is Gothic revival at its very best."[21]

It also marked the fulfilment of an act of faith by successive generations
of clergy and laity. As the Official Guide to the Cathedral sums up "The zeal
of great Primates had inspired the work but it would never have been done
without the loyalty and devotion of priests and people. Priests had gone all
over the world to collect money, and at home the people had answered every
appeal, particularly in the historic parish of Armagh. The Papal Legate at the
consecration rightly hailed them as a generous and faithful people."

NOTES

1 Op. Cit. p.547
2 Clarkson. Op. Cit. pp.15-16
3 Ibid. p.17
4 Ibid. p.18
5 Ibid. p.18
6 Ibid. p.18
7 JH Whyte, *The Course of Irish History*, p.250-251
8 Ibid. p.255
9 Msgr R Murray, *A History of the Archdiocese of Armagh*, p.71, published by Editions Dr Signe, Strasbourg, 2000
10 Ibid. p.71
11 The Reverend Ambrose Macaulay, pp.2-3 *William Crolly, Archbishop of Armagh* 1835-49, published by Four Courts Press, 1994
12 Ibid. pp.140-141
13 Coleman. Op. Cit. pp.444-445
14 Macaulay. Op. Cit. pp.455-456
15 Coleman. Op. Cit. p.445
16 Macaulay. Op. Cit. p.456
17 John Cooney, *Sunday Times*, 19 December 1999
18 Maire Ni Chearbhaill. pp.4-5 "*Irish Cardinals 1866-1977*", published by Elton Press, Sandycove, Dublin 1983
19 Coleman. Op. Cit. p.445
20 Maire Ni Chearbhaill. Op. Cit. p.12
21 Galloway. Op. Cit. p.20

*'No person of taste, who had travelled much,
would consider it exaggeration to give the City
of Armagh a leading place among the most
delightfully situated inland towns of the United
Kingdom...Armagh is a thriving city....'*

George Henry Bassett
County Armagh: A Guide and Directory 1888

In the latter part of the nineteenth century, Armagh enjoyed a period of relative peace and prosperity. There were occasional outbreaks of violence associated with the political issues of the times, but they were relatively insignificant compared to the enormous upheavals of earlier centuries.

This was a period when Armagh developed as a market centre for the surrounding area, and the physical character of the city which had been determined by Archbishops Robinson and Beresford and others continued to provide an air of architectural distinction to this ecclesiastical capital of the island.

It was also noteworthy that while the two main Churches and their Archbishops continued to give a spiritual and moral lead to the community at large, the overall dominance of the old-style political prelate and of the religious establishment in Armagh, though still-influential, had begun to diminish. The work and example of St Patrick, and the best efforts of his successors, had ensured that Armagh would remain the spiritual capital of Ireland, but the age of increasing industrialisation and political sophistication underlined how far the secular power had been moving elsewhere.

The sporadic violence was nevertheless worrying. Towards the end of the previous century there had been sectarian violence between Protestant "Peep o' Day Boys" and Catholic "Defenders". Matters came to a head in September 1795 at the Battle of the Diamond near Loughgall, when the "Peep o' Day Boys" routed the Defenders. That evening the victorious Protestants marched into Loughgall and formed the "Orange Society", later called the Orange Order, to maintain their own interests and to protect the Protestant ascendancy.

> "During the next few months the Roman Catholics of Armagh and the neighbouring counties were subjected to a violent persecution, which drove thousands of them to take refuge in Connaught. It is very uncertain how far the members of the new society - the 'Orangemen' - were directly involved in these outrages; but they were held responsible for them all, and stories, often exaggerated, of the cruelties that the refugees had suffered at their hands spread throughout the country."[1]

Such outrages were a depressing mirror-image of the atrocities perpetuated

THOMAS WYNNE & CO.,

Linen Manufacturers,

Dyers and Finishers,

LISLEA,

ARMAGH.

Manchester Agency: 22 CHATHAM BUILDINGS.

"BERESFORD ARMS" HOTEL,

ARMAGH.

IN order to meet the greatly increasing business, the Proprietor has just completed an additional Wing, containing a large number of Bed-rooms.

Commercial gentlemen have both Sitting and Dining-rooms.

'Bus attends all Trains.

Two Billiard Rooms.   Posting.

WM. CAMPBELL,

PROPRIETOR.

WM. H. ADDEY & CO.,

P. L. LINEN MANUFACTURERS AND FINISHERS,

ALLISTRAGH MILLS,

ARMAGH.

MY object in giving the above Drawing is to show the position of my House in Market Square, so that those who have not yet favoured me with a visit may be induced to do so.

My aim is to treat customers well, so that they will not only come back themselves, but bring others with them.

In this I have succeeded so far, my business having increased steadily, and new customers are almost daily coming in on the recommendation of others who have already tried my Goods and found them reliable. This in itself is a proof that the value must be good.

I keep a Large Stock of General Drapery Goods, suitable for the various Seasons as they move round, and will esteem it a favour should you kindly give me a trial.

W. J. LENNOX,
43 MARKET SQUARE, **ARMAGH.**

Advertising pages from Bassett's *Guide and Directory of County Armagh*, 1888.

against Protestants by the Defenders several years earlier, in the merciless tit-
for-tat spiral of violence that has so disfigured Irish history. Unfortunately the
sectarianism continued in Armagh. Coleman records that Archbishop Crolly
"had many trials to bear from the Orangemen", and there was serious rioting
by Protestants in the city in July 1845, when a Roman Catholic was
murdered. In 1873, during the Primacy of Archbishop McGettigan, a number
of visitors who had been invited to the dedication of the Roman Catholic
Cathedral were attacked on their way home by Protestant extremists.[2]

Armagh Gaol which was built on
the site of the old barracks erected
in 1736. G.H. Bassett wrote in
1888 that "the cells ... are in
perfect condition...."

Fortunately, however, such distressing incidents were sporadic, and life in
the city and surrounding areas was lived in comparative peace and harmony.
One invaluable insight into community life in the last quarter of the 19th
century is provided by George Henry Bassett's *Guide and Directory of County
Armagh*, and reprinted by The Friar's Bush Press in 1989. In his Directory,
Bassett covers a wide spectrum of life in the county in general, and of
Armagh in particular, about which he writes fulsomely. He records that it had
a population of just over 10,000 in 1881, and continues;

> "No person of taste, who had travelled much, would consider it exaggeration to
> give the City of Armagh a leading place among the most delightfully situated
> inland towns of the United Kingdom. A cluster of hills, rising gently out of a
> beautiful valley, form the site upon which striking architectural effects have been
> produced.
> "Three of the hills are crowned by imposing Church edifices, including the
> ancient and modern Cathedrals of St Patrick, and the Church of St Mark. A
> fourth hill bears upon its summit an Observatory, the green domes of which
> contrast most agreeably with the neighbouring towers and spires. The Royal
> School occupies the fifth hill, the military barracks the sixth, the Catholic
> convent the seventh, and the eighth is divided between the Union Workhouse
> and Sheil's Institution for persons of reduced income."[3]

The thoroughfares of the city "have the narrowness that is so suggestive
of sociability and good feeling between the occupants", and the shop fittings
and the arrangement of merchandise show "artistic instinct and good
sense." Allowing for the fact that his publication was funded partly by the
advertisements of local traders, Bassett may have taken a slightly rosy view,
but there is no doubt that Armagh was prospering.

> "As a market for farm produce, considering the population, it is one of the best
> in Ulster. Manufacturing and other industries give extensive employment, and
> numerous advantages are derived from being the capital of the County. The
> Assizes are held twice a year; its gaol receives prisoners from all the towns and
> villages, and from Cavan, Monaghan, and portions of Down and Fermanagh. It is
> also a regimental district and militia headquarters, and has the County Lunatic
> Asylum and County Infirmary."[4]

Armagh had become a fashionable place, and was attracting "cultivated
people" as well as the families of former civil servants and military men who
had been stationed there. Several of the wealthier merchants had "expended
a large amount of money in bricks and mortar", in other words they built
bigger houses. The picture of Armagh as a comfortable and somewhat genteel
neighbourhood , after all the rigours of the past, was further emphasised by
the description of The Mall.

> "The Mall proper is really the city park, a well-planted and handsomely

The Mall c.1900. This picture was taken some two years after George Bassett wrote: "All classes of the inhabitants freely use this breathing -space, and it is a perfect paradise for children". In this picture the grandly- attired lady, left, and the nursemaids and children (centre) are a strong contrast to the girl with a wicker basket and shawl.

Armagh County Museum is located on The Mall. With the appearance of a little Greek Temple it is the oldest County Museum in Ireland with extensive collections based on specimens gathered by the Armagh Natural History and Philosophical Society during the nineteenth century.

enclosed green vale of eight acres. It is surrounded by a broad foot-way, well-shaded and amply provided with seats. All classes of the inhabitants freely use this breathing-space, and it is a perfect paradise for children."[5]

As a market-centre, Armagh was the centre for regular fairs. "The great market continues to be held on Tuesday down to the present, for all kinds of produce, with the exception of grain and grass-seed. These are sold in the season on Wednesday and Saturday. Every Tuesday throughout the year the principal thoroughfares are crowded in every part by country people. There is a splendid limestone Market House in Market Street, built by the Hon William Stuart DD in 1811, eleven years after he became Primate. The market places are, for flax, in Irish Street; poultry and eggs, Dobbin-Street; butter, Dobbin-Street; grain, grass-seed , pork, hay and straw, the Shambles, Mill-Street; live pigs, Gaol Square. There are two weigh-bridges at the Shambles, and one in Gaol square."[6]

Armagh was also at the heart of the Apple Blossom County, which developed a deserved reputation as an important apple-producing region, and which was reflected in the sale of produce in the local shops and fairs. As a market centre with a large agricultural hinterland, it was no surprise that Armagh was the focus for county shows. In 1888 it held a Flower, Dog and Poultry Show, in which there was also "a department for butter, in which several prizes were offered. It gave an opportunity for a lecture to the farmers and their wives and daughters by Canon Bagot, whose work in this field has proved valuable in Munster and Leinster."[7] This was genteel living indeed.

Armagh also had an Ornithological Society, which was formed in 1883, just three years after a similar Society was formed in Lurgan. "Both societies hold annual shows for poultry, pigeons and cage-birds, and thus far, have been most successful in their objects." There was also ample opportunity to sample the delights of the rural life, including fishing and hunting.

However, Armagh was not exclusively agricultural. It also had a thriving

Armagh is at the heart of
the apple blossom country.

community of traders, and their forceful business approach was typified by a
Mr Lennox who advertised his drapery business thus, with a full-page
advertisement in Bassett's Directory, complete with a drawing of his premises,
with elegant lades in coaches outside;

*"My object in giving the above Drawing is to show the position of my House in
Market Square, so that those who have not yet favoured me with a visit may be
induced to do so.*

*"My aim is to treat customers well, so that they will not only come back
themselves, but bring others with them.*

*"In this I have succeeded so far, my business having increased steadily, and new
customers are almost daily coming in on the recommendation of others who have
already tried my Goods, and found them reliable. This in itself is a proof that the value
must be good.*

*"I keep a Large Stock of General Drapery Goods, suitable for the various Seasons
as they move round, and will esteem it a favour should you kindly give me a trial".*

With such a direct, yet charming, approach, Mr Lennox was bound to do
well! (See page 110).

Armagh also had a number of manufacturing industries, and Bassett
records that in the city and its vicinity there were four power-loom linen
weaving factories, and two power-loom coarse linen weaving establishments,
one at Allistragh and the other at Lislea.

"There is also a large flax-spinning mill at Armagh. On the Armagh side of the
Blackwater, at Benburb, there is a power-loom factory for weaving course linens,
and one also of a similar kind at Dundrum , Tassagh."[8]

Despite their busy lives in making money from the land and from
industry, the citizens of Armagh had time for a wide range of recreations.
Lawn tennis and archery were popular, and the local tennis club (which
included archery) had 100 paid-up members in 1888. At the annual meeting
that year, it was decided to hold two tennis tournaments and two archery

Tennis Tournament 1892. An Armagh Tennis Club was established in 1878, and a decade later it had one hundred paid up members, one subscription levy being sufficient for an entire family. Sartorial style was obviously of great importance, irrespective of individual skills at tennis.

competitions. Archery was established first, in 1862, and in 1878 the tennis club was started, eventually offering five grass courts.

Cycling was also popular, though no club existed, and "At Armagh the ladies have taken to the tricycle with a show of enthusiasm which promises well for the success in the immediate future."[9] Cricket was well-established, and a club had been formed in 1859. By 1888 there were one hundred and twenty members, paying an annual subscription of ten shillings each. "A portion of The Mall green is rented at £25 a year, and maintained in excellent order. There is a good pavilion, and seats for guests. The club is really 'an institution' of Armagh. It has some good men, and its matches, being open to the public, are usually witnessed by a large number of people."[10] The Armagh Rugby Club had also been long-established by 1888, and shared the Mall grounds with the cricket club, many of whose members were also rugby players. Rugby was also played at the Royal School.

For those who were not sports-minded, there were many other opportunities for recreation, including the Armagh County and City Club, presumably for 'gentlemen', the Armagh Natural History and Philosophical Society, the Philharmonic Society, the Young Women's Christian Association, and the Catholic Reading Room.

This vignette of Armagh shows a society which was prospering and at ease with itself, though there were always individual tragedies. Bassett tells the earlier story of a soldier hanged for murder in Armagh, after a quarrel with a fellow-officer. A Major Alex Campbell, who was descended from an ancient Highland family, was convicted of murdering Captain Alexander

Boyd in a duel. Boyd apparently had accused Campbell of giving an incorrect order when on parade. The quarrel continued throughout the evening, and Campbell-stung by the perceived insult and somewhat the worse for drink-rushed to his room, returned with loaded pistols and insisted on immediate 'satisfaction.' A shot rang out behind closed doors and Boyd was seriously wounded. As he lay dying in the arms of his wife, Campbell begged his victim to acknowledge that the duel had been fair. "Yes" said Boyd "But you are a bad man. You hurried me."

"Having gasped out the completion of the sentence, he expired. Major Campbell, after some time, gave himself up. He was tried, found guilty of murder, and sentenced to death by Judge Mayne. A great deal of sympathy was excited for him: but, although respited, his friends were unable to save his life. At the execution, a company of his old regiment formed the gaol guard".[11]

The year after the publication of *Bassett's Guide and Directory*, there was a community tragedy on a large scale when eighty-eight people died and some four hundred were injured in what came to be known as the Great Armagh Railway Disaster. On Wednesday, 12 June 1889, there was a collision at Killuney, near Armagh, between the runaway rear section of a Sunday School excursion train en route for Warrenpoint, and a following passenger train on its way to Newry. The Armagh tragedy remained the worst in the British Isles for twenty-six years, until the Quintinshill train crash in Scotland in 1915 which claimed two hundred and twenty-seven lives, and remains one of the worst in railway history in Britain and Ireland.

The railway first came to Armagh in 1848, with the completion of a line from Belfast by the Ulster Railway Company, which had started building the track from Belfast and had reached Portadown in 1842.[12] It took another six years, including the complexities of bridging the River Bann, before the line reached Armagh. The official opening on 1 March was greeted less than enthusiastically by the *Armagh Guardian*, at a time when many vested interests including landowners and canal companies were opposed to such developments, as were the Churches which denounced Sunday travel as an affront to God. The story is told of one old Presbyterian preacher in County Antrim whose long prayer against such infernal new contraptions on the Sabbath was interrupted by a long blast on the engine's whistle. Whereupon the deeply-offended cleric said with vehemence "There, Lord, sure ye can hear it for yerself!"

As yet there was no connection between Armagh and Newry, a town which was increasing in importance. However in 1853 the Newry and Enniskillen Railway Company, later known as the Newry and Armagh Railway Company, began to construct a line between the two centres, and after eleven years of hard labour and difficulty, work on the track halted roughly one mile outside Armagh. Negotiations took place with the Ulster Railway Company which, not surprisingly, was worried that goods would now be transported to the port of Newry rather than to Belfast. However, agreement was reached, and the line between Newry and Armagh was completed in 1865.

Unfortunately the Newry and Armagh Railway Company did not

The Great Armagh Railway disaster which occurred on 12 June 1889. Eighty-eight people died and around four hundred were injured.

prosper financially, and in 1879 it was merged with the new Great Northern Railway Company. Seven years later the Newry-Warrenpont line, in existence since 1849, also became part of the GNR system. Warrenpoint had the added bonus of a tramway line to the seaside village of Rostrevor with its beautiful surroundings, and these were obvious attractions for day-trippers from other parts.

One particular attraction for many towns and villages in rural Ulster was the Sunday School excursion, often known as the "Wee trip."[13] This involved weeks of planning, not only by Sunday School teachers, but also by parents and other relatives or guardians. Well-scrubbed children were dressed in their best clothes, and after a short meeting and prayers in the local Church or church hall, they paraded with their parents (and indeed most of the village) down the main street to the station, behind the local flute or accordion band. Wide-eyed children boarded musty passenger carriages, with their horsehair stuffed seats, while the bellowing steam and hissing jets of the huge engines helped to create a cacophony of clanking as rail-stock was hitched and unhitched under the watchful eye of the all-powerful engine driver, while his invariably coal-blackened firemen stoked the roaring boiler. It was a scene which inspired hundreds of small boys to make instant vows to become engine-drivers, and which accounts for the continuing nostalgia for the age of steam among now middle-aged and older "men", who really ought to know better.

So it was in Armagh on that fateful day in June 1889. It was variously estimated that between eight hundred and nine hundred and forty men, women and children would take part in the excursion organised by the local Methodist Church, though in the event it is thought that the figures were much higher, and the *Belfast News Letter* claimed that at least 1,200 passengers were on board the train. About 9.00 am the Sunday School day-trippers made their way to the station, parading behind the Band of the 3rd Battalion of the Royal Irish Fusiliers. The excursion train was due to leave at 10.00 am but was delayed for fifteen minutes, partly due to the huge crowds who wanted to go on board. When it eventually pulled out of the station it was crammed to capacity, with many carriage doors locked on both sides, thus trapping the passengers inside. This was to add to the fatalities and injuries when the collision occurred.

All went well, until some three miles out of Armagh it was discovered that the struggling locomotive was unable to haul the carriages to the top of a steep gradient. The driver applied the vacuum brake when the train came to a halt. It was decided, unaccountably, that the train should then be divided and that the first few carriages should be taken to a siding in Hamiltonsbawn and left there, in order to allow the engine to return for the remainder. However, during this complex manoeuvring, the first part of the divided train pressed back and jolted the rear section into motion, thus over-riding

FEARFUL RAILWAY DISASTER NEAR ARMAGH.

APPALLING LIST OF KILLED AND WOUNDED.

THE CITY IN MOURNING

THE RAILWAY OFFICIALS ARRESTED.

MESSAGES OF SYMPATHY.

On last Wednesday, the city of Armagh was thrown into a state of the most terrible horror and consternation by the occurrence within a couple of miles of the city, of a railway accident, certainly the most dreadful that it has ever been our painful duty to record which perhaps has

Several family groups perished, including James and Margaret Cleeland and their three sons. The family's headstone is in St Mark's Graveyard, Armagh.

Church of the Immaculate Conception, Tullysarran. This photograph of the construction of the Church was taken on 5 November 1920. Cardinal Logue dedicated the Church, which replaced an eighteenth century building.

and nullifying the hand-brake in the guard's van. The carriages crunched over the stone left at the rear of the guard's van, as an added precaution, and began careering downhill and backwards along the line, with disastrous consequences.

Meanwhile, the regular 10.35 am passenger from Armagh to Newry was chugging up the same track. The horrified driver and helper saw the danger but could only slow their own speed before the runaway carriages smashed into the oncoming train at an estimated speed of forty miles an hour, and, with hundreds of passengers trapped inside, the result was utter carnage.

The collision occurred on the steeply-graded embankment and "A fearful noise resulted, clearly audible to the despairing people running down from the front portion of the excursion train. No 9 engine of the 10.35 am train stopped dead, quivered, and rolled over on her side on top of the embankment. The guard's van and the last three flimsy wooden coaches of the runaway disintegrated completely, pieces being flung like matchwood in every direction. The bodies of the unfortunate occupants suffered a similar fate. The other carriages remained upright, but some were derailed, and in these many people were also injured."[14]

One graphic eye-witness account from a Captain Preston was published in the *News Letter* of 15 June. When informed by the police of what had happened, he rode to the scene on his horse, with a large flask of brandy and other articles which he thought might come in handy. The sights, he said, were appalling.

"When the soldiers of the Royal Irish Fusiliers arrived, we organised a sort of ambulance corps, and got the bodies into rows under the hedges, so as to be out of the sun. The smell that had arisen from them was already injurious. In one row we laid out twenty-seven dead, and in another row on the other side of the hedge, I counted twenty-three. Altogether before I left the place I counted fifty-seven dead.

"One poor little fellow, about five years of age, was horribly mangled at the bottom of the embankment. I asked a man who was near to assist me put the

body under the hedge. The man put his hands under the lad's head, and I caught him by the feet. The feet came off in my hands, and the head in the hands of the man. We placed the body in three pieces under the hedge."

"Immediately afterwards I saw two little children on the grass and went up to them and said: 'Well, little ones, were you on the train?' They were plucking daisies, as if nothing had happened. 'Yes, sir' replied a girl of about six 'and she was too', pointing to the dead body of a little sister, who had a smile on her face, a few yards off. The dead little girl had a black mark on her forehead, but was not mangled."[15]

Where the ages were known, nineteen of the victims were under 15 years, twenty-seven were between 15 and 20, thirty were between 21 and 60, and two were more than 60. According to the *Armagh Guardian* of 21 June, 34 of the dead were Church of Ireland, 19 Presbyterian, 18 Methodist and nine were Roman Catholic - thus showing the ecumenical nature of relations in the city long before the term had been invented.

Several family groups perished, including James and Margaret Cleeland and their three sons, aged 14, 12 and 8. A long succession of funerals took place through a devastated city, and on one day alone, no fewer than 35 of the victims were buried. Within a few days of the disaster, local churchmen and prominent citizens opened a relief fund, to which Queen Victoria gave £50, and the Lord-Lieutenant of Ireland £100, with the GNR giving only £200. Afterwards, however, the Company had to meet a major bill of £145,000 for compensation claims and expenses..

A Board of Trade Report attributed the immediate cause of the accident

Enthronement of Dr John Baptist Crozier, Church of Ireland Archbishop of Armagh 1911-1920. The ceremony, on 17 March, was so crowded that several hundred people had to remain outside.

Irish Street, Armagh, Flax Market 1913. The growing of flax continued on farms until after the First World War. Here in the market yard off Irish Street farmers and buyers meet at one of the Tuesday markets.

to the inability of the brake in the rear guard's van to hold the rear ten coaches of the train when they were dealt a severe blow by the front portion. The Report strongly recommended the introduction of a better braking system, and within a few days of the Armagh disaster, the Government announced a Bill to bring railway safety law up to date. On 30 August 1889, the Regulation of the Railways Act came into force, thus setting out binding safety laws on all companies. It could be said, therefore, that the Great Armagh Disaster helped to change railway history in the British Isles.

"..... those who died in the Armagh Railway Disaster did not die in vain. It served a noble purpose by causing those in authority to pause, think and act for the common good. Many another such calamity must have been avoided through the lessons learned on that dreadful day in June 1889."[16]

The pain and loss was felt by the entire community in Armagh for a very long time. Despite the relative peace and prosperity of the times, it seemed as if tragedy and suffering were never far away, and the railway disaster with its huge loss of lives and widespread injuries seemed a portent of worse to come.

As the century and the Millennium drew to a close, the war clouds began to gather again. The seeds of a European conflict were sown, and the complex political alliances across the continent led to almost inevitable conflagration on a massive scale. At home the political upheavals surrounding the passage of the Home Rule Bill led to sustained tension and the possibility of widespread violence throughout the Province, where the Protestant majority vowed to oppose such a measure, and by force of arms if necessary.

Dedication of the Boer War Memorial in the Mall, Armagh 1906 – attended by, among others, one hundred officers and men of the 1st Battalion The Royal Fusiliers whose headquarters were in Armagh.

McCann's shop 1918, at the junction of Albert Place and Railway Street. Charles McCann, was Chairman of the Armagh County Board GAA from 1911 – 1916.

The differing views throughout the Province and the island were mirrored in Armagh. Archbishop Crozier, the Church of Ireland Primate, was deeply involved in the Home Rule controversy and was pictured outside the Palace on 4 October, 1913, when he entertained the political leaders Sir Edward Carson and Sir James Craig, both of whom were wearing their Unionist badges.

Over on the other hill,

"Cardinal Logue wavered between asserting the rights of the Church to intervene in politics where there was a question of morality (as he saw it) and an ardent desire to hold the peace even if to do so meant accepting direct rule from Britain. He always feared that a new political solution in Ireland would leave northern Catholics under the power of Unionists, and Catholic education would suffer."[17]

Civil war was averted by the outbreak of the First World War in 1914, when the entire Ulster Volunteer Force, which was formed to oppose Home Rule, joined the British Army as the 36th (Ulster) Division, and John Redmond, the leader of the Irish Parliamentary Party, offered the services of the Irish Volunteers in the South. Young men from both the Unionist and Nationalist communities in and around Armagh, and many thousands throughout Britain and Ireland, joined the call to arms. Britain declared war against Germany in August 1914, and during the initial air of euphoria, many thought that the fighting would be over by Christmas. How wrong they were.[18]

As the war dragged on, and the euphoria was turned into disillusion in the mud of Flanders and elsewhere, it became clear that the suffering would touch almost every household in Ulster. During the first two days of the Battle of the Somme in 1916, some 5,500 men of the Ulster Division had been killed, and many others wounded. On 12 July all work was suspended at noon, as a mark of respect for the dead and injured, as the people of Ulster tried to come to terms with the cataclysmic shock of such casualties. That year the "Twelfth celebrations" were abandoned. The terrible carnage at The Somme, and the sacrifice of Ulstermen, would remain a deep darkness in the Ulster psyche, never to be forgotten.

Two soldiers from the Armagh-based Royal Irish Fusiliers were awarded posthumous VC's in the First World War. The first was won by Private Robert Morrow of the 1st Battalion at Messines on 12 April 1915

"... when he rescued and carried to safety several men who had been buried in the debris of trenches wrecked by shell-fire. Private Morrow carried out this gallant work on his own initiative and under heavy fire from the enemy."

The second was won by Lieutenant Geoffrey St George Shillington Cather of the 9th Battalion at the Battle of the Somme when

"From 7.00 pm till midnight, he searched No Man's Land and brought in three wounded men. Next morning at 8.00 am he continued his search, brought in another wounded man and gave water to others, arranging for their rescue later. Finally at 10.30 am he took out water to another man and was proceeding further on when he himself was killed. All this was carried out in full view of the enemy, and under machine gun and artillery fire. He set a splendid example of courage and self-sacrifice."[19]

The men's regiment, the Royal Irish Fusiliers, were raised in Dublin in 1793, and known as the "Faughs", from their Gaelic battle-cry "Faugh-a Ballagh", literally "Clear the way". Their forerunners were the 87th and 89th Regiments of Foot, recruited in the counties of Armagh, Cavan, Monaghan, Louth, Meath, Wexford, Waterford and Limerick. During Army reforms they were combined in 1881 to become the 1st and 2nd Battalions of the Princess Victoria's Royal Irish Fusiliers, with their depot in Armagh. Shortly afterwards their strength was increased by three more battalions from what had been the Armagh, Cavan and Monaghan Militia Regiments.[20]

The Royal Irish Fusiliers endured extreme conditions and suffered heavy losses during the Boer War, and for the first time its soldiers wore khaki camouflage uniforms. A memorial to the Royal Irish Fusiliers who died in this war stands in the Mall in Armagh near the Regimental Museum which is open to the public. Commemorated on the War Memorial is Drummer Peter Durcan from Dublin, who was one of several generations of his family to serve with the Regiment. He was killed in October 1899 at the Battle of Talana.

During the First World War, the Regiment which had been greatly expanded to meet this emergency, gave distinguished service. Altogether it won 44 Battle Honours, over twice as many as during all its previous service, but in the process it suffered terrible casualties, with 3,181 men dead and more than 15,000 wounded.[21]

Such stark statistics help to convey the degree of suffering and loss felt in many homes in Armagh and surrounding districts from which a large proportion of the young men had joined the Regiment. Those who survived the horrors of such conflict returned to a country which had changed greatly since they left, and which was to witness yet more violence and political upheaval.

The shadow of violence which had hovered for so many centuries over St Patrick's city was to remain in the years immediately after the "War to end all wars" as Britain and Ireland struggled to come to grips with new realities. A war had been won abroad, but another war was to rumble on at home, with deadly consequences. The light of St Patrick's example burned on, for those who had eyes to look for it, but the darkness threatened to crowd in all around.

NOTES

1 Professor JC Beckett, *The Making of Modern Ireland 1603-1923*, published by Faber and Faber, 1966, p.257

2 Coleman, Op. Cit. p.301 and p.316

3 Bassett, *The Book of County Armagh*, 1888, p.59

4 Ibid. p.61

5 Ibid. p.61

6 Ibid. p.73

7 Ibid. p.39

8 Ibid. p.25

9 Ibid. p.53

10 Ibid. p.105

11 Ibid. p.117

12 The details of the disaster are contained in a comprehensive publication, written by Mr Damien Woods, and published by Armagh Council, in association with Armagh County Museum, on the 100th anniversary of the accident

13 The author had first-hand knowledge, as a boy in his native village of Bessbrook in County Armagh, of the excitement of such a day at the seaside!

14 D Woods. Op. Cit. p.18

15 Ibid. pp.21-23

16 Ibid. p.38

17 Msgr R Murray, Op. Cit. p.82

18 The author's grandfather Thomas McCreary joined the Royal Irish Fusiliers to "replace" his younger brother Sandy who had joined under age. He served as a stretcher-bearer at the Somme, and was later captured by the Germans. During his long life he rarely talked about his war services, and like most men who had known the horrors of conflict, he never believed in "the glories of war"

19 Amanda Moreno, *A Short History of the Royal Irish Fusiliers.*

20 Ibid.

21 Ibid.

Further advertisements from *Bassett's 1888 Guide and Directory of Armagh* reflecting a busy commercial scene.

THE ARMAGH COACH FACTORY

[ESTABLISHED OVER A CENTURY.]

The Show-rooms, Workshops, Painting-shops, Drying-lofts and Storerooms contain an area of over 14,500 feet Covered Floor Space.

TAYLOR ∴ BROTHERS,

THE MALL,

ARMAGH.

Telegraphic Address—"Taylor, Armagh."

[Established over Half a Century.]

FRIZELL'S

Cabinet and Upholstery Warehouse,

THE SEVEN HOUSES,

ARMAGH.

Every description of Cabinet Furniture, Bedding, &c.

Importer of the latest designs in Artistic Furnishings from Paris and London.

A LARGE STOCK TO SELECT FROM.

Funeral Undertaking—
All Requisites.

DONNELLY & SOMERVILLE,

PLUMBERS,

Gasfitters, Bellhangers, Locksmiths, &c.,

BARRACK STREET,

ARMAGH.

Special Features :

SANITARY PLUMBING.

HOT WATER APPARATUS FOR DWELLINGS, CONSERVATORIES, &c.

THE FITTING OF ELECTRIC AND CRANK BELLS.

Repairs of Rifles, Fowling Pieces, Revolvers, &c.

CHARLEMONT ARMS HOTEL,

ARMAGH.

J. H. MANN {LATE OF LONDON AND GLASGOW.} **PROPRIETOR.**

This Hotel is in the best business centre, and has been remodeled and refurnished throughout.

ELEGANT COMMERCIAL AND WRITING ROOMS STRICTLY RESERVED.

'Bus Attends all Trains.

Public Dinners, Suppers, &c., on the shortest notice.

Hot and Cold Luncheons always ready.

TURKISH AND OTHER BATHS.

POSTING IN ALL ITS DEPARTMENTS.

Carriages, Broughams, Waggonettes, Phætons, &c., always ready.

✢ TURKISH BATHS. ✢

LADIES : Monday and Friday, 2 to 6 p.m. ; Wednesday, Thursday and Saturday, 10 to 12 noon.

GENTLEMEN : Monday and Friday, 7 a.m. to 2 p.m., and from 6 to 9 p.m. ; Tuesday, 7 a.m. to 9 p.m. ; Wednesday, Thursday and Saturday, 7 a.m. to 10 a.m. ; 12 noon to 9 p.m.

Sulphur and other Medicated Baths, and full Hydropathic treatment as at any of the famous sanitariums.

Michael Collins, 1921 front right. Collins had been elected M.P for Armagh in the new Northern Ireland Parliament and shown here at a large Sinn Fein demonstration at Armagh on 4 September 1921. Less than a year later he was killed in an ambush in Co. Cork.

'Go to Armagh and let us see the linen mills there – closed down, unfortunately, and the poor workers unemployed, and most of them starving.'

Senator Thomas McLaughlin, a member of Armagh Council, speaking in the Northern Ireland Senate during a debate on 27 November 1935

Those who returned to Armagh, and those who stayed, had to adjust to a radically new order, after the end of the First World War, which had brought its own immense suffering. The 1916 Easter uprising in Dublin set in train a series of events which led to the establishment of a Southern Parliament in 1919, the Anglo-Irish war of 1919-21, and the 1920 Government of Ireland Act, which set up separate legislatures and governments in Northern and Southern Ireland.

On 22 June 1921, King George V opened the Northern Ireland Parliament. Both parts of Ireland, Unionist and Nationalist, were moving along different paths, but these differing loyalties and aspirations continued to be cherished by the Protestant and Roman Catholic communities in the North at local level, including Armagh. Whatever the proposed merits, or the demerits, of such an arrangement, it was to prove a divisive influence which cast a long, dark shadow over community relations for the rest of the century.

To add to the complexities and challenges, Northern Ireland's major areas of employment – shipbuilding, linen and agriculture – were affected by adverse economic developments world-wide. Agriculture was particularly badly-off, compared not only to Britain but also to the industrial sector in Northern Ireland.[1]

Armagh itself began to feel the chill wind of change. There was a gradual decline in population, partly due to migration to areas of greater opportunity including Belfast. As well, the increased competition from manufacturers in and around the capital city adversely affected a number of rural settlements, including Armagh, which was overtaken in size by Lurgan in 1871 and by Portadown, at the prosperous centre of a railway hub, some two decades later.[2]

Politically there were significant changes also. Armagh was one of the ten urban councils which came under Sinn Fein-Nationalist control for the first time, in 1920. A year later Michael Collins, who had been elected MP for Armagh in the new Northern Parliament, attended a Sinn Fein demonstration in the city in September 1921. More than 20,000 people came to Armagh to witness this historic event. Some twenty-one local authorities controlled by Nationalist-Sinn Fein coalitions, including Armagh, had no allegiance to Stormont or London, and their functions were taken over by Government commissioners in April 1922. Politically and economically, the times were indeed changing in the city of St Patrick.

The *Armagh Guardian* reported "Armagh Sensation – City Council Kicked Out", and stated "Last year Armagh City Council, paying more

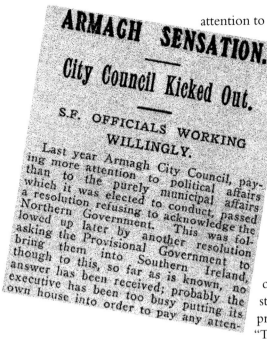

ARMAGH SENSATION.

City Council Kicked Out.

S.F. OFFICIALS WORKING WILLINGLY.

Last year Armagh City Council, paying more attention to political affairs than to the purely municipal affairs which it was elected to conduct, passed a resolution refusing to acknowledge the Northern Government. This was followed up later by another resolution asking the Provisional Government to bring them into Southern Ireland, though to this, so far as is known, no answer has been received; probably the executive has been too busy putting its own house into order to pay any atten-

Report from the "Armagh Guardian" on the dissolution of Armagh City Council by the new Northern Ireland Government. The Council had passed a resolution refusing to acknowledge the Northern Government and a second resolution requesting the Provisional Government in the South to put the city under the control of the Irish Government.

attention to political affairs than to the purely municipal affairs which it was elected to conduct, passed a resolution refusing to acknowledge the Northern Government."

It continued.

"Then, at last, the Northern Government, long forbearing, took action. On Saturday morning the police guard on the City Hall was augmented, and shortly afterwards Colonel H Waring arrived, and presented the Clerk with a sealed order dissolving the Council, and appointed him as Commissioner to carry on business in its stead.

"He took over possession of the Hall and all the books of the Council, and shortly afterwards all the documents were removed to the Co Courthouse, where an office was opened in the Sheriff's room for the transaction of Council business."

The newspaper reported reassuringly that no change had taken place in the work of the city, and in a style typical of the times when facts and editorialising were presented together it continued:

"The scavengers carry on their duties as formerly, the Clerk and all the other officers, Sinn Fein though they may be, have elected to work under the Commissioner, and the duties of the Council will probably be carried out more expeditiously by one man than by a faction-divided Council, whose meetings of late were lengthened by debates by Republicans and Sinn Fein Treaties as to what should be done, while the few Unionists present sat quiet and voted or did not vote, as seemed best to them."[3]

These were desperate times, and the local newspapers were full of reports about murder and mayhem in and around Armagh. The *Guardian* reported the attacks on two young men, one of them a B Special constable, Joseph Steenson, who was hauled off his bike, shot and left for dead. But he survived and "walking, falling, crawling, rising and walking, only to fall again, he made his way back to the house he left."

Another young man – Robert Milligan – was not so fortunate. He, too, was hauled off his bike, dragged into a field, shot in the mouth and chest, and later died, where "the hounds of hell left him". These killings, according to the anonymous reporter was "characteristically the work of gangs of slayers who have disgraced the fame of Ireland."[4]

Some of these reports were distressingly similar to those of more recent times when violence and bloodshed so disfigured daily life in Ulster, and other parts of the island. However, normal life went on as far as possible – then as now – and one significant source of information about Armagh and district is the Allison collection of photographs dating from the turn of the century until the end of the Second World War.

The pictures provide a unique insight into Armagh at work and play, and cover a vast canvas – from shops, streets and country houses, to schools, churches, agriculture, industry, transport and, the police, bands and recreation. Despite the political upheaval and the economic setbacks of the first few decades of the 20th century, the Allison collection conveys a sense of normality about the daily life of the city.

The C.B Cafe. Irwin's C.B Cafe with the tables set for afternoon tea was a popular rendezvous for meetings. This picture was taken in 1936.

There are pictures of Irwin's City Bakery Cafe in the mid-thirties with the tables set for afternoon tea, a study of Woolworth's "3d and 6d Stores" around the same period, as well as Zwecker's hairdressers, Guy's bicycle shop and Short's Piano Warehouse. The life of the two main communities in Armagh is well represented in *The Way We Were*, a book featuring a selection of pictures from the Allison collection.

For example, there is an historic picture of a GAA practice at St Patrick's College, with the President – the Very Reverend E J Cullen – acting as referee, and mounted on a horse. Two pages later there is a photograph of rugby being played at The Royal School Armagh, on a particularly agricultural-looking pitch.

The Armagh branch of Woolworth's 1935.

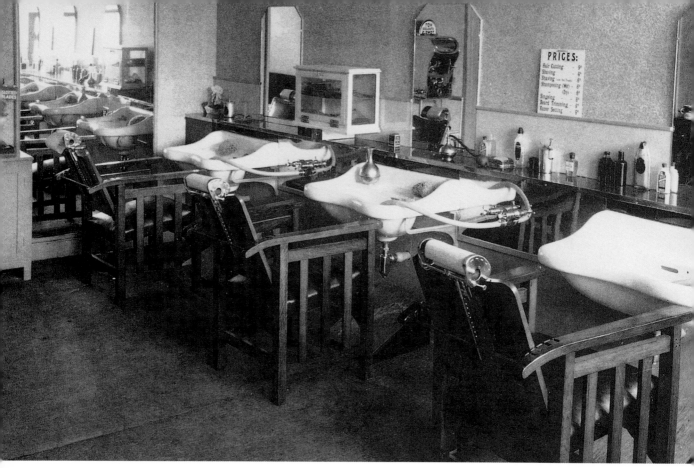

PRICES:
Hair Cutting
Shaving
Shaving — on the Teeth
Shampooing (Wet) —
(Dry)
Singing
Beard Trimming
Razor Setting

The Gentleman's Saloon in Zweckers c.1937.

Further on there are two striking portraits of church leaders in Armagh – one of Archbishop Charles D'Arcy, Church of Ireland Primate from 1920 until 1938, and on the opposite page Cardinal D'Alton, who was translated to Armagh in 1946, created Cardinal in 1953, and died some ten years later. And to further underline the role played by both communities in Armagh, there is a picture of a Unionist "A" snooker team which won the local league in 1947 by only two points from the Hibernian team, and, opposite, a photograph of the Hibernian team which won the same trophy several years later.[5]

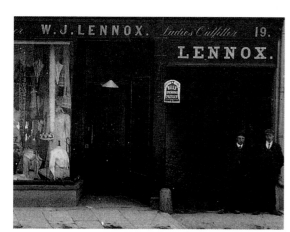

W.J. LENNOX. Ladies Outfitter 19.
LENNOX.

In 1867 Mr Lennox opened in Market Street as a draper and ladies and gentlemen's outfitter. This picture was taken in 1906.

The affairs of the Council continued to give concern, and in March 1934 its business was taken over again by a Commissioner, due to financial irregularities. The *Armagh Observer* noted, on 10 March;

"The news which we publish elsewhere of the drastic action taken by the Ministry of Home Affairs in dissolving the Armagh City Council and replacing it by a Governmental manager came as a great shock and disagreeable surprise to many – in fact, to most citizens of the Primatial city."

The Council was prorogued for more than a decade, and this led to a long dispute between non-Unionist members of the Council and the Government. Senator Tom McLaughlin, an Armagh businessman and Chairman of the Council at the time, believed that the suspension could have been avoided if other members, including the Unionists, had accepted a Council request for a public inquiry.

He believed that the affairs of the Council had been "practically cleared up" when the Commissioner was appointed, and that there was "practically

The Armagh Guardian Office, 1928. The Trimbles were a notable publishing family, one branch being the proprietors of the *Impartial Reporter* in Enniskillen, while Delmege Trimble took over the *Armagh Guardian* and Printworks in 1893.

no reflection on the existing city council". He raised the matter regularly in the Northern Ireland Senate.

On 25 October 1938 he stated

"The local council will have been abolished five years in March next, and surely the time has now come when the people of Armagh, and particularly the majority of the citizens whom I represent, should have their local government franchise rights restored to them."[6] Senator McLaughlin said that he objected to the appointment of a Commissioner from a financial point of view, and claimed that this cost the ratepayers 4d in the £.

He set out an alternative by which the citizens "could elect a council of ratepayers who would give their time and services free and do their best for the welfare of the city and its people. It is time that the Commissioner went, and the people of Armagh allowed to elect an urban district council."[7]

Predictably, this view was not shared by the next speaker Major Boyle, a Unionist, who also expressed an interest in the city of Armagh. He claimed that at the time of the take-over by a Commissioner "a state of chaos existed, and I understand that irregularities were rife". The then Ministry of Home Affairs, which had the power to appoint a Commissioner, had found financial discrepancies. "As a result the rate collector was arrested, and was eventually lodged in His Majesty's prison for twelve months. In addition, the clerk of the markets was short to the extent of £200 in his lodgements, and I think the sum of these shortages amounted to between £3,000 and £4,000."

Major Boyle claimed that, contrary to Senator McLaughlin's allegation, the Commissioner had saved the citizens a great deal of money. He added, "The rate is now 10s 8d in the £, and I hope that when the new rate is struck, it will be even less. The city has undoubtedly better managed since it came into the hands of the Commissioner."[8]

Some 18 months later, Senator McLaughlin was still on the attack. On 14 March 1940, he told the Senate:

Senator Tom McLaughlin, a former member and chairman of Armagh Council, who strongly criticized the abolition of the Council.

A mechanized apple sprayer 1938.

"In the city of Armagh we have had a Commissioner or a dictator for the past six years. Why? Because the majority of the voters of the city of Armagh are Nationalists and Catholics, and the Commissioner, who costs the ratepayers 4d in the £, is kept there for the purpose of depriving the citizens of Armagh of exercising the franchise, thus preventing a majority Nationalist council from functioning."[9]

Senator McLaughlin further claimed that arrangements were well underway "for the gerrymandering of the city by way of the extension of the city boundary". He alleged that "Conferences of the Unionists have already been held in the Armagh City Hall to consider the gerrymandering scheme and to make sure that the gerrymandering is well done."[10]

He went on to claim that gerrymandering had taken place elsewhere.

"A similar thing occurred in the cases of the Nationalist majorities in the City of Derry, Omagh, and the counties of Tyrone and Fermanagh, where the Nationalists have been victimised. Could anything be worse even under Hitler? You talk of the occupation of Poland, but what of the occupation of the County of Tyrone by a Unionist County Council representing the minority. In that county the Nationalists have a majority of the population of 15,000, and they can return only eleven county councillors against the majority's sixteen."[11]

Sir Joseph Davison, a Unionist Senator, in a reply that has a familiar ring concerning the level of debate about Northern Ireland affairs even today, said,

"I am sorry to hear Senator McLaughlin quoting figures purporting to represent injustices done to his Party."

He also referred to Senator McLaughlin's oft-repeated complaint about the cost of a Commissioner in Armagh and stated

"If there had not been a wrong administration in the City of Armagh it would not have been necessary for the Minister of Home Affairs to put in a Commissioner. The Commissioner will remain there, I presume, until the Minister of Home Affairs is satisfied that the properly elected representatives will

carry out their duty in a proper manner."[12]

There were other matters exercising the minds of the people of Armagh, and not least the local economy which was languishing in a severe depression. In a Senate debate on 27 November 1935, Senator McLaughlin spoke passionately about the demise of the linen business. He said,

"Go to Armagh and let us see the linen mills there – closed down, unfortunately, and the poor workers unemployed, and most of them starving. I think we have only one going at the present time so far as Armagh is concerned, and that is the one in the direction of Milford. We have Gillis's Mill closed down, and Campbell's Mill closed down, and Milford working half-time. That is what the Government calls prosperity."[13]

The Second World War brought food rationing and other shortages, the 'black-out', travel restrictions and other vexations, but it also led to an economic improvement shared by Armagh, as Northern Ireland and its people contributed to the war effort. The arrival of the US servicemen, in preparation for the D-Day assault on Europe and its aftermath, brought a new dimension of internationalism and prosperity to the Province, where American "candies" and cigarettes went a long way to woo the local population.

A large number of the newcomers were stationed in County Armagh, and their general welcome to the Province was echoed in a Senate speech on 3 February 1942, just a week after the first American troops disembarked at Belfast. Senator William Ernest Stevenson, attired in morning dress, replied to the King's speech which had been read out by the Governor, the Duke of Abercorn, and said "It is a matter of great satisfaction to know that American troops have landed in Northern Ireland. They will be a very welcome addition to our fighting forces, and it goes without saying that as our visitors they will be treated by all with courtesy, (and) kindness, and will receive that hospitality for which Ireland is famed."[14] So it proved, though there was less

British troops at The Mall, Armagh with fixed bayonets and gas - masks in September 1939.

133

WITH COMPLIMENTS AND THANKS

H. B. Rui

MANAGER. Chairma

ILITARY BALL - 16th JUNE. 1944
EWCASTLE SALUTE THE SOLDIER WEEK.
T THE SLIEVE DONARD HOTEL. NEWCASTLE

The Band of the Royal Irish Fusiliers at a military ball in the Slieve Donard Hotel, Newcastle. The ball took place on 16 June 1944, during the "Newcastle Salute the Soldier week". Between the Union Jack and the Stars and Stripes in the background, are the pictures of Churchill, Roosevelt and Stalin and Chiang Kai Shek.

than a fulsome welcome from the male population of the Province who found it hard to compete for young females against the novelty of the newcomers, bearing not only the gifts mentioned earlier, but silk stockings as well!

As in the First World War, the people of Northern Ireland paid a heavy price in the numbers of Service personnel who were killed and wounded in the War, including those from the city of Armagh and the surrounding districts. The local regiment, The Royal Irish Fusiliers, distinguished itself as it had done previously, and both Battalions – the 1st and 2nd – won high praise for their bravery in the various theatres of war in Europe.

During the retreat to Dunkirk the 1st Battalion was awarded a Distinguished Service Order, five Military Crosses, two Distinguished Conduct Medals and three Military Medals. Field-Marshall Earl Alexander of Tunis, in a letter to the Regiment in 1945, noted "I can say without reserve that the 1st Battalion Royal Irish Fusiliers is among the finest that it has been my privilege to have under my command."[15] A total of five hundred and one members of the Regiment were killed during the Second World War.

After the war, Northern Ireland which had been socially deprived compared to other parts of the United Kingdom, began to share in the benefits of victory, partly as of right, and partly as a result of the Province's loyal war effort, which was appreciated by a grateful British Government.

Field Marshall Montgomery reviewing a Royal Irish Fusilier Guard of Honour in Austria during the Second World War.

The Attlee Administration also guaranteed Northern Ireland's constitutional position within the United Kingdom, and the post-war years heralded an era of unprecedented peace and prosperity in the Province.

Roger Weatherup, the former curator of the Armagh County Museum, notes:

"Public money was to be provided to establish a better future for everyone, and 'free' (actually paid for by taxation) health care and education, and a better standard of living, were to be available to all. The funding was to be found by Central Government, and the local authorities were to manage it as directed.

In Armagh, the County Council through its Health and Education Committees and the Surveyor's and Planning Departments were to manage the improved services, while the Urban and Rural Council received grants towards improving housing, sanitation and other matters.

"Government departments directed major projects including the design and construction of new and improved roads, including Friary Road, and the building of new hospitals and schools. The

A 1938 seal of The Northern Ireland Senate, with a "summons" addressed to Senator Tom McLaughlin to attend the opening of Parliament at Stormont, 1938. Significantly the name of King Edward VIII has been replaced hastily by that of George VI following the Abdication.

introduction of new industries, and the provision of suitable factories were also undertaken by the central authorities. To expedite the provision of much-needed modern rented dwellings, the Northern Ireland Housing Trust was created to supplement the building programmes of local Councils, and around Armagh new estates including The Folly, Daire's Willows, Duke's Grove, and Orangefield began the encroachment of the city into the surrounding countryside."

However, there was a downside to some of this development, as Roger Weatherup notes.

"The centralisation of much of the planning, and some of the implementation of the developments, led to unimaginative standardised designs which completely ignored the diversity of architectural styles and local building materials, not only

Tom McLaughlin who followed in his father's footsteps in local government in Armagh, and was himself a leading supporter of the Campaign for Social Justice.

SUCCESS STORY OF ARMACHIAN AND FIRM

Now Northern Bank Director

ARMAGHMAN Mr. T. G. McLaughlin is again highlighted in the news, both personally and by the advancement of the firms which he runs.

Son of the late Senator T. McLaughlin, of Armagh, he now mainly resides in the picturesque Antrim coast town of Cushendall of which his wife is a native.

He has always loved Armagh and its people, where his business and philanthropic interests lie, but his main hobbies are close to indeed on the sea.

We learn that the Northern Bank pleased to announce the appointment of Mr. McLaughlin, of Armagh & Cushendall, as a Director of the nk. He was educated in Armagh and at St. cent's College, Castlerock, and is irman of a group of family businesses luding Thomas McLaughlin Ltd., ter Crown Corks Ltd., Barcroft rniture Ltd., and McLaughlin (Catng Supplies) Ltd. in Northern land, and Thomas McLaughlin eland Ltd.), in the South. In addin, he is chairman of the board of magh Shoes Limited.

St. Patrick's College, Armagh, and is associated with the Transport Holding Company and City-bus.

A past captain of County Armagh Golf Club, he also maintains an interest in sailing, and is Commodore of Cushendall Boating and Sailing Club. He is widely known and respected in drama circles for his achievements, both as an actor and as a producer, which have earned him many awards at various drama festivals.

COMPANY DIRECTORSHIPS

The Board of Messrs. T. McLaughlin Ltd., the manufacturing and distributive firm to the Hotel & Licensed Trade in Ulster and the Republic of Ireland, have announced the following appointments to take effect as and from February 1st, 1974 : Messrs. Charles P. O'Neill and Patrick V. Daly will become Managing Directors the firm and other associate Companies in Ireland.

Under the present Chairman, Mr. Thomas McLaughlin, this firm has grown from very small beginnings to become one of the two top firms in its field in the British Isles.

Head offices and factory are located at Cathedral Road, Armagh, with sales and showroom at Don Street, Belfast.

The Southern-based Company McLaughlin (Ireland) Ltd., depots, distribution and sales cer in Dundalk, Dublin, Kilkenny Donegal.

in Armagh but in the towns elsewhere. A devotion to the latest ideas and the use of new, and often untested, building materials left many centres with unsympathetic structures of steel, concrete and glass.

"The desire to imitate mainland practices led to the closure of much of the railway system, often before the upgrading of roads had been completed, and to the establishment of 'new towns', or the accelerated expansion of a few existing ones, whereas the money would have been better spent in generally improving the existing urban centres."

The comparative peace of the post-war years was broken by an IRA border campaign. It began with a raid on Gough Military Barracks in Armagh in June 1954, during which a large quantity of arms was eventually located and stolen (after an episode slightly reminiscent of the Keystone Cops) and driven across the border. The official IRA campaign began in earnest in 1956, though previously there had been attacks by Northern militants on an RUC barracks at Rosslea and on several customs posts. In September, 1957 the Vogan Window in St. Patrick's Church of Ireland Cathedral in Armagh was destroyed, and all the windows on the south side of the Cathedral were extensively damaged by an IRA bomb-blast which had targeted a nearby police-station.

The campaign, however, never achieved the momentum of that of the Provisional IRA from the early Seventies. The Fifties and early Sixties campaign was confined to the border, it lacked widespread popular support, and the police on both sides of the border were well-informed and active in their counter-revolutionary measures. With most of the main participants either dead or behind bars, the uprising gradually fizzled out, and was called off in February 1962.

Nevertheless, the troubles were by no means over. Since the formation of the State, the Northern Ireland Government had failed to deal adequately with the grievances of the Roman Catholic minority over housing, civil rights and other matters, and while the Province appeared relatively peaceful in the post-war decades, a head of steam was building up towards a massive explosion which would take place at the end of the Sixties.

This was foreshadowed by the formation of a number of bodies, including the Campaign for Social Justice which was established in January 1964. Its stated objective was "to collect comprehensive and accurate data on all injustices done against all creeds and political opinions, including details of discrimination in jobs and houses, and to bring them to the attention of as many socially-minded people as possible."

The aims of the Association were intended to transcend party politics but its members would

"feel free to approach, from time to time, any political party anywhere which we think is likely to help us. Whilst we know that the majority of Northern Ireland people, both Protestant and Catholic, are warm-hearted and humane, a minority continues to make life difficult and embarrassing for the rest, and to repress continued appeals for fair play by men of goodwill. Our aim is, we think, both basic and Christian, but nevertheless has not been realised here for hundreds of years–namely–equality for all."[16]

Less than three months later, similar sentiments were expressed at a meeting of the Campaign for Social Justice in Rostrevor by Tom McLaughlin, an Independent member of Armagh Urban District Council, and the son of Senator McLaughlin who had spoken out so vociferously about minority rights a generation earlier.

Councillor McLaughlin referred to the vexed question of the allocation of houses by local authorities.

"I would feel that the local body should then take steps to provide houses on a basis of need, and this is the important word–need. In the many figures quoted during recent months 'so many houses for Catholics, so many for Unionists', the question of need has not been mentioned.

"Surely if 500 Catholic families, and 100 Protestant families, require housing, the Local Authority by building 100 houses for Catholics and 100 houses for Protestants has not given justice. This factor of need must be taken into account before any judgement can be given on any housing situation."

He concluded,

"This Campaign for Social Justice must therefore be above political parties. It must be aimed against any form of injustice carried out by any group or individuals, Protestant or Catholic, Nationalist or Unionist, Orange or Green.

"We must make everyone aware of their obligations to their fellow creatures. If we are Christian then we must practise the great virtue of charity. We must strive to create a new 'image', a community where 'discrimination' will never be thought of, a forward, progressive community, proud of itself and its members, Protestant or Catholic, a community in which a person's religious beliefs are not used as his ticket to a job, house or other privilege."[17]

In other words, a society of which St Patrick himself would have thoroughly approved.

Armagh Urban District Council, like all others in Northern Ireland, was labouring under great difficulties. This point was underlined by Don Ryan,

Don Ryan, former Clerk of
Armagh Urban District
Council.

who was Clerk to the Urban District Council from 1963 until 1972,
shortly before the whole system of local government in the Province was
completely re-organised. He says,

"The huge difficulty they all faced was a lack of money. It was hard for any
Council to do other than to make ends meet. After the re-organisation of 1973,
when so much authority was removed from the Councils, what had been the
Cinderella subjects, such as tourism and culture, became major operations.
Housing was the nightmare for all Councils, not only because of the political
overtones but also because of the enormous drain on the rates fund."

Housing was provided for both main communities, with their political
representatives deciding where they wanted houses built, which tended to
be in their own parts of the city. Sadly however, future generations in
Armagh had to live with the polarisation of housing into Unionist and
Nationalist areas as a result of this "understanding" within the Council.

Don Ryan says "I don't recall that there was any problem about the
houses being built, but there was no obvious criteria applied, such as a points
system, to their allocation." Both sides had their own way of dealing with the
situation, but Don Ryan tells a story about Unionists deciding on their
housing allocation prior to the next Council meeting.

"One Councillor stood up to put forward the name of a certain person for a
house. The Chairman replied testily 'You will do no such thing. Sit down.' The
Councillor, greatly taken aback, asked 'Mr Chairman, have I got it wrong?' To
which the Chairman replied 'Indeed you have!' That was democracy."

The Councillors were men and women of their time, with similar virtues
and vices to those members of other Councils grappling with the hangover
of history – and some of them doing it not too well. Don Ryan recalls "As
a group of people, the Councillors in Armagh got on well, and there was a
fairly harmonious relationship, with one or two exceptions.

"At times there were heated exchanges, but nothing of a particularly
serious nature. Some of the non-Unionists protested regularly at what they
felt was the unfair way in which the Unionists were controlling things.
However, once a fair allocation system for housing was drawn up by the
Government, it became mandatory, and all my Council accepted it, and
other measures, without demur. All they needed was enlightened
leadership."

The Armagh, and the Province, of the Sixties was very different to that
of today. Don Ryan had moved from Belfast to take up his post as Clerk with
the Armagh Council. He says

"The city felt remote from Belfast, and in a way it was. At that stage the
motorway extended only to Lisburn. Armagh was, and still is, far enough away
from Belfast to remain an entity in its own right. Other centres organised 'Civic
Weeks', but Armagh never seemed to feel the need to do that. There was never
any sense of an 'identity crisis'. Other places jumped up and down to try to tell
the world they were there, but Armagh never felt it had to do that."

It was a city with a special pride, even a touch of arrogance.

"Armagh goes back a long way. In those days they would have regarded
themselves as a cut above most other centres in Northern Ireland. This went back
to the legislation of the previous century, where the focus was on Dublin and
Belfast, with Armagh as number three. For example, the title of one Railway Act
referred to the town of Belfast being connected to the city of Armagh, and not

the other way round."

Armagh was also a closely-knit place, but with a distinct sense of hierarchy. Don Ryan remembers:

"Because of my job as Clerk to the Council, like a bank manager, I became part of the local 'society' overnight, but some of my other contemporaries found it a very unfriendly place, which did not seem to accept strangers in a warm-hearted way. I could never say that about Armagh, but there was a great formality about the place. Shortly after we arrived, my wife received invitations to morning coffee, but never on the telephone. People sent out calling cards, it really was as formal as that."

Armagh, which had weathered so many storms, was little enough aware of what the next few decades would hold, nor indeed were people in most parts of Northern Ireland. They knew that many things were not right, including the allocation of housing, but when Captain Terence O'Neill succeeded Lord Brookeborough as Prime Minister in 1963 it looked as if the 'old guard' would be pushed quietly into the past. O'Neill, despite his lack of the common touch which had so benefitted the conservative Brookeborough and his supporters, set out to build bridges between the two communities, and to further enhance the Province's growing prosperity.

Tragically, he discovered that he was able to achieve too little, too late. The liberal wing of Unionism was not sufficiently soundly-based to see off the 'old guard' who interpreted any concessions to the minority as weakness and a sell out. O'Neill was unable to deliver on his promises to the minority, and as a civil rights campaign was progressively overtaken by the newly-formed Provisional IRA, the Province gradually slid into a deep pit of violence.

The too brief period of comparative peace and increasing prosperity would quickly come to an end, and the city of Armagh, like the rest of the Province, would have to suffer some of the worst decades of violence in the entire history of the island. The light of St Patrick would be all but crowded out by the prevailing darkness.

NOTES

1 David Johnson *An Economic History of Ulster 1820-39*, published by the Manchester University Press

2 Jonathan Bardon *A History of Ulster*, published by Blackstaff Press, p.397

3 *Armagh Guardian*, 24 March 1922

4 Ibid.

5 *The Way We Were* was published in 1993 by Friar's Bush Press, in association with the Public Record Office of Northern Ireland, which holds the original prints. A comprehensive commentary is provided by Desmond Fitzgerald and Roger Weatherup.

6 *Northern Ireland Senate Debates Vol. XXI*, 1 March – 24 November 1938, pp.294-295

7 Ibid.

8 Ibid.

9 *Northern Ireland Senate Debates Vol. XXIII*, 19 December – 18 February 1939-41, page 102

10 Ibid.

11 Ibid. p.103

12 Ibid. p.106

13 *Northern Ireland Senate Debates Vol. XVIII*, 26 November 1935 – 12 November 1936, p.32

14 *Northern Ireland Senate Debates Vol. XXV*, 3 February 1942 – 16 February 1943, p.7

15 *A Short History of the Royal Irish Fusiliers*, pp.10-13

16 Press Release issued by the Campaign for Social Justice, on 17 January 1964

17 Archives of Tom McLaughlin

'... today I blush and fear exceedingly to reveal my lack of education; for I am unable to tell my story to those versed in the art of concise writing – in such a way, I mean, as my spirit and mind long to do, and so that the sense of my words expresses what I feel.'

St Patrick's *Confession*

Despite St Patrick's embarrassment about his lack of education, in the centuries following his mission Armagh gained a deserved reputation not only as an ecclesiastical headquarters but also as a centre of learning. The religious schools which thrived in Armagh and elsewhere in Ireland emphasised the importance of education and helped to lay the foundation for the spread of Christianity and of education throughout western Europe.

> "Irishmen went out in pilgrimage, 'seeking salvation and solitude', but they also evangelised pagan peoples; they built up libraries on the continent, wrote works of scholarship and helped to make ready for the flowering of learning which was to follow in ninth century Gaul."[1]

It was ironic that the city of St Patrick, who had been so painfully conscious of his own comparative lack of education, helped to lay the foundation of a vast education network throughout Ireland and greater Europe. It was also fitting that Armagh itself, down the ages, witnessed the significant development of education within its boundaries.

The Royal School Armagh traces its origins back to 1608 when the Privy Council of James I issued a decree that "there should be one free school, at least, appointed in every county, for the education of youths in learning and religion."[2] Incidentally the Royal School shares its birth-date with another well-known Ulster institution – The Old Bushmills Distillery – which can also trace its origins to the year 1608.

The Privy Council decree of that year paved the way for a number of similar schools to educate the children of the newly-arrived Planters, following the Flight of the Earls the previous year. Although Archbishop Ussher, the Church of Ireland Primate, was given 600 acres of land at Mountnorris, near Armagh, to endow the new school, a Royal Charter was not forthcoming until 1627, in the reign of Charles I. Nevertheless, it is recorded that as early as 1608 an Oxford graduate John Lydiat was teaching in the Armagh school.

The school was later moved to the relative security of Armagh City, and situated in the redundant abbey of St Columba in Abbey Street. Here it remained until the arrival of Archbishop Robinson, who turned his attention

Opposite: A window in St Patrick's Church of Ireland Cathedral which displays Archbishop Robinson's contribution to Armagh, with The Royal School featured, as well as the Palace, the Primate's Chapel and the Observatory.

141

The Royal School, Armagh - *A Christmas Scene* painted by Darryl Hutchinson (Head Boy 1994/95).

to improving the Royal School, and – as has been noted earlier – much of Armagh itself.

What is now known as "the old building" was completed in 1774 at a cost of £5,078, a substantial portion of which was provided by the then headmaster Dr Grueber. This building included the present boarding wings and the single central storey of what is now the library. Dr Grueber, by all accounts, was a popular figure.

Evidently the Headmaster lived in style, and in 1776 his income was £400 per annum, which was a large sum in those days. He also had the income from the four hundred apple trees in the walled garden at the back of the School. There was also a field, now a car park, where a large herd of cows added a rustic touch to this scholarly institution. The Headmaster's drawing-room is now the School's Board Room, and at one stage there were twelve servants in the School, including Robert Graham, who worked there as a butler in 1888.

The School had gained a reputation in the eighteenth century, and its pupils included Isaac Corry, who became Speaker of the Irish Parliament, Richard Wellesley, who was twice Lord-Lieutenant of Ireland and also Governor-General of India, his younger brother Arthur, Duke of Wellington who defeated Napoleon in 1815 and later served as British Prime Minister, Leonard Gillespie, Surgeon and Physician to the Fleet under Admiral Lord Nelson, and Lord Castlereagh, British Foreign Secretary at the time of the Battle of Waterloo, and a significant figure in the reconstruction of Europe in the post-Napoleonic era. The youthful Castlereagh described how the boys in the School enlivened their playtime by re-enacting such historic events as the storming of the Bastille and other noteworthy events of the French Revolution.

The School made steady progress and in 1849 it was enlarged, mainly with money donated by Archbishop Beresford. At this time there were sixty-three pupils, more than three times the number registered some sixteen years earlier, and a number of new buildings were added. Fortunately, the School had sufficient land for such expansion, and the extensive estate allowed it to be reasonably self-sufficient in agricultural produce. This, in turn, gave pupils a practical education in agriculture and environmental matters, and the boys were encouraged to cultivate their own plots, as well as those of prefects and the Headmaster.

Indeed, land was used for this purpose during the two World Wars – a practice carried out in other places. During the Second World War, for example, the quadrangle and part of the front lawn at Queen's University were turned into vegetable plots, as part of the Government's "Dig for Victory" campaign. It was alleged that staff acting as air wardens on night duty on the roof of the main Queen's building spent much of their time looking after their vegetables in the allotments.[3]

At the Royal School Armagh, the new buildings erected in the later part of the nineteenth century included the present Reid Hall, and more dormitories and classrooms which made the exterior of the old building largely what it is today. By 1879 the School had one hundred and eleven pupils and thirteen teachers. Its success was such that the Inspector of Grammar Schools noted in 1881 that it was "the most successful boarding school in the north of Ireland and believed Armagh was probably the most suitable place for a Royal School in Ireland."[4] The curriculum was basic, with all Forms I to VI studying Mathematics, English, French, Latin and Greek.

However, there was also time for strenuous recreation, and Armagh Royal won the inaugural Ulster Schools' Cup for rugby in 1877. This sporting achievement augured well for the future, and down the years the School has enjoyed a sound sporting tradition, particularly for cricket and rugby.

The School witnessed significant changes in the 20th century.

"Compulsory mass education had made the school more accessible, but the real change came with the 1947 Education Act which opened what was seen as an elitist institution to those who were successful in the 'qualifying examination' or '11-plus'. In response, more buildings were erected to add to the new Preparatory School opened in 1940. A new teaching block was opened on the site of the Headmaster's orchard in 1966, and by the early 1970's, there were over 500 pupils, including 150 boarders – a small proportion of whom came from overseas to enrich the cultural mix."[5]

In the late 1970's a number of pupils from Armagh Girls' High School attended the Royal School for shared classes and in 1986 the amalgamation of both schools took place – Armagh Girls' High School having been founded as a private school in Russell Street in the early 20th century. The amalgamated school underwent further construction and refurbishment in 1990, and more work was needed shortly afterwards following the explosion of a terrorist bomb at the Courthouse.

In the Church of Ireland Cathedral there are three windows which are

St Patrick's Grammar School, Armagh.

of significant interest in the history of The Royal School. Two of these depict Archbishop Robinson's contribution to Armagh, including the School itself, and the third is the impressive Old Armachian Memorial Window "In honoured memory of the valiant sons of the Royal School of this city, who gave their lives in the Great War 1914-1918". A total of sixty-two pupils died in the First World War and thirty-one in the Second World War. The Old Armachians have placed two memorials in the School – the First World War Memorial is in the Hallway beside the Library, and the Second World War Memorial is attached to the wall of the Cricket Pavilion.

Significantly, The Royal School Armagh has had a direct link with the Archbishops of Armagh since its establishment in 1608, not only through the generous funding from Archbishops Robinson and Beresford, but also through the tradition of appointing the Archbishop 'in situ' as Chairman of the Board of Governors. The School's annual Carol Service is held in the Church of Ireland cathedral, thus perpetuating and symbolising the direct link between St Patrick and Armagh as a centre of learning.

Another direct link to the Patron Saint is St Patrick's Grammar School, which was officially opened in October 1988 by the late Cardinal Tomas O'Fiaich, then Chairman of the Board of Governors. This "new" school was the result of the amalgamation of two of the Province's oldest grammar schools – Christian Brothers' Grammar School and St Patrick's College, both of which had distinguished traditions.

St Patrick's College had been established as a junior seminary on Sandy Hill by Archbishop Crolly. This was under the direction of Diocesan Priests until 1861 when the Vincentian Order was invited to take charge of the school. The Vincentians continued their apostolate in Armagh until the amalgamation, and generations of St Patrick's College students, from all over Ireland and beyond, owe a debt of gratitude to the Vincentians for providing an excellent all-round education.

The Irish Christian Brothers came to Armagh in 1851 at the invitation of Archbishop Cullen, later to be Ireland's first Cardinal. Within a short time, a site was acquired at Greenpark, and primary and secondary schools were established. The Christian Brothers' School steadily built up a strong academic and sporting tradition.

When the Vicentian Order indicated their intention to withdraw from Armagh, Cardinal O'Fiaich asked the Christian Brothers to become joint trustees of the new amalgamated school. Thus the visionary work in

education which was started by Archbishop Crolly in 1838 was to continue on Sandy Hill. Cardinal O'Fiaich was succeeded as Chairman of the Board of Governors by Cardinal Daly in 1991, and by Archbishop Brady in 1997.

The "new" St Patrick's Grammar School proved to be a vibrant institution, not only academically but on the sporting field including Gaelic football and hurling, golf, athletics, swimming and ski-ing, and many Ulster and All-Ireland titles have been won.

Archbishop Cullen, who had invited the Christian Brothers to Armagh in 1851, also issued an invitation to the Society of the Sacred Heart. He remarked pointedly at the time "This town … is a Babylon for the want of religious education for young girls." Some eight years later, after numerous challenges and tribulations, the Society of the Sacred Heart acquired the land covering the present Convent grounds on Windmill Hill. On 30 April 1859, Archbishop Dixon laid and blessed the first stone of the Convent of the Sacred Heart, which was dedicated to Saint Catherine of Siena. The hill was renamed Mount Saint Catherine.

An historic picture of a GAA practice game at St. Patrick's College, with the President, the Very Reverend E.J. Cullen acting as referee and mounted on a horse.

St Catherine's College, Armagh, Convent of the Sacred Heart.

The Society of the Sacred Heart built up a strong tradition, and this is carried on today by Saint Catherine's College, which has a distinguished record of achievement not only academically but also in cultural, sporting and community activities.

It was founded in 1973, with the fusion of the Sacred Heart Grammar School and the Sacred Heart Secondary Intermediate School into a new, non-selective and all ability school catering for Catholic girls from 11-18 years. The

St Brigid's High School, Armagh.

School is committed to "a sound, balanced, Catholic education which promotes the all-round development of each pupil." This reflects the first Plan of Studies formulated by the Society of the Sacred Heart in 1805; "No matter what the direction of her studies, we must aim at the formation of the whole child with a view to her vocation in the age and circumstances in which she has to live."

One of the two other secondary schools in the city is St Brigid's High School at Windmill Hill, near St Catherine's. It was opened in 1971 and caters for boys. St Brigid is said to have been born in Faughhart, Co Louth. Her father Dubhthach was a pagan chieftain and her mother was a Christian named Brocessa. According to legend, the St Brigid's Cross was made as she sat beside the bedside of a dying chieftain. As she wove the cross from rushes on the floor she explained what it meant to be a Christian. According to tradition, St Brigid was a friend of St Patrick.

The City of Armagh High School was formerly Armagh Secondary School at Lonsdale Road, and was relocated in new premises at Alexander Road, where it was opened officially in 1995 by Her Majesty the Queen. It caters for girls and boys. In both schools – St Brigid's and Armagh High – there is a strong emphasis on Christian principles. Both offer a wide range of extra-curricula activities, with St Brigid's featuring Gaelic football and hurling, and the City of Armagh High School including rugby football, cricket and hockey.

Pupils from City of Armagh High School in the Home Economics Room.

The Armagh College of Further Education at Lonsdale Street (still known by some people as "The Tech") has a direct link with the Archbishops of Armagh. It was established in 1900 as the Municipal Technical School under the control of the then Armagh Urban District Council. This Council formed a Technical Instruction Committee, and the first co-opted members were the two Primates, Cardinal Logue and Dr Alexander. This was an auspicious start to an institution which, since its establishment, has served the whole community in its own distinctive way as a centre for Continuing Education.

In Archbishop Robinson's vision of a University in Armagh, the Royal School was meant to be the basis of a School of Classics, while a newly-endowed Library, envisaged in 1771, would accommodate a Faculty of Theology. It was established by an Act of Parliament published in 1773 and titled "An Act for settling and preserving the Publick Library in Armagh for ever ..." It named the institution "The Armagh Public Library", the official title by which it should be known. The commonly-used titles "The Robinson Library" and "The Church Library" are incorrect.

The Library was overseen by a Board of Governors and Guardians, with the Archbishop of Armagh "for the time being" presiding. The Governors were clergy from the Church of Ireland, and it was not until 1886 that a layman was appointed. The Librarian or "Library Keeper" was to be appointed by the Archbishop and had to be a Presbyter of the Established Church and to hold an MA degree from an English or an Irish university.

The Armagh Public Library, an
Archbishop Robinson creation which
was established by Act of Parliament
in 1773.

The distinguished Dublin architect Thomas Cooley designed the Library
in its initial form. It was a simple but well-proportioned two-storey building
with a central door in the North Facade which gave access through the
Keeper's house to the book room on the first floor. The Library's income and
the Keeper's emoluments were provided from grants of land in the county.

In 1845, Archbishop Beresford enlarged the Library, with a Mr Monserrat
winning a prize for the best design submitted. The building was extended at
each end by a new two-storey bay, and a new entrance – created at the East
end – gave direct access to the Book Room. Above the entrance there was a
Greek inscription which is translated as "The healing place of the soul". It
was not until 1914, however, that the installation of a spiral staircase gave
access to the Gallery without going through the Keeper's private apartments.

Archbishop Robinson left his extensive personal library to form the basis
of the collection, and this was supplemented by gift and purchase to form a
good research base which has been of considerable benefit to scholars down
the years. Before the First World War, the library became a centre for fiction,
as an agent for Mundies Lending Library.

This public service was revived in the middle of the twentieth century,
through the Times Book Club. With the development of the local Council's
free library facilities, this practice was discontinued. To mark the Bicentenary
in 1971, the building was renovated. The exterior stonework was cleaned, the
roof was repaired and the woodwork was painted. The interior was also
cleaned and repainted, and the Library remains today as one of the long-
standing examples of the extraordinary vision of Archbishop Robinson.

The Observatory circa 1885.

Another outstanding example of Robinson's legacy to Armagh was the establishment of an Observatory which would provide a School of Sciences for a proposed University. The earliest recorded astronomical observations in Armagh were made by members of the religious colleges in the area during the early Middle Ages, and were later compiled in the Annals of Ulster.

The construction of the Observatory began in 1789, from plans drawn by the celebrated Armagh architect Francis Johnston. Describing it only a quarter of a century or so later, Stuart writes "It bears the concise and sublime inscription 'The Heavens Declare the Glory of God'. The walls are constructed with beautiful hewn limestone, in the most firm and durable manner. Tasteful plantations, which adorn the sloping sides of the hill on which the observatory stands, have flourished exceedingly, and already the building is almost embosomed in trees."[6]

The first Director of the Observatory was the Reverend Dr James Archibald Hamilton, who was appointed on 24 August 1790. Archbishop Robinson endowed land to the astronomer, and such was his political influence that this procedure was sanctioned shortly afterwards by an Act of Parliament signed by King George III. Following Robinson's death in 1794, money was scarce but nevertheless, the Director was able to purchase a state of the art equatorial telescope made by the celebrated firm of John and Edward Troughton, and this – together with a pair of outstanding clocks made by Thomas Earnshaw of London – remained the main piece of equipment in the Observatory for many years.[7]

Another cleric, the Reverend Dr William Davenport succeeded Hamilton who died in 1815. He, in turn, was succeeded in 1823 by the Reverend Dr Thomas Romney Robinson, a well-known astronomer and meteorologist, who made his mark over a long tenure of office. Robinson held office for a remarkable fifty-nine years. He extended the building, and

acquired important new instruments, including a transit instrument in 1827, and a mural circle four years later.

With his assistants, he compiled the Armagh Catalogue with "The Places of 5,345 stars observed from 1828-1854 at the Armagh Observatory", and a later and more accurate list on the placing of 1,000 stars. He also invented, among other things, the Robinson Cup Anemometer, which transformed the recording and measurement of wind speed and direction.

Robinson died in 1882 and was succeeded by a Dane, Dr J L E Dreyer, who was an assistant at the Dunsink Observatory, near Dublin, which was founded in 1785, some four years before construction work began in Armagh. During his tenure of office, he installed in 1885 a 10-inch Robinson Memorial refractor manufactured by Grubb of Dublin, and produced for the Royal Astronomical Society a scientific report on nebulae and star-clusters which is still used by astronomers world-wide.[8] A personal copy of Dreyer's report, with the author's hand-written corrections and comments, is still in the Observatory's Library, which also houses an extensive collection of contemporary and historic textbooks, many of them provided by Dr Romney Robinson. The oldest dates from 1499.

Patrick Moore, author and broadcaster, who was Director of the Planetarium in the 1960s.

In 1916 Dreyer went to Oxford to continue his work and was succeeded by Joseph A Hardcastle who died in November 1917 even before he moved to Armagh. The Reverend Dr W F A Ellison became the Director in 1918, but due to a lack of money the activities of the Observatory were greatly restricted.

The Observatory's significant development began with the appointment of Dr Eric M Lindsay in 1937. Born at Portadown, he studied astronomy at Queen's University and later at Harvard. With help from the Northern Ireland Government at Stormont, Lindsay helped to put the Observatory on a sound financial basis, and also added to its growing international reputation.

Dr Eric Lindsay, Director of Armagh Observatory, 1937-1974.

Professor Mark Bailey, the current Director of the Observatory.

After the Second World War he worked with Dunsink and Harvard to establish the first international observatory as a portent of further developments.

"Under his leadership ... the Observatory grew from an essentially one-man enterprise into a modern astrophysical institute with a staff of about ten. Sophisticated instruments for measuring the photographic plates from the southern hemisphere site were acquired and international collaborations extended."[9]

The reputation of the Observatory was further enhanced by Dr Ernst Julius Opik, an Estonian refugee, who joined the staff in 1948. He was one of the most outstanding astronomers of the twentieth century, and arguably the most accomplished astronomer to work at Armagh. Despite many tempting offers to work elsewhere, he stayed at Armagh for the rest of his working life – though taking regular leave to work as a part-time Professor at the University of Maryland.

His philosophy about work and financial reward was neatly summarised in a letter to Lindsay before his arrival. He wrote "... questions of salary and personal ambitions have never played a part in my life, at least have never influenced my decisions. Given the possibility for research, I do not think that I shall feel inclined to look for anything else." His interests ranged from such topics as meteors, comets, asteroids and the planets to interstellar matter, stellar interiors and distances to other galaxies. A minor planet discovered by astronomers in 1977 was later named after Dr Opik, in honour of his eighty-fifth birthday in 1978.

Dr Lindsay, whose untimely death occurred in 1974, was also honoured by the International Astronomical Union in 1977 which named a crater on the near side of the Moon after him. Following his death, Ernst Opik was Acting Director until 1976, when Dr Mart de Groot, a Dutchman, took over.

Incidentally Dr Opik's approach to science was neatly summarised in a collection of short essays first published in 1956 and presented for the general reader. Writing in the third person he stated "while all his original viewpoints may not pass to posterity, he will consider his purpose fulfilled if his efforts inspire others in the search for truth, or make them feel the beauty of the cosmos and the mystery of our existence."

Dr Mart de Groot , who was Director until 1994, helped the Observatory to stay at the leading edge of research and scholarship. Computers were introduced, staff numbers increased slightly, "and the modern era with its frequent use of overseas observatories and satellites began."[10] The expansion of the Observatory, initiated by Lindsay and continued by de Groot, with Government support, has made it one of the leading astronomical institutes in the British Isles.

It has for long been part of a sophisticated international network. The astronomers at Armagh work regularly with colleagues in Australia, South Africa, the USA, South America, and Europe including the Canary Islands, Hawaii, Russia and Japan, as well as satellites with ground stations in Spain, Germany, and America. Staff at the Observatory also work closely with scientists at Queen's University, Belfast and with colleagues at the Dublin

Opposite: The 2 1/2 inch equatorial telescope by Troughton in its original dome on top of the Observatory's main building.

The Armagh Planetarium

Dr Tom Mason, Director of Armagh Planetarium. " We have an important role in communicating science, but we are also in show-business".

The Armagh Planetarium was founded in 1968 by Dr Eric Lindsay, the then Director of Armagh Observatory, as a public outreach facility for the Observatory. It was the first Planetarium in Northern Ireland and one of the first in the United Kingdom.

The role of the Planetarium is to provide up-to-date information about astronomy and other disciplines, including earth science, geology and environmental science to as wide an audience as possible, both nationally and internationally.

Armagh Planetarium at dusk with the planets Venus and Jupiter in the night sky.

The aim is to enable as many people as possible to increase their enjoyment and understanding of the natural world and to appreciate the rich astronomical and scientific heritage within Northern Ireland. As such, the Planetarium is one of the leading visitor attractions in Northern Ireland and in Armagh City and district.

Director Dr Tom Mason says, "The Planetarium is essentially a shop-window for astronomy. Given the prevailing weather in Northern Ireland, it is not possible for people always to see the stars, and our role is to simulate a starry sky to enable them to learn more about the subject."

He is refreshingly direct about the challenges of promoting and communicating science in the modern world. "We are taking off the 'magic white robes' which the scientists liked to wear and putting science on white screens. In the spirit of Buckminster Fuller who said that there are no 'departments' in nature, we are also tackling non-astronomical subjects such as stone age technology, minerals and rocks and other basic sciences-the subjects many teachers would love to tackle but do not always have the time to do so."

The Planetarium is visitor-based. "The more people who come through our doors the better it is for us, but we also reach out to the local community with a series of talks for up to 10,000 school-children each year, and anyone else who wants to listen." A favourite presentation is that on the "Star of Bethlehem", which includes the use of computer graphics showing, among other things, pictures of the coinage of King Herod's time."

Another important aspect of the work is to reach out to the underprivileged in the local community. "Our role is to be pro-active, particularly in areas of social need, and this programme is now paying dividends."

Dr Mason sums up "The onus is on the scientists to communicate. There is no point talking at a group all evening in a monotone. They will switch-off, and you might as well just go home. People are very tactile. They love to 'touch' science. Just think of the thrill of actually holding in your hand part of a 4 billion year old meteorite!

"You have to fire-up people with enthusiasm for science, to be very much 'hands on' and consumer-friendly. We have an important role in communicating science, but we are also in show-business!"

Institute for Advanced Studies.

The current Director Professor Mark E Bailey, a Cambridge graduate, says

"During more than 200 years of development, Armagh Observatory has touched upon virtually every aspect of modern Astrophysics. Our current activities focus on three broad areas – Stellar Astrophysics, including star formation, stellar jets and outflows, the Sun and other topics; Solar System Astronomy, including the origin and evolution of comets and asteroids, and Solar System-Terrestrial Relationships, including investigations into solar variability and climate."

As part of this work, scientists have found that although higher global temperatures may have occurred in recent years as a result of the enhanced 'greenhouse' effect, most of the global warming of the twentieth century can be attributed to solar activity. Scientists are also aware of the potential devastation from asteroids and comets impacting on the Earth, and a recent Government Task Force Report on this subject has recommended measures to try to combat this – an area of science where Armagh Observatory is at the forefront.

The Observatory is, in fact, a remarkable institution with a long, colourful history, an impressive record and a deserved international reputation as one of the foremost scientific institutions in these islands. Still principally housed in the premises constructed by Archbishop Robinson, the Observatory itself is a listed building of great architectural merit and historic interest. In the Board Room are portraits of Robinson and the other Archbishops, as a reminder of its clerical foundation, while not far away the scientists continue to research into the heavens with the most up-to-date equipment.

The Observatory is tucked away in attractive landscaped grounds that include the Armagh Planetarium, founded in 1968 and a scale model of the Universe known as the Astropark, founded in 1994. It is one of the jewels of Armagh, and a credit to its founder and to the generations of distinguished scholars and scientists who have made it what it is today.

In turn, the Observatory has recognised its benefactors by making it possible to have a Minor Planet named "Deni" in recognition of the support given by the former Department of Education for Northern Ireland, prior to its disappearance in the re-organised Northern Ireland Civil Service following the Good Friday Agreement.

The Observatory has also been instrumental, together with the International Astronomical Union, in the naming of two asteroids, one for the city and the other for the Observatory. The former was named, appropriately, "Ardmacha", and the latter was called "Armaghobs". Both were discovered by the distinguished American astronomer Eleanor 'Glo' Helin, a good friend of the Armagh Observatory who is based at the Mount Palomar Observatory in the USA.

The link between the Observatory and Queen's pre-dated the establishment of a University campus at Armagh, but it underlined that the city of St Patrick has a long and historic claim to be a centre of learning. The struggle by Armagh and its people to establish a university in the city would almost entail a book in itself, and some of the early initiatives, and disappointments, were well-chronicled by the late T G F Paterson, a former Curator of Armagh County Museum.

Charles Wood

Charles Wood, the distinguished musician and composer was born in Armagh in 1866, and received his early musical education as a chorister in the Church of Ireland Cathedral. When he died in 1926, he left a legacy of over 250 sacred works, plus a large number of hymn tunes. An annual Charles Wood Summer School is held in Armagh.

Paterson notes that in 1583 there was a proposal for the establishment of universities in Armagh and Limerick.

"Both cities had excellent historical backgrounds but Armagh had special claims. It was then, as now, the ecclesiastical capital of Ireland. It had long been a seat of learning, and life and thought in many countries had been influenced through the teachings of its students."[11]

A much more serious proposal emerged at the end of the eighteenth century, following the death of Archbishop Robinson in 1794. He had stipulated in his Will that a bequest of £5,000 should be given to the establishment of a university at Armagh, provided that it be completed within five years of his death. However it was not until August 1798 that the subject was brought to official notice, which meant that there was little over a year left before the legacy would elapse.

On 24 August an official request was forwarded to Lord Cornwallis, the then Lord-Lieutenant of Ireland, stressing Armagh's claims, including the provision of Armagh Public Library and the Observatory, plus a further bequest of £1,000 for a Chapel "That would answer to the College". Cornwallis took this seriously, and in July 1799 forwarded a plan for the proposed university to the Prime Minister, the Duke of Portland, requesting that he ask the King himself to approve the scheme. It was important that its incorporation would be drafted by October of that year, otherwise Robinson's legacy would become legally void.

The scheme proposed that the revenues of the five Royal Schools in Ulster should be put towards the salaries of the headmasters but also the salaries of Professors and Scholars at the new university, as well as the maintenance of its students and the upkeep of the buildings.

The Dean of Armagh was to be appointed Provost, and the Librarian of Armagh as well as the Astronomer, were to be Fellows. Professorships were to be established in Classical Learning and History, Mathematics and Experimental Philosophy, Moral Philosophy and Church Law, Divinity of the Church of England, and Divinity for Dissenters. There were to be five Junior Fellows and forty Scholars, and dissenters were eligible for any post, apart from that of Provost.[12]

However, this ambitious plan failed to win the approval of the Prime Minister, who declined to recommend it to the King. Instead he proposed that the funds of the Royal Schools could not be used in this way, and that Robinson's legacy should be allowed to lapse. Portland felt that the better classes in Ulster should receive part of their education at the schools and universities of England, contrary to Robinson's view that a local university at Armagh would be such that "nothing would tend so much to conciliate and soften down the minds of the various sectaries in the north of Ireland and bind them to the common interests of the Empire".

Subsequent events have shown Robinson's view to have been optimistic. Even with the later establishment of two large universities in the province of Ulster the mistrust between "the various sectaries" still remains.

It was not until 1845 that the claims of Armagh were considered seriously, when the Queen's Colleges were being established in Ireland. The two main contenders were Armagh and Belfast, where there was already a strong tradition of higher education. The Scottish universities had educated many Ulster folk, mainly Presbyterians, and the Irish colleges in continental Europe had provided education for young Roman Catholics long before the establishment of Maynooth College in 1795.

The foundation of the Belfast Academical Institution in 1810 (and from 1831 the "Royal" Belfast Academical Institution) had been providing a university level education, though it could not award degrees. As well the city of Belfast itself was growing rapidly, from some 20,000 in the year 1800 to nearly five times that figure by the middle of the 19th century.

Undaunted by such opposition, Armagh lobbied vigorously for a university, and a meeting of its prominent citizens took place on 7 August 1845. It was attended by the Roman Catholic Archbishop Dr Crolly who spoke in favour, and Primate Beresford, who was unable to be present, nevertheless offered the sum of £1,000 towards the establishment of a Chair in Divinity.

The Reverend Pooley Shuldham Henry, who was ordained and installed in First Armagh Presbyterian Church in 1826. Some local people were confident that he would be the first President of the University at Armagh, but to their consternation the Queen's College was established in 1845, not in Armagh but in Belfast with the Reverend Henry as its first President.

Later on, a memorial was drawn up and presented to the then Lord-Lieutenant Lord Heytesbury. Among the advantages listed by Armagh were two that had been presented previously – namely the existence of a fine Public Library and a good Observatory. However, other advantages were listed.

They included Armagh's "central position"; the fact that it was a Metropolitan City and the place of residence of the two Primates; that it was "One of the healthiest parts of Ireland and no large manufactories near"; that it was "more conducive to the moral and intellectual attainments of students than a trading manufacturing or sea-port town where incitements to vice were numerous", in other words a direct dig at Belfast; and that the city had a population of "Church Protestants, Roman Catholics and Presbyterians in equal proportions."

St Patrick himself could not have made the case better, if he had been alive, though the break-up of the church he had founded this would in itself have caused him considerable sorrow. Nevertheless, Armagh faced an uphill battle to establish a university. The Lord-Lieutenant received a deputation from the city but rebuffed the Roman Catholic Archbishop who was lobbying hard for Armagh by declaring that a college built there might "offend the Presbyterians" in the rest of the Province.[13]

The war of words raged on. Belfast poured scorn upon Armagh's pretensions as the ecclesiastical capital. Armagh replied that such arrogance came with a peculiarly bad grace from a town of mushroom growth noted only for its spinning-jennies and factories. *The Morning Herald* fanned the flames by stating that 'Armagh was more academical than her alluvial neighbour'. Belfast retorted by asking what Armagh had ever done for education. Swiftly came the reply: "That is a story that began fourteen centuries before the smoking chimneys of Belfast had emerged from the mud."[14]

Right to the end there was confidence in Armagh that the new university would be established in the city, and one letter-writer to the *Armagh*

Sir Gordon Beveridge, Vice -
Chancellor of Queen's University
Belfast 1986-1997, who first mooted
in public the establishment of an
outreach campus in Armagh,
with Lady Beveridge.

Guardian was certain that the local Presbyterian Minister the Reverend Dr Pooley Shuldham Henry would be its first President. One can imagine the consternation in Armagh when the Government eventually announced that the new Queen's College would be established in Belfast, with others in Cork and Galway, and that the new President in Belfast would be none other than Dr Henry, who was also an "old boy" of the Belfast Academical Institution.

Henry served as President from 1845-79. Professor J C Beckett, the first Professor of Irish History at Queen's from 1958 until his retirement in 1975, wrote of Henry that "he was not a man of academic distinction, but he was a good administrator, he had considerable experience of public affairs, and he inspired confidence both inside and outside the college."[15]

Armagh had to wait a long time before the prospect of a new university was raised again. This occurred in the 1960's when the Northern Ireland Government recognised the need for a further institute of higher education to meet increasing number of students, and set up a Committee chaired by Sir John Lockwood, Master of Birkbeck College. It was decided – to the surprise of most educationalists and the anger and dismay of Londonderry and Armagh respectively, which were thought to have much better historical and educational claims – that a new university should be established at Coleraine. This was viewed by many people as a most unsatisfactory decision which had been made on political rather than on educational grounds.

Armagh's hopes were dashed yet again, and the city had to wait until the mid-1990's before Archbishop Robinson's vision became a reality. Following discussions between Queen's University and representatives of Armagh City and District Council from the early 1990's it became apparent that the establishment of an outreach by the University in Armagh could be feasible.

The idea was considered by senior figures within Queen's and first mooted in public by the then Vice-Chancellor Sir Gordon Beveridge, who

President Mary Robinson, who visited Armagh during the "Armagh Together" celebrations.

The first graduates from the Queen's University at Armagh, in July 2000. Also pictured are, at rear left to right, Professor Bob Cormack, Pro Vice-Chancellor, Desmond Mitchell, Clerk and Chief Executive of Armagh City and District Council, Mr Richard Jay, Director at Armagh, and Dr Tess Maginess, Student Support Officer.

already had a close connection with the city as the first Chairman of the Navan Fort Initiative Group. When preparing his Graduation Speech for 4 July 1994, he was considering suitable themes and on the advice of one of his speech-writers he devoted his address to the theme of "Vision in the Context of Higher Education". He stated:

"The first part of my vision is based on four key issues. Firstly, there is the huge, unsatisfied demand from well-qualified school-leavers across the Province and cross-border. Second, the number of part-time students will rise significantly, especially given the reduction of full-time student maintenance grants.

"Third, as far as the south and the west of Ulster are concerned, there is a barren landscape of university provision, unlike the fertile concentration of the north and east. Fourthly, the Queen's approach of modular-based degrees facilitates part-time student study.

"These taken together make me believe that there is a pressing need for Queen's to take education out to these students, who will be primarily part-time, and thus I foresee the setting up of Queen's campuses in one or more selected towns in the south and west of the Province; already Queen's has been approached by interested and concerned citizens from Armagh and Omagh, indicating that potential accommodation already exists.

"This aspiration could be actively enhanced by the participation of students from across the border, perhaps linking up, too, with a sister institution, University College Galway, not only as a symbolic link which we have shared in the past, but to meet a real need in the world of today. This is an important challenge and

a practical response, although to make it a reality there is a need for an equally imaginative response from Government and its agencies in Northern Ireland."

The Armagh campus opened its doors to the first generation of students in September 1995, during the University's year-long Sesquicentennial celebrations. It was fitting that almost exactly one hundred and fifty years after the announcement of the establishment of Ulster's first University in Belfast and not in Armagh – as the locals had hoped – the wheel had come full circle with the opening of Queen's University at Armagh.

President Mary McAleese at Armagh with the Mayor, Councillor Tom Canavan and the Lady Mayoress, Mrs Roisin Canavan.

To accommodate the new outreach institution, the refurbishment of the old City Infirmary built by Archbishop Robinson in 1774 had been completed with commendable speed. Though launched in 1995 by the then Pro-Vice-Chancellor of Queen's Professor Mary McAleese (now President of Ireland) who had been a driving-force in the work to establish the outreach at Armagh, the campus was not officially opened until 1997 by Sir Ron Dearing, author of the seminal Dearing Report on Higher Education.

Since its establishment, Queen's at Armagh has made significant progress. It began with a 50-seat lecture theatre fitted with the latest electronic equipment, including facilities for distance-learning. There was also a small library, a student common room, three seminar rooms, a resource centre with direct computer-contact with Queen's, Belfast, office space and an attractive entrance hall. The initial staff comprised two administrators, two clerical staff, a computer technician, and three Queen's lecturers on a part-time basis.

The academic programme reflected the philosophy of the project which was to widen access to Higher Education. At the core of the academic activity was the Bachelor of Arts Degree through part-time study, which was tailor-made by the Queen's Institute of Continuing Education (now Lifelong Learning) for adult and mature students, as well as a range of one-year certificates. These included Counselling, Community Work, Women's Studies, Computer Information Systems, Marketing, Advertising and Public Relations, Disability Studies, and other subjects.

Queen's at Armagh also offers a degree in Early Childhood Studies, as well as post-graduate courses in Computer-Based Learning, Irish Studies, Religion and Society, and education. Short courses for the development of IT skills have been heavily in demand. In 1996 the first students were accepted onto an undergraduate pathway in Irish Studies, and in the same year Queen's at Armagh, in conjunction with Dublin City University, launched a Master's Degree in Science Communication, the first of its kind in Ireland. This was aimed at helping to address the perceived communication gap between modern science and the public at large, and students on the course spend their time equally in Dublin and Armagh.

In 1999, Queen's at Armagh signed an agreement with the Dublin Institute for Public Administration to develop a Doctorate in Governance, designed for senior public officials in Northern Ireland and the Irish Republic. In the same year, plans for the regeneration of the rest of the site were drawn up, and extra teaching and office space was planned.

Professor Sir George Bain, Vice - Chancellor of Queen's University. "We continue to value our partnership with Armagh. There is an important job to do here".

This involved the expansion and re-siting of the library, to include a reserve collection for the library of Cardinal Daly, Emeritus Archbishop of Armagh and a former Queen's student and member of staff. The Cardinal Cahal Daly Library was officially opened at Armagh on 19 September 2001. Two Queen's partnership projects were also established. One, under Professor John Brewer, was on the Social Study of Religion, which was linked to the Council's Centre for Religion, and the other, under Andy Pollak, was the Centre for Cross Border Studies, a policy research unit funded by the European Union, through the Education Departments of both Governments in Belfast and Dublin, and run by a Board including representatives of Queen's, Dublin City University and the WEA. The University also agreed to provide space in its recently-refurbished building to help accommodate the new Secretariat to the North-South Ministerial Council, which was established under the Good Friday Agreement.

In October 1999, Professor Sir George Bain who had succeeded Sir Gordon Beveridge as Vice-Chancellor at the beginning of the previous year, made a keynote speech to Armagh City and District Council and underlined the University's commitment.

He said:

"We continue to value our partnership as a benefit to both parties and to the people of Armagh. Because of Armagh's history, its intellectual and cultural resources, and its location in the border area, we believe that we have an important educational and developmental job to do here." He added "Queen's, Armagh is putting down roots and is here to stay as long as Armagh and the surrounding region demonstrate a significant demand for our services."

Professor Bain identified new areas of development, and four keys to the University's future academic outreach – social inclusion; heritage, culture and tradition; the enhancement of local skills, especially in IT, for economic and social development; and cross-border activities.

Queen's University at Armagh is now well-established, and promises much for the future. Mr Richard Jay, the Director, says "Some 300-400 students cross our threshold each year on a variety of studies ranging from one year full-time postgraduate courses, five or ten week introductory courses for those with few conventional entry qualifications, right through to five year part time degrees.

"Many students travel a considerable distance, a good proportion coming from Monaghan, Dundalk and further afield. Many students have passed through, but one of the most heart-warming events was a special formal presentation in July 2000 for 15 part-time mature student graduates, including one male, who had joined the campus when it first opened in 1995."

Professor Bain, the Vice-Chancellor, put in context the considerable achievement of Queen's at Armagh in its first few years

"The modern campus, recently expanded and re-decorated, lies at the heart of a flourishing complex of educational and administrative activities which have transformed the site, and is a key point in the regeneration of the city centre.

"It is perhaps a testimony to the Queen's vision of outreach that in July 2000, Mr Michael Woods, the Irish Minister of Education, spoke warmly of using the outreach model to expand Higher Education in a number of areas of under-provision in the Republic. Queen's at Armagh has come a long way, and its development is an achievement of which we can all be proud. No doubt Archbishop Robinson himself would be immensely pleased that his vision for a University at Armagh has become a reality."

No doubt St Patrick, who set so much store by education of all kinds, would concur. The development of education and of learning in the city where he founded his main church would give him much cause to rejoice.

NOTES

1 Kathleen Hughes, *The Course of Irish History*, p.90
2 *The Royal School Past and Present*, a Millennium History of the Institution from 1608 – December 1999
3 *Degrees of Excellence: The Story of Queen's, Belfast 1845-1995*, Walker and McCreary, p.68, published by the Institute of Irish Studies at Queen's
4 *The Royal School Past and Present*, p.5
5 Op. Cit. p.6
6 Stuart. Op. Cit. p.523
7 Dr Mart de Groot, *The Way To The Stars*, published by The Armagh Observatory in association with Armagh District Council, p.7
8 The full title of the report is *New General Catalogue of Nebulae and Clusters of Stars* – de Groot, Op. Cit. p.9
9 de Groot, Op. Cit. p.9
10 de Groot, Op. Cit. p.9
11 TGF Paterson, *Harvest Home: The Last Sheaf*, p.57. *Proposals for a University at Armagh*, published by the TGF Paterson Memorial Fund Committee, Armagh County Museum 1975
12 Paterson. Op. Cit. pp.60-61
13 Ibid. pp.67-68
14 Ibid. p.68
15 Walker and McCreary. Op. Cit. p.3

Cricket on the Mall, an Armagh institution.

Armagh at Play

The City of Armagh and the surrounding area have a long tradition of achievement in sport. Reference has been made earlier to George Henry Bassett's vignette of 1888, by which time lawn tennis and archery were popular, and the local club had 100 paid-up members, with one subscription "being sufficient for an entire family". Archery had been established in 1862, followed by lawn tennis in 1878.

Cycling was also popular, particularly with the ladies who rode tricycles. A cricket club was formed in 1859, though the sport was played at The Mall as early as July 1845. The sight of cricket whites against the green back-drop of The Mall is still a familiar and welcome summer sight in Armagh.

The Rugby Club was formed in 1875, and in the Centenary History, recently reprinted, the then President of the Ulster Branch, Noel Henderson, mentioned three outstanding memories of playing in Armagh – "tough but fair opposition, the most beautiful pitch in Ireland at the Mall, and the tremendous evenings at the Beresford Arms."

In 1972, the Club moved to new premises at the Palace Demesne, and although the brain-drain of young players to the rest of the United Kingdom poses a problem, Armagh Rugby Club still has a distinctive role. Soccer is also strong in the area at a number of levels, and the Armagh City club, with Senior status, has an impressive record, picking up a local award recently as Senior Team of the Year.

Hockey is one of the most successful sports in Armagh, with strong representation by both men and women. During the 2000-01 season, the Armagh men's senior team won promotion to the Ulster Senior Two League – a remarkable achievement given that the club was founded only in 1994, though there is a fleeting mention in the Ulster Branch minute book of an Armagh club in the year 1901-02. It is also worth noting that the City of Armagh High boys and girls Under-16 hockey teams won their respective Ulster Schools titles in the season 2000-01.

The County Armagh Golf Club, situated on the Markethill to Newry Road, is also a thriving institution which celebrated its centenary in 1993 and which continues to make headlines in the sporting press. It has one of the most beautiful parkland courses in Ireland, with panoramic views of the city, including the two cathedrals, and the Palace Demesne.

Gaelic football, hurling and camogie have always been strong in Armagh and district, and the first reference to the GAA in Co Armagh appeared in the 2 October 1886 issue of Sport, which stated that "Frank Brassil Dineen and John Boyle O'Reilly, both members of the central executive of the GAA, were busy recruiting members and organising branches in Armagh."[1] There is also "little doubt that football and hurling of a kind had been played in Co Armagh long before the foundation of the GAA."[2] Over the years, Gaelic sport has been strong in the city and county, and recently the Armagh Gaelic team distinguished itself greatly by winning the Ulster Senior Championship two years in succession.

Perhaps the most distinctive sport to be associated with Armagh, however, is Road Bowls, also known as Bullets, Bowl-Playing or simply Bowling. The sport is played with a 28oz solid iron bowl, the circumference of which is approximately 18 centimetres. Two contestants match their individual skills in throwing the bowl with optimum speed, controlled delivery, and intentional accuracy along a carefully-considered and tactically-selected play-path, and over a pre-determined course distance of normal roadway.

The winner is the player to reach the finishing line in the least number of throws or shots. Course distances vary, but are usually around 4 km in length. A score, or a match may be watched by anything from several dozen to perhaps thousands of spectators. The sport is most prevalent in Armagh and Cork[3], and it is also played in Dagenham, Essex.

The journalist Martin Fletcher, writing in The Times of London, stated: "It is sport in its purest form – a genuine community event undefiled by professionalism or commercialism, although thousands of pounds change hands in bets. It is played on the public byways. It is played not for money, but for love and glory by men and women whose fathers, grandfathers and great-grandfathers would have passed their Sundays in the same way."[4]

NOTES

1 Con Short, Peter Murray and Jimmy Smyth Page 20 Ard Mhacha 1884–1984 *A Century of GAA Progress,* published by the Armagh County Board.
2 Op. Cit. Page 24
3 Brian Toal *Road Bowling in Ireland* Page 1, published in 1996.
4 *The Times*, Page 19, 22 May 1999.

Top:
Armagh RFC at Ravenhill for the Junior Cup Final.

Centre:
The Armagh County Team 1999 which won the Ulster GAA Championship.

Below:
Armagh Road Bowls – "A sport in its finest form".

'It was the best of times, it was the worst of times ...'

Charles Dickens *A Tale of Two Cities*

These words aptly summarise the story of Armagh in the last decades of the twentieth century. It suffered the worst of times through the conflict involved in terrorists' campaigns and security counter-measures, yet it also looked forward to the best of times through the visionary developments – artistically, ecclesiastically and architecturally – which enriched the city as it moved towards and into the new Millennium.

Throughout its history, Armagh has been a centre of political activity, not least during the latest round of what is termed euphemistically in Northern Ireland "The Troubles". The civil rights movement was strong in Armagh, and one of the major confrontations between civil rights supporters and loyalists took place in the city on 30 November 1968.

The civil rights supporters in Armagh had been given permission to march through the centre, but from around 2 am that morning, loyalists had been converging on the city. Don Ryan, the then Clerk of the Urban District Council, recalls "The atmosphere was dreadful. I was down in Armagh during the morning, and shopkeepers were boarding up their premises in anticipation of trouble. Loyalists seemed determined to prevent the civil rights marchers from going beyond the nationalist area. There was a minor riot on the outskirts of Armagh, and relations between the two communities went downhill after that."

The People's Democracy, which had grown out of left-wing politics within the student body at Queen's University was active in Armagh. Don Ryan remembers when PD supporters crowded into Council meetings. "We were invaded for several weeks. At that time there were no proper rules governing the admission of the public. However, when we did draw up a set of rules, members of the PD stopped coming. I suppose there was no fun in it any more."

Armagh suffered widespread damage from a systematic bombing campaign by the Provisional IRA, and buildings in the commercial area were prime targets. The destruction of Armagh City Hall in 1972 is remembered vividly by Desmond Mitchell, at that time the deputy Clerk of the Council.

"The City Hall was the seat of political power in Armagh, and therefore its destruction by the Provisional IRA was a political statement."

He was in the building when the alarm was raised.

"I did not hear clearly the police warnings about getting out, so I ran to the nearest exit I could find. On my way out towards the front door I jumped over a brown suitcase, which I later learned had contained the explosives. I ran so hard

Desmond Mitchell - as Clerk and Chief Executive of the Council he was a prime mover in the development of Armagh. "We wanted the city to be imbued, as far as possible, with St Patrick's spirit."

Charles Armstrong Chairman of Armagh Council in November 1983 when he was killed by a Provisional IRA booby-trap bomb in the car park of the Palace Demesne. His portrait hangs in the Mayor's Parlour which is named in his memory.

that my watch came off my arm and smashed to the ground. The Provisionals claimed that the bomb was a considerable success technically. It demolished the whole building."

The destruction in the city continued through the Seventies and Eighties, and into the Nineties. In September 1993 a massive bomb badly damaged Armagh court-house, and the adjoining property in the Mall. There were repeated attacks on the local RUC station, which have continued almost up to the present. It was ironic that the buildings and fabric of Armagh which had so often been burned and destroyed by warring factions down the centuries, again bore the brunt of the Provisional IRA bombing campaign.

Tragically, many human beings were in the front line, and many were killed or injured in the violence. One of the early casualties was John Taylor, the Armagh politician who survived a murder attempt on his life on 25 February 1972. Then aged only 34, he had a successful political career already, and was a Cabinet Minister in the Unionist Government at Stormont.

Following a business meeting in Armagh which ended after 5.50 on a Friday evening, Mr Taylor returned to his car, a green Humber, and switched on the ignition. He recalled the incident later, in graphic detail:

"Immediately, there was a tremendous bang. I lost all sense of feeling in my legs, and my foot went down heavily on the accelerator. The car was not in gear and the roar of the engine was deafening. I thought it was a booby-trap, but then I realised that the roar was coming from the engine. This was all happening in split seconds, but I also realised that shooting was coming from the direction of my right ear and that I was in the process of being shot.

"I remember the blood gushing out, and I also remember being slumped back in the seat. That probably helped to save my life because I believe that several bullets whizzed past my nose. If I'd stayed upright, even more bullets would have passed through my face and head. I also remember the terrifying feeling of not

Bomb damage at the Armagh Branch of the Trustee Savings Bank, 1973.

being able to lift my leg off the accelerator. It felt like a ton weight."[1]

Taylor had been ambushed by Official IRA gunmen who fired a hail of seventeen machine-gun bullets which shattered his jaw-bone. He was taken to Armagh City Hospital where the medical staff tried urgently to find a vein suitable for a blood transfusion. John Taylor recalls "I still have this picture of a large and determined nurse cutting me at the bottom of my leg with a razor, and having found a suitable vein, they connected me up."[2]

He was later transferred to the Ulster Hospital Dundonald for further treatment. On the way to Belfast he was read a comforting message from the Archbishop of Armagh, Dr George Simms. He recalls "This gave me the determination to try to overcome what had happened to me as best I could, though I did feel that it would be only a matter of time before I would die."[3]

However, he had luck on his side in that he was still young and fit, and he received excellent care from the surgical and nursing staff at the hospital. After a long period of painful recuperation, he made a good recovery, and he was eventually able to return to his business interests and to his public life as a senior Unionist MP. Others were not so fortunate.

John Taylor, now Lord Kilclooney of Armagh, who was injured in an Official IRA ambush in 1972.

Armagh at the height of the Troubles had a fearsome reputation for violence, and it became known with neighbouring areas of Tyrone as part of a "Murder Triangle". Of the 2,037 civilians killed between 1966 and 1999, there were 228 from County Armagh, third only to West Belfast with 436, and North Belfast which had 396. Around half the civilian deaths for this period occurred in Belfast, "though per head of population, Armagh has been the most dangerous county". Of the total of 3,636 deaths associated with the Troubles, within the British Isles and Europe, 1,647 occurred in Belfast. The second highest total was for County Armagh, with 510.[4]

Police figures for the RUC Armagh sub-division, which included the city and the nearby towns and villages of Keady, Loughgall, Markethill, Middletown and Tandragee, show that 141 people died in this area between the outbreak of violence in 1969 and the end of 2000. Many more died along the border areas with the Irish Republic where paramilitary and military activities were particularly intense.

Civilians who joined the Ulster Defence Regiment as part-time soldiers or were associated with the police, were murdered by the Provisional IRA. A number of these were also Unionist Councillors. In December 1972, William Johnston, a local businessman who was an Ulster Unionist member of the Armagh Urban District Council, a member of the Police Authority, and also an Orangeman, was kidnapped with an employee and taken over the border by armed members of the Provisional IRA.

After they were interrogated, they were taken back across the border. The employee was released, but Mr Johnston was shot twice in the head and left lying on the road. He was aged forty-eight, and married. It is believed that he was murdered because of his involvement with the Police Authority.[5]

In August 1975, another Unionist Councillor – Joseph Reid – was shot dead by an IRA gunman who came to the door of his farm-house near Keady. One of his teenage daughters opened the door, following a knock by a stranger who asked for her father by name. Mr Reid was a part-time soldier in the UDR, and as he came down the stairs of his home he slipped a

revolver into his pocket. Shots rang out. Mr Reid was hit five times in the chest and stomach, and died soon afterwards. He was aged 46, and left a wife and five children.[6]

In November 1983, Charles Armstrong was killed by an IRA booby-trap bomb soon after he left an Armagh Council meeting at the Palace Demesne. After a device exploded under his car, he died at the scene. Mr Armstrong was the Ulster Unionist Chairman of the Council, a senior member of the Orange Order and Royal Black Perceptory, and a part-time major in the Ulster Defence Regiment. Aged fifty-four, he left a wife and eight children.[7] The Mayor's Parlour in the Council offices is named the "Armstrong Room" in his memory.

People from all backgrounds became part of the grim litany of deaths and injuries, and some died in particularly controversial circumstances. On 12 December 1982, two Armagh men Seamus Grew and Roderick Carroll, both members of the outlawed paramilitary Irish National Liberation Army, were shot dead in a car on the Killylea Road, in an incident involving an RUC Mobile Support Unit. This was alleged to be part of an RUC "shoot-to-kill" policy. Two years later an RUC officer was brought to court to face charges, but was acquitted.[8]

The range of deaths in Armagh and district is recorded in full in the definitive book "Lost Lives", which provides a moving account of those who died as a result of the Northern Ireland Troubles. The list for County Armagh is tragically comprehensive, and a reading of two consecutive pages of entries for the year 1982 underlines by its very understatement the range of deaths which affected the entire community, and further afield.

"Peter Corrigan, Armagh, civilian, Catholic, 47, married, unemployed, a Sinn Fein election worker ... killed by the UVF. Sean Quinn, Armagh, RUC, Catholic, 37 married, 3 children. The Sergeant was one of three police officers killed by an IRA landmine at Kinnego embankment, Oxford Island, near

Lurgan. (The others were Alan McCloy, Protestant, 34, married, 2 children, and Paul Hamilton, Protestant, 26, who had been married for one month.) ... Gary Ewing, Fermanagh, RUC, Protestant, 31, married, 2 children, Helen Woodhouse, Fermanagh, civilian, Protestant, 29, single, recreation officer. Charles Spence, Armagh, UDR, Protestant, 44, married, 3 children, customs officer."[9]

During the worst of the Troubles in Armagh and the surrounding districts, a number of atrocities stood out – including the massacre of ten Protestant workmen gunned down by a group calling itself the Republican Action Force at Kingsmills, near Bessbrook on 5 January 1976, allegedly as a reprisal for the murder of Roman Catholics a short time previously. On 21 January 1981, Sir Norman Stronge, aged 86, a prominent Unionist and former Speaker of the Stormont Parliament, was murdered together with his son James, when armed intruders forced their way into their home at Tynan. After shooting dead the two men, the terrorists started a fire which destroyed the building.

On 18 May 1994, two students from the Armagh College of Further Education, both Catholics, were shot when a UVF gunman opened fire on a taxi depot in Lower English Street, Armagh. Gavin McShane, aged seventeen, from Richview Heights, Keady was playing a golf video game with his friend Shane McArdle, also seventeen, from Coolmillish Road, Markethill. Gavin died instantly, and Shane died in hospital the next day. Gavin's mother had lost an eye in 1976 when she was caught up in a bomb-blast. At the time she was pregnant with Gavin and referred to him as her 'miracle boy'. A taxi-driver was wounded in the arm during this terrible incident.[10]

On 3 March 1998, Philip Allen, a Protestant, and his best friend Damien Trainor, a Catholic, were murdered by LVF gunmen in a bar in Poyntzpass. These horrific killings, and all the others, traumatised the community, but they also made people even more determined to continue with the kind of inter-community bridge-building which the two dead men had so graphically symbolised by their friendship.[11]

There were many more deaths, each of which represented an immense human tragedy for family and friends, and clergy of all denominations had first-hand experience of the widespread suffering among their people, as they ministered to the families of the bereaved and to those who had been injured. Lord Eames, reflecting on the trauma of his years at Armagh, felt that the area

> "had probably received more blows and received more undermining of confidence than anywhere else in Northern Ireland. I find evidence of this in the deep, deep hurt in the hearts and minds of people in both communities. I had been Bishop of Derry and Raphoe in some of the years after Bloody Sunday, and in the Bogside and on the other bank of the river I thought I had seen what hurt and scars there were. But I honestly now feel that the depth of the reaction to the Troubles that I came across in Armagh surpassed even that."[12]

Yet in the worst of times, the light of hope was not extinguished. With courage and resilience the people on all sides carried on with their lives, as best they could. Central and local government, and their agencies, and the European Community, and the private sector, provided financial, human and other resources not only for rebuilding, but for laying the foundation for a better community future.

The re-organisation of local government in 1973 led to the amalgamation of the old District and Urban Councils into the new Armagh City and District Council, including the territory of the former urban councils of Keady and Tandragee, and part of Tandragee Rural Council. In political terms this meant that the new Council had a small Unionist majority.

In the early seventies the Nationalists boycotted the Council for a short period due to the political situation, but in due course Armagh helped to show the way in the implementation of power-sharing. This balance was reflected in the Council's employment policy, and by the early 1990's the work-force matched the religious background of the local community. Over the years the Chairmanship and important posts on the Council have been held by representatives of both the main Protestant and Catholic communities, including the Ulster Unionists, the Democratic Unionists and the Social Democratic and Labour Party, though prior to the 2001 local government election, Sinn Fein had not held major posts.

The tourist potential of Armagh was underlined in the early nineties by the establishment of the Navan Centre, to the west of the city on the Killylea Road. Housed within a building which was specially designed to become an integral part of the landscape, the Navan Centre provides the visitor with a rich understanding of the multi-faceted history of the area.

Once inside the complex, the visitor is introduced to pre-Christian Ireland and to the world of the Celts. The central feature is an exhibition explaining how archaeology has uncovered many of Navan's secrets, and this helps people to understand how the site was used throughout its long history, as well as the significance of the objects which were found during excavation.

This centre has been an important visitor attraction, though in May 2001 there were worrying reports of a drop in numbers due to the continuing political unrest, the outbreak of foot-and-mouth disease, and other factors. In June the centre was closed abruptly due to lack of funds, though local MP and Deputy First Minister Seamus Mallon said that he was seeking ways in which Navan would be re-opened on a viable basis. He said " There will have to be changes, but it will and must re-open." Eamonn O'Neill, Chairman of the Northern Ireland Assembly's Culture, Arts and Leisure Committee, echoed the disappointment and fears of all who recognise the significance of Navan. He said "Its loss would simply be inexplicable to the rest of the world. It is not an exaggeration to say that it would be the equivalent of New Grange being closed down. Such a move would cause a national outcry elsewhere."[13]

Bearing in mind the importance of tourism for the local economy, the Council – which had given some assistance to Navan, though it was not essentially a Council project – pioneered other imaginative developments and strategies to develop the city's infrastructure and tourist potential.

One of the prime movers was the Clerk and Chief Executive of the Council, Desmond Mitchell who had been assistant Clerk from 1968-72 and who returned as Chief Executive Officer in April 1988, after five years as

Chairman George MacCartney, with Jacques Delors, the President of the European Commission, laying the foundation stone of St. Patrick's Trian on 3 November 1992.

CEO in Omagh. Dessie Mitchell is a self-effacing man, but his important contribution to the welfare of Armagh has been widely recognised. His former boss Don Ryan says "Much of what Armagh is today, is due to Dessie Mitchell. I cannot speak highly enough of his abilities."

Kevin Myers of the *Irish Times* noted that

"Armagh was fortunate ... in the person of the city's Chief Executive Officer, Dessie Mitchell, who spent his career running towns around Northern Ireland at a time when the IRA was doing its level best to level them. In one of the most inspired examples of optimism in Irish urban history, Dessie Mitchell in the 1980's began to assemble the ingredients which would make Armagh the pleasant place to visit that it is today."[14]

Mr Mitchell says that he felt himself drawn back to Armagh because it was, and is, such a special place.

"It has a wonderful architectural heritage, and a unique history, though its ecclesiastical position has not always been fully recognised or articulated. My vision for the city was based on these assets, and the objective was to try to create an Armagh that would fulfil more of its potential not only to its own people, but also to people beyond its boundaries as a beacon of all the good that can be found in our society."

He pays tribute to the work of the Council in helping to make much of this vision a reality. "Councils are often criticised, and it is not easy being a Councillor, particularly if you take the long view. The short-term view can

Prime Minister John Major with Chairman Pat Brannigan and Vice-Chairman Heather Black in Armagh, at the opening of St Patrick's Trian.

sometimes be easier and more populist, but not self-sustaining in terms of the quality of life for the city."

The Council produced an imaginative Tourist Development Plan, and central to this was the concept of St Patrick and Armagh. "This was the place where he established his first main church. In one sense Armagh was his adopted home, and we wanted the city to be imbued as far as possible with his spirit, so that all which was best about St Patrick could be articulated and could be made more easily accessible to all sections of our society."

One of the prime developments is St Patrick's Trian, which derives its name from the ancient division of the city into three districts, or "Trians". They were known as Trian Mor "The Great Third" (to the south and west), Trian Massain "The Massain Third" (to the east) and Trian Saxon, "The Saxon Third" (to the north).

The Trian visitor complex is an imaginative tourist and educational centre which presents the story of St. Patrick and Armagh in a novel form. The foundation stone was laid on 3 November 1992, by Jacques Delors, the then President of the European Commission which provided much of the funding, and it was officially opened on 31 March 1994, by the then United Kingdom Prime Minister John Major.

In the Trian, three permanent exhibitions relate the story of Armagh from ancient times to the coming of St Patrick; the life and work of the Saint and his connection with Armagh; and "The Land of Lilliput", based on the book *Gulliver's Travels* by Jonathan Swift, who once spent some time in the Armagh district. Taken together, all three present a comprehensive and vivid account of Armagh's history from the earliest times.

Dessie Mitchell explains.

"At the heart of the concept was the Council's desire to develop the city centre by using buildings that had become derelict, and to bring them back into life.

Eames' plea for Gulliver's return

CHURCH of Ireland Primate Archbishop Robin Eames has appealed for the safe return of the remaining missing treasures, including a first edition of Gulliver's Travels, taken when armed raiders plundered the Robinson Library in Armagh on December 14.

His renewed plea follows the weekend interception by Gardai at Dublin Airport of two men – as they were heading for San Francisco. Five manuscripts were recovered.

Philip Joseph Monks, believed to be in his 40s, from the Druids Villas area of Armagh, and Arthur McShane, with an address at Clondalkin, Dublin, appeared at a special sitting of Dublin District Court accused of handling stolen property.

Monks was remanded in custody. His co-accused got bail.

Keeper of the Library Dean Herbert Cassidy and Chief Librarian Harry Carson travelled to Dublin on Saturday to identify the valuable articles.

Now back in safe-keeping are the hand-painted Book of the Hours, printed in Paris in 1518; a Flemish Missal from the 15th Century, belonging to Archbishop Boulter, an Archbishop of Armagh who was responsible for the erection of the first four houses at Vicar's Hill in 1726; a 13th century Gregorian manuscript; a Breelin Bible, dated 1611, and Vol 1 of the Polygot Bible, which is in eight languages.

Two solid-silver Corporation maces, dating back to 1656, were recovered just before Christmas, lying in a bag on the footpath outside Ballbriggan Garda Station.

Gulliver's Travels, written by Dean Jonathan Swift, contains his own handwritten notes and amendments. The two volumes, which date back to 1726, are worth in the region of £35,000.

The robbery, when a female librarian was tied up and locked in an office by the two raiders who conned their way into the building, left the Church of Ireland hierarchy devastated.

Dean Cassidy says he is very happy to have the articles back and is hoping that their recovery may lead to more being found.

Archbishop Eames says he is thankful that some of the articles have been recovered.

Describing the remaining books as "part of our heritage", he appealed to anyone who has knowledge of their whereabouts to help.

Police are understood to have swooped on two houses in Armagh following the arrests. Nothing is believed to have been found.

The objective of creating St Patrick's Trian was to provide a much-needed tourist amenity to tell the Armagh story to the world, but it had the added value in that it was part of the Council's plans for widespread urban regeneration."

"The heritage of Armagh was an important dimension in the tourist develop plan for the city. We assisted with the development of the Navan Fort Heritage Centre, and we also involved both Cathedrals with their enormous potential for tourism, as well as the Observatory and the Planetarium. We set out to attract funds where we could, and we were particularly successful in Europe. We also went out to win the backing of the tourist authorities in Northern Ireland, and the then Minister Richard Needham and the Tourist Board were most helpful."

Armagh's well-known association with Dean Swift made local and national headlines in December 1999 when raiders entered the Armagh Public Library, tied up a female assistant and locked her in an office before making off with priceless treasures, including a first edition of Gulliver's Travels, dating from 1726. The two volumes, worth an estimated £35,000, were missing for some time, though other valuable artefacts were recovered. These include the hand-painted *Book of the Hours*, printed in Paris in 1518, a Flemish Missal from the 15th

"Land of Lilliput", at St Patrick's Trian, Armagh, based on the book *Gullivers Travels* by Dean Swift.

century, belonging to Archbishop Boulter, a 13th century Gregorian manuscript, a Breelin Bible dated 1611, and Volume 1 of the Polyglot Bible, in eight different languages.

Two solid-silver Corporation Maces, dating from 1656, were found in a bag lying on the road near Dublin. Police arrested two men at Dublin Airport

Georgian scene at the Palace Stables Heritage Centre.

on their way to San Francisco, and they were later charged with handling stolen property. Fortunately the two-volume first edition of *Gulliver's Travels* was recovered by the Gardai and handed back to the Very Reverend Herbert Cassidy, Dean of Armagh and Keeper of the Library, in the summer of 2001.

On a happier note, the Georgian Period in the history of Armagh is brought to life in the Palace Stables Heritage centre in the former Demesne of the Church of Ireland Archbishop. After the re-organisation of local government, the new Armagh Rural and Urban Council needed bigger premises. The Archbishop's Palace and Demesne came on the market, partly due to the cost of the upkeep of the buildings. These were sold to the Council, despite the objections of those people who did not wish to see such treasured buildings moving out of the ownership and control of the Church of Ireland. One of the many advantages to the Council, however, was the availability not only of larger buildings but also the possibility of developing some of these as tourist attractions.

Accordingly, The Palace Stables Heritage Centre was centred in the former Georgian stables and courtyard on the Archbishop's estate, and the entire complex has been carefully restored to create an impression of stable life in the eighteenth century. An exhibition titled "A Day in the Life" recreates a typical day in the stables on 23 July 1776, when Archbishop Robinson entertained Arthur Young, the famous agriculturist, and other guests.

Staff in period costume add to the historical effect, and give the exhibition a dimension of "living history". There are also telling quotes, such as that from Arthur Young: "The tables of people of fortune are very plentifully spread; many elegantly differing in nothing from those of England ... Claret is the common wine of all tables, their port in incomparable, so much better than the English."

The Palace Stables Heritage Centre is part of a well-established "Pilgrim's Trail", which also includes St Patrick's Trian, the two Cathedrals, Armagh Public Library and Armagh County Museum, and the Museum of the Royal Irish Fusiliers-all of which, individually and collectively, underline the rich heritage of the city of St Patrick.

An impressive new Market Place theatre and arts centre, adjacent to St Patrick's Trian, was opened in 2000. It represents the final part of the Tourist Development Plan, and it has been well-received by the public and by architectural observers alike. *The Sunday Times* noted that it "has given the city a civic building worthy of comparison with Archbishop Robinson's glory years". Writer Shane O'Toole states that "With wraparound seating on three levels and in the pit, it is the nearest thing in Ireland to the Royal Shakespeare Company's Swan Theatre in Stratford-upon-Avon."

He notes that, according to the architect Glen Howells, the Council was prepared to offer as much money and time as was needed to produce the best results. "At a final cost approaching £6 million, the Market Place represents incredibly good value for money."[15]

Other important developments in recent years have emphasised Armagh's importance as an administrative centre, including the establishment of the

The Market Place Theatre and Arts Centre, Armagh.

Armagh Mayor Jim Speers with Prime Minister Tony Blair, at St Patrick's Trian. Also pictured are from left, Mrs Margaret Mitchell, Desmond Mitchell, Deputy First Minister Seamus Mallon, Deputy Mayor Joe McGlennan, Jim Speers Junior and Mayoress Mrs Elizabeth Speers.

A GATHERING FOR PEACE

Headquarters of the Southern Education and Library Board in the city. As well, the administrative offices of the Southern Health Board have moved to Tower Hill in Armagh.

The Council has also made a major investment in the development of school buildings in the city, and in its comprehensive housing programme it has been conscious of the need to blend the new architecture with the best of the old. In this context, the city's Conservation Area has been reviewed and extended. In 1988 the old Armagh Gaol, which latterly housed women prisoners, was closed and its inmates transferred to the then comparatively new Maghaberry Prison. Two years later the controversial Drumadd Barracks, often criticised by members of the nationalist community because of the interrogation procedures used there, became the base for the security forces' border operations.

Following the Good Friday Agreement in 1998, and the later establishment of cross-border institutions, the Council property at the Demesne was used for the first meeting of the cross-border Ministerial Council. This underlined Armagh's ancient influence in all-Ireland political, as well as ecclesiastical, affairs. It should be noted, however, that the full-scale display of Irish Ministers' Mercedes-Benz saloons sweeping to and from the Council buildings on that day was a less than thoughtful gesture to their Unionist counter-parts, who were taking considerable political criticism for attending the meeting.

During the later years of the twentieth century and into the new Millennium, Armagh has been a focus for many important visitors – including the Queen and other members of the Royal Family, United Kingdom Prime Ministers, successive Irish Heads of State and leading politicians including the Taioseach of the day, noted European dignitaries, and-one of the most newsworthy visitors of all – the US President Bill Clinton who visited the city in 1998 and gave a keynote address. (This was

President Clinton addresses the crowd. From left are Seamus Mallon MP, Deputy First Minister. Robert Turner, Mayor of Armagh, Sharon Haughey, Tony Blair, Prime Minister. Hilary Rodham Clinton, Dr Marjorie Mowlam, Secretary of State for Northern Ireland, and David Trimble MP, First Minister.

First meeting of North-South Ministerial Council at Armagh. Left to right: Irish Prime Minister Bertie Ahern, First Minister David Trimble and Deputy First Minister Seamus Mallon.

Opposite: Prince Charles meets the people at Armagh.

The Queen shares a joke with Cardinal Daly, at a reception in the Palace, Armagh. The others pictured are the Mayor Jim Nicholson and Sir Gordon Beveridge, Vice-Chancellor of Queen's University.

beamed live across the United States and Europe – including Heidelberg where this writer arrived just in time to catch Clinton's speech on CNN, after having been delayed by several hours because of the arrival of the President's aircraft at Belfast International Airport. He had travelled direct from Russia where he had been meeting the then Russian President Boris Yeltsin.)

John.B.Vallely.

Visits by people of this status in public life have helped to keep Armagh on the political map, and the Council is anxious to remain outward looking. It has established strong economic, academic and civic links with Virginia in the United States, and also with the underprivileged people of Razgrad in Bulgaria. Desmond Mitchell says

"This outreach to Eastern Europe is part of the spiritual legacy of St Patrick, in the sense of bearing goodwill to your neighbours, and your neighbours are essentially where you find them. There have been a number of visits of Armagh people to Razgrad, and vice versa, and we hope that this important link will continue."

As well as pursuing a policy of outreach internationally, Armagh is conscious of its continued need for outreach within the wider local community, particularly as it lies near the heart of the apple industry. Armagh plays an integral role, with Loughgall and Richhill, in the annual Apple Blossom Festival each Spring, and it also has close ties with its neighbouring centres of Keady and Tandragee.

One of the continuing problems facing Armagh, however, is the lack of manufacturing industry. Despite the best efforts of the Council, and others, much remains to be done. Desmond Mitchell says

The Travelling Piper
J.B.Valley's paintings reflect his skill not only as an artist, but also as a musician, and are in great demand. His family has been associated with the Armagh area since Pre-Christian times.

"This issue is being addressed by a local economic development group, which includes representatives of the Council and also the private sector and other community interests. The main aim is the development of new industries, particularly in the field of IT, but this is not easy to establish in the face of intense competition from other areas. The lack of a good manufacturing base in Armagh is a major problem, and it is one which has to be tackled thoroughly to help secure the future. There is also an urgent need for a greatly-improved roads infrastructure for the city."

Whatever the problems of manufacturing, Armagh retains its strong local identity in the arts and sporting circles. The spectrum of musical ability ranges from classical and choral, with the Armagh City Choir regularly performing with the Ulster Orchestra, to – at the other end – a vibrant folk culture, personified so well and for so many years by Tommy Makem, from nearby Keady, and many others steeped in traditional Irish music.

The arts have been well-represented also by the artist and Irish traditional musician J B Vallely, an accomplished instrumentalist on the flute and uilleann pipes. With his wife Eithne, he founded more than thirty years ago the annual William Kennedy Piping Festival, organised by the Armagh Pipers' Club. His

Opposite top: The Queen at Armagh when she handed over a new Charter to the city.

The Armagh Rymers are one of Northern Ireland's most colourful folk theatre ensembles, carrying on a tradition dating back 2500 years.

superb paintings – combining both his love for art and music – are internationally acclaimed, and remain in great demand. At one time, some people thought that the artist "JB" and the musician "Brian" were two different people, but they are the same one talented man.[16]

One of the most accomplished poets to have emerged from the Armagh area was W R Rodgers, whose poem title simply "Armagh" remains a classic observation of the city:

"There is a through-otherness about Armagh
Of tower and steeple,
Up on the hill are the arguing graves of the kings,
And below are the people.

Through-other as the rooks that swoop and swop
Over the sober hill
Go the people gallivanting from shop to shop
Guffawing their fill.

And the little houses run through the market-town
Slap up against the great,
Like the farmers all clabber and muck walking arm by arm
With the men of estate.

Raised at a time when Reason was all the rage,
Of grey and equal stone,
This bland face of Armagh covers an age
Of clay and feather and bone.

Through-other is its history, of Celt and Dane,
Norman and Saxon,
Who ruled the place and sounded the gamut of fame
From cow-horn to klaxon.

There is a through-otherness about Armagh
Delightful to me,
Up on the hills are the graves of the garrulous kings
Who at last can agree."[17]

What of the future of Armagh? The city has survived well in a physical sense the trauma of the past thirty years of violence, and although the scars of community upheaval and conflict will take a long time to heal, the signs are encouraging. As Kevin Myers points out in *An Irishman's Diary* "The various factions within Armagh accepted the need for the city to come to terms with its history and its factionalised legacies. Armagh in its own way has become an emblem of people coming to terms with rival pasts, disputing identities …"[18]

Council meetings, as elsewhere in Northern Ireland, were often very contentious, but in the mid-Eighties it was agreed that motions circulated

Noel Sheridan,
former Sinn Fein Councillor.

Brian Hutchinson, DUP
Councillor.

Heather Black, DUP Councillor.

from other Councils, which were often contentious in themselves, would not be debated, but simply marked "For information". One of the results was that debates then centred on the main business concerning Armagh and district, with a noticeable lowering of tension compared to previous years.

Although the Councillors have strong party political views, as might be expected in any Council, they share in common a deep affection for Armagh and a desire to promote its best interests. They also demonstrate an awareness of the importance of St Patrick in the history of the city – even if they, like most other people, admit to a lack of a detailed historical knowledge about him.

Democratic Unionist Councillor Heather Black, a former Mayor, has been on the Council for twelve years, like her late husband Tom who also served for twelve years in the Cusher Ward. She says "St Patrick is our Patron Saint, and I appreciate that. I still hold on to my Church of Ireland teaching that he was a good Christian." DUP Councillor Brian Hutchinson, who has served for eight years and whose father Douglas was a long-time Council member, describes Patrick as "A type of preacher who brought Christianity to Ireland before there were Roman Catholics or Protestants. I respect him for that."

Councillor Noel Sheridan, the longest-serving Sinn Fein member on the Council until he failed to gain a seat in the 2001 local government elections, says "Lots of people use Saint Patrick for all kinds of things. To some extent they take him for granted. They say 'Sure he's our patron saint', and they leave it at that. I think that people should see him as cross-community, not as belonging to the one side or the other."

Councillor Pat Brannigan, the first SDLP Chairman of the Council and later Mayor of Armagh, has served in local government for nearly a quarter of a century. He sees Patrick as "an inspirational figure" but believes that he could not have been in all the places which claim a connection with him. "Most of the stories would be mythical but they have made an impression on the people of Ireland to the extent that Christianity has survived up to the present time."

He notes, however, that there is a "certain diminution" in some of the religious practices associated with the celebration of St Patrick's Day. "As a person who goes to church regularly, I believe that St Patrick would be disappointed at the number of people who seem to be forgetting God. To my mind, St Patrick's challenge in the Christian message is still as relevant as ever."

Official Unionist Councillor Jim Speers, also a former Mayor who has served in local government for nearly 25 years, regards St Patrick as

"a zealous missionary in terms of propagating the Gospel in his time, and, I suspect, someone who was a strong individual. It is important to stress that Armagh is where he established his main church, but I honestly feel that this has not been a focus in the minds of our people as much as it could and should be."

All five Councillors recognise the need for the continued promotion of Armagh. Mrs Black says

"The city has lost some of its dignity in a rush for popularity. The Council works hard, but there is a need for people on all sides to work harder, especially for civic pride."

Brian Hutchinson believes that

"We don't need more tourist attractions, but we should let people know more about what we do have here. We also require more industrial development but in a way that will not detract from the beauty of the city."

Noel Sheridan feels that Armagh needs more tourist facilities not only to attract people to the city,

"but also to make sure that they stay on. We need more night-life in the city centre. Armagh after 5.30 pm is a ghost town. The last thing we need is a 'quick-fix'. What is required is a focal point in the middle of the city."

Pat Brannigan believes that the city and its people need a period of consolidation.

"We need peace and stability so that Armagh can develop to its fullest potential. We also need jobs. When I joined the Council in 1977, the unemployment rate was nearly 18 per cent, and now it is 5.3 per cent. Though unemployment in some wards could be around 8 or 9 per cent, the figure for Armagh and district overall is lower than the average for Northern Ireland.

"However, we need to do more. Among other things, we are developing a Monaghan-Armagh digital corridor to help provide jobs for the long-term employed. In the city centre we are going through a bad period, like some other towns, but I think it will turn again. We do not need big multiple stores, but more theme shops, and small businesses offering high quality. I believe that Armagh will fulfil its true potential."

Jim Speers says "In terms of archaeology, history, heritage and the environment, Armagh has a great deal to offer, but the Troubles have prevented us from capitalising on this. There are also challenges in business. We have to compete with bigger centres such as Craigavon, Newry and Lisburn, where there are big multiple stores.

"In business, however, competition is the life-blood of trade, and in Armagh we have an opportunity to create an individualistic approach, with the development of shops and stores that can provide a different experience. There is an opportunity to develop niche markets with quality. I am optimistic. Armagh is a special place, in fact to me it is the centre of the Universe, and I think that we have the potential for a very good future."

As has been noted earlier, Armagh needs much more inward investment to provide new jobs in the manufacturing industry, and its links with the major road networks need to be improved. One of its best hopes for the future still lies in developing its tourist industry and in concentrating even more on its unique attraction as the ecclesiastical capital of Ireland. However, it was extremely depressing for those who treasure the city's architectural heritage to discover in June 2001 that Green's Barber shop and house at 34, Upper English Street - a most historic building-had been demolished without warning, despite proposals for its restoration.

In essence, the future of Armagh depends also on the attitudes of its people. Some are positive, and see a glass half-full where others see it as half-empty. To prosper, Armagh requires not only investment and a continued focus on tourism, but also a greater realisation by its people of the richness of their heritage.

This point is reinforced by Dessie Mitchell.

"There is a danger that people in and around Armagh have become so accustomed to the richness of their environment and history that they have almost forgotten about its importance. It is those who come from outside who are really amazed at the place.

"I suppose it is a matter of trying to re-awaken the Armagh people to the richness of their unique history. I think that the take-off will happen, but much depends on the political situation in the Province generally. However, given political progress and stability in the long-term, I am convinced that the example of St Patrick and the vibrancy of his message will be the driving forces for a new vision of Armagh."

NOTES

1 Alf McCreary, *Survivors*, published by Century Books 1976, p.210
2 Ibid. p.210
3 Ibid. p.211
4 *Lost Lives* by David McKittrick, Seamus Kelters, Brian Feeney and Chris Thornton, published by Mainstream Publishing, p.1481
5 Ibid. pp.307-308
6 Ibid. p.570
7 Ibid. pp.962-963
8 Ibid. p.292
9 Ibid. pp.918-919
10 Ibid. p.1361
11 Ibid. pp.611-614; 849-850; and 1428-1431
12 Interview with Alf McCreary
13 *News Letter*, 25 May 2001, p.10
14 *Irish Times*, 6 May 1995, p.13
15 *Sunday Times* Culture Section, 24 September 2000
16 Neil Johnston, *Belfast Telegraph*, 27 November 2000
17 Copyright, WR Rodgers, *Poems* (1993) The Gallery Press, Oldcastle, Co Meath
18 *Irish Times*, 6 May 1995, p.13

Clinton visits Armagh

President Clinton visited Armagh in September 1998, where he addressed a large cross-community audience at a "Gathering for Peace". He said "Armagh is a city on a hill in every sense. Your faith and tolerance are making a new era of peace possible. For yourselves and all the world, in every act of genuine reconciliation you renew confidence that decency can triumph over hatred. You have inspired the rest of us to aim a little higher.

I thank you, and America thanks you, for the precious gift you give us all, a gift of hope redeemed and faith restored.

Armagh has stood for these better aspirations throughout its long history. If there is a recurring theme to this seat of learning and religion, it is the largeness of the human spirit. Here, a Briton, Saint Patrick, devoted himself to the cause of Ireland and left a legacy of faith and compassion. Here, the *Book of Armagh* preserved his gentle message and the power of the Gospels.

Today, the two cathedrals dominate the landscape. Two proud traditions can exist side by side, bringing people closer to God and closer to each other – never underestimate the impact you can have on the world. The great English poet and clergyman, John Donne, wrote those famous lines, 'No man is an island. We are all a piece of the continent, a part of the main'."

'And if my own people do not know me, a prophet has no honour in his own country.'

St Patrick's *Letter to Coroticus*

One of the most striking aspects of the City of Armagh is the outline of the two Cathedrals, perched on their respective hills. From a distance they are literally outstanding silhouettes on the skyline, and even in the narrow streets of Armagh itself they are visible, singly or together, from the turn of a corner or from one or other of the scenic points in this hilly city. There is no doubt that Armagh is an ecclesiastical city. Its two Cathedrals and other splendid church buildings are a constant reminder of the spiritual amid the secular.

However, there is another dimension to Armagh. While the two Cathedrals are a witness to the worship of God, they are also a reminder of the divisions within Christendom. Each represents a distinctive theology and style of worship, and even though there has been a thaw in inter-church relations since the bitter divisions of the Reformation and the coldness and religious apartheid of succeeding centuries, a number of fundamental differences remain. Many ecumenists argue, with justification, that the Protestant and Roman Catholic Churches have more in common than that which divides them, but they are definitely not "the same". They are part of one Christian body, in the broad sense to which St Paul aspired, but they are definitely not "one body".

Each Cathedrals bears witness to the distinctiveness of its tradition. A visitor from those parts of the world where Cathedrals are regarded more as museum-pieces than as places of worship, would find little difference between the Church of Ireland and Roman Catholic Cathedrals in Armagh. Both are beautiful in their own way, each was built to glorify God and to provide a central place of worship for its own tradition, and each is respected even in an increasingly secular world.

The Protestant Cathedral is neat and compact, and encompassed by its historic surroundings, whereas the Roman Catholic Cathedral seems larger, more filled with light, and with a grand sweep in the multitude of steps which lead up to its imposing exterior. One of the most impressive aspects of the Roman Catholic Cathedral is the view from its front steps across the valley to the other Cathedral on the hill of Saint Patrick. Conversely the Roman Catholic Cathedral is visible from that same hill, but with difficulty. There is eye contact across the valley, but communication across the ground from both sides is a little more indirect. This in itself is perhaps symbolic of the broad history of Christianity in St Patrick's island and city, though the "eye contact" of today is indubitably more Christian in spirit than the cold stares of the past.

Both Cathedrals, not surprisingly, have numerous reminders of St Patrick, and chiefly in their magnificent stained-glass windows. In the Roman Catholic Cathedral there is a notable example of bridge-building, in a stained-glass window depicting St Patrick, and also a picture of its Church of Ireland counterpart. One writer noted, observantly, that "the Catholic Cathedral's Saint Patrick is the familiar patriarchal figure with flowing white hair and a long white beard dressed in early seventeenth century bishop's robes and carrying a jewelled crozier surmounted by a cross, with the serpents writhing at his feet beneath a few sprigs of shamrock."

In the Protestant Cathedral, however, he is depicted as much younger, with short, dark hair and a neatly-trimmed goatee beard, a Roman-style cloak and "elaborate Roman sandals. The same writer also pointed out that the heraldic shield over his head displays the St Andrews's cross, rather than that of St Patrick himself and notes: "It is difficult to establish exactly why and when the Church of Ireland opted for a young, Roman and often clean-shaven Saint Patrick, but it is most likely that this image originated during the latter part of the nineteenth century, when antiquarians were rediscovering the truth behind the legendary figure."[1]

Mrs Elizabeth Shannon, the widow of a former US Ambassador to Ireland, visited Armagh and described the city as "so lovely and proud and gray, sitting high on a hill overlooking the green rolling countryside. We visited the Protestant and Catholic cathedrals, both magnificent churches built to honour Christ and to glorify the Christian spirit, a spirit now defiled by the hatred and divisiveness that religion has 'inspired'. The red hats of former cardinals hang in solemn rows from the ceiling of the Catholic Cathedral. To me they symbolise the bloodshed spilled in Northern Ireland under the name of religion."[2] The English journalist Martin Fletcher also visited Armagh – 'A small but elegant old city which was chosen by St Patrick as the site of his principal church in AD 445, it has remained Ireland's spiritual and ecclesiastical capital ever since'.[3]

Some years previously on a visit to Armagh, I wrote that the Protestant Cathedral is a treasure-house of history, with fascinating stone carvings, a remarkable collection of books and manuscripts, and the chancel which is out of alignment with the nave. The Catholic Cathedral is a more modern and extremely beautiful church ... 'The nave is dominated by a large white sculpture with a dove in the middle and two large prongs symbolising community togetherness. The locals refer to it, unkindly, as 'The extracted tooth' ... I wonder how many Protestants come here to appreciate the beauty of this Catholic Cathedral, or how many Catholics appreciate the Protestant Cathedral on the other hill'.[4]

However, on more recent visits a new dimension has become more apparent to me, which outsiders and first-time visitors might not notice immediately. Yet it provides a clue to the subtle but important ways in which each Cathedral represents not only Christianity in general, but also its own flock in particular.

As if to underline its historical authenticity, there is a large stone carved on the outside wall of the North Transept of the Protestant Cathedral. This marks the burial place of Brian Boru with the words 'Near this spot on the

Opposite: The interior of St Patrick's Church of Ireland Cathedral.

187

Different Views.
St Patrick is depicted in the Roman Catholic Cathedral as a Patriarch. (Right-middle panel). There is also an ecumenical dimension to this window, with both Cathedrals featured near the top. In the Church of Ireland Cathedral he is a much younger figure, in Roman style attire. (Opposite page, right-hand panel). The blue and white saltire above his head seems more typical of St Andrew than St Patrick.

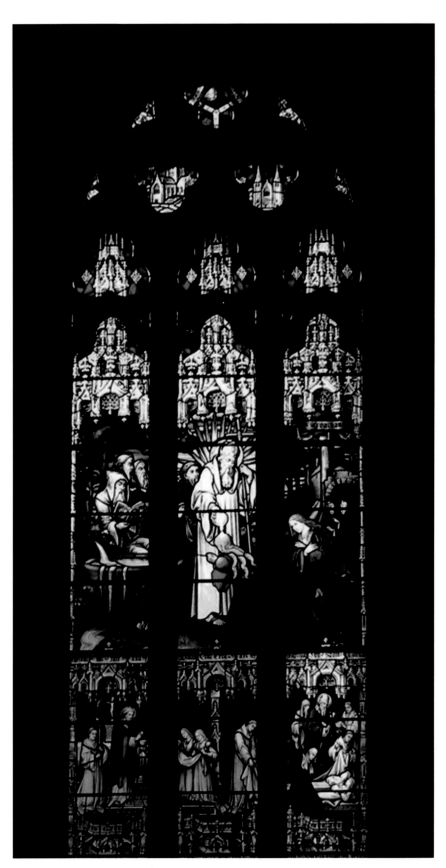

St. Patrick's Roman Catholic Cathedral.

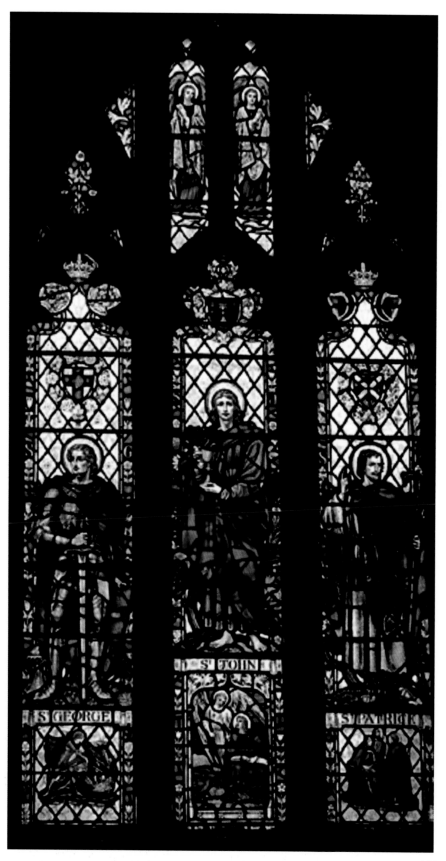

St. Patrick's Church of Ireland
Cathedral.

Burial plaque of Brian Boru at St Patrick's Church of Ireland Cathedral, with Paul Condylis, an American writer and actor. "This city exudes a sense of history".

A painting in St Patrick's Trian showing the establishment of Armagh's two great Cathedrals.

North side of the Great Church was laid the body of Brian Boroimhe, Slain at Clontarf AD MXIV'. And to emphasise its claim as the site of St Patrick's principal church, there is a large list inside the building of all the Abbots, Bishops and Archbishops of Armagh in unbroken sequence from Patrick himself. The Protestant cathedral also has a military chapel, and a number of regimental flags hang in the church.

Over at the Roman Catholic Cathedral there is no military chapel, and no list of Archbishops of Armagh is displayed. However, a number of slowly decaying red hats of former Cardinal Archbishops of Armagh are featured in the church, and on the outside of the building there is a statue of St Patrick, flanked by one of St. Malachy. Within the broad sweep of ecclesiastical history, the conclusion is inescapable – one God, one Patrick, two Cathedrals, and two traditions which are definitely not the same.

Down the years the Archbishops were strong characters who imprinted their personality on their church. Reference has been made to a number of these Primates in earlier times, but in recent years there were also noteworthy Primates from each tradition.

There have been seven Roman Catholic Archbishops since the early 20th century – Cardinal O'Donnell 1924-27; Cardinal MacRory 1928-1945; Cardinal D'Alton 1946-63; Cardinal Conway 1963-77; Cardinal O'Fiaich 1977-90; Cardinal Daly from 1990 until his retirement in 1996, and Dr Sean

 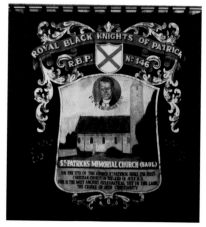

These banners used by the Ancient Order of Hibernians, and the Royal Black Perceptory illustrate how St. Patrick relates to both traditions.

Brady from 1996 until the present.

The sense of pride within the Archdiocese at the appointment of their Archbishops as Cardinals was echoed in an *Irish News* report of 24 November, 1929 concerning Cardinal MacRory;

"Ireland will rejoice at the tidings from Rome at the Pope's decision to number the Archbishop of Armagh amongst the great ones of the church who are to be elevated in December to the dignity of seats in the Sacred College. The news comes fast after the decision that the world Eucharistic Conference of 1932 will be held in Dublin.

In Down and Connor, no less than in the Archdiocese of Armagh, the announcement of the elevation of Dr MacRory to the exalted position of a Prince of the Church will be received with joy. For thirteen years his Grace ruled with wisdom over the ancient diocese of St. Malachy. During the terrible years when the Catholics of Belfast and indeed of the entire diocese were menaced with possible extinction, his Grace stood by them and protected them by voice and pen against the dangers that then beset them...

On the occasion of his departure from Belfast, Dr MacRory said 'Peace and goodwill reign here now between all creeds and classes, and I hope and pray that they may long continue. Quarrelling and fighting upon the score of religion between Christians, all professing to be the followers of the Prince of Peace, is something very hard to beat for absurdity. Moreover, it is a flagrant violation of the spirit and law of Him Who bade us love even our enemies.'"

His words today seem immensely sad, given what has taken place since then, and in many areas prevails today.

Lord Eames, who became Church of Ireland Primate and Archbishop of Armagh in 1986, has worked closely with three Catholic Primates. He says:

"When I went to Armagh, Cardinal O'Fiaich was the Archbishop. I had a great regard for him as a person and as a historian, and I learned a great deal from him about the history of Armagh. I found him at all times the friendliest of people. I was often in his home, and he in mine.

"He was very much identified with the Nationalist side of the Irish tradition. As a churchman he was a very devout and devoted liturgical scholar, and the great range within the Tomas O'Fiaich Library and Archive bears testimony to the depth of his learning.

"He was succeeded by Dr, later Cardinal, Cahal Daly who had a great yearning to understand Protestant minds. He brought gentleness yet firmness to the See of Armagh, and he was a person with whom I felt much in common.

St Mark's Church of Ireland on the Mall, Armagh.

Down the centuries the Cathedral was also the parish church of
Armagh, although a Chapel of Ease and garrison church,
dedicated to St Mark, was built on the East side of the Mall in
1811. It was largely rebuilt and enlarged in 1830, and in 1866
the chancel and extensions to the aisles were added. Some thirty
years later during a further refurbishment, new pews and a pulpit
were installed. The pulpit is reputed to be the most lofty in
Ireland, the preacher being at the level of the gallery. Although
it served the majority of city families it did not replace the
Cathedral as the parish church until 1972 by which time
Armagh had ceased to be a garrison town.

With the emergence of the four church leaders over the years he put himself into that heart and soul, and he was often at the centre of our discussions.

When he retired he was succeeded by Archbishop Sean Brady, whom I had not known previously, but whose quiet manner, sense of humour and friendly nature make it a pleasure to work with him. I have a high regard for Archbishop Brady, and I believe that as the years go by, people will come to see in him a richness and sensitivity, and a pastoral caring for his flock".

On the Anglican side, there have been eight Church of Ireland Archbishops since the early 20th century – Dr John Baptist Crozier from 1911-20; Dr Charles Frederick d'Arcy from 1920-38; Dr John Godfrey Fitzmaurice Day from 1938-9; Dr John Allen Fitzgerald Gregg, who succeeded Archbishop Day and who resigned in 1959; Dr James McCann who served for ten years until his resignation in 1969; Dr George Otto Simms who was Archbishop from 1969 until 1980; Dr John Ward Armstrong, who served from 1980 until 1986; and the current Archbishop, Lord Eames.

Archbishop Eames, as well as reflecting upon his Roman Catholic counterparts, also spoke about some of his own predecessors. He said

"I remember James McCann, an Ulsterman who was very interested in the rural life of the diocese and who made many friends with his tremendous physical impression. He was a big man, and he was loved for his pastoral care of the clergy. "Then there was George Simms, who found it difficult to come to terms with the demands of Northern Ireland at that time. Those who worked with him spoke of the difficulty which he had with the Troubles. In retirement he rejoiced in being able to return to Dublin. He was scholarly, and he wrote a very good book on St Patrick. Historical themes occupied a great deal of his time.

"My immediate predecessor John Armstrong was born and bred in Belfast and was a former Dean of St Patrick's Cathedral in Dublin. He had to fight against ill-health, but he is remembered with great affection for the care of the clergy of the Diocese.

The Cardinal Tomas O'Fiaich Memorial Library and Archive on the Moy Road, Armagh, which was opened in 1999. The Cardinal's papers and books form the nucleus of this collection, with substantial additions from the records of the Archdiocese of Armagh, including materials owned by the Cardinal's predecessors, and the Micheling Kerney Walsh Collection. The Library Collection consists of over 15000 books mostly from Cardinal O'Fiaich's own library, as well as more than 450 periodical titles, many of which are now rare.

Archbishop John Allen Fitzgerald
Gregg.

Archbishop George Otto Simms.

Archbishop John Ward Armstrong.

My predecessor who is most often remembered is Archbishop Gregg. People say that he was rather austere and withdrawn, but a total figure in terms of leadership, and he is remembered with great admiration and affection."

While Armagh derives its title as the ecclesiastical capital of Ireland from the work and example of St Patrick and also the Primacies of successive Archbishops, there is also the important tradition and Christian witness of the Non-Conformist churches in the city. These include the Presbyterians and the Methodists who have made a significant contribution to ecclesiastical life in Armagh and to this island.

There are also the other denominations, including the Baptist Church, the Elim Church, the Free Presbyterian Church, the Pentecostal Churches and the Reformed Presbyterian Church. In the words of an ecclesiastical exhibition in St Patrick's Trian "All are inheritors of the Gospel of Christ brought by St Patrick to Ireland."

According to James Stuart a census of Armagh taken in 1817 established that there were 2,001 members of the Church of Ireland in the city, 1,596 Presbyterians and others, and 3,413 Roman Catholics, but in this estimate the Methodists were included partly among the Episcopalians and partly amongst the Presbyterian Protestants.[5]

Methodism, according to Stuart, was introduced into Armagh by the indefatigable John Wesley himself. Wesley, he stated, had made frequent visits to Ireland before he endeavoured in person to make any converts in the city of Armagh. He had received shelter and hospitality in various places nearby, including Tandragee and Lurgan, before proceeding to Armagh on 15 April 1767. He had been offered accommodation in a Church Lane boarding house, run by Eleanor Russell, an Athlone woman who had heard Wesley preach in Clonmain.

About a half-hour before he was due to preach in the Market House a town constable went to him and said 'Sir, the sovereign orders me to inform you, that you shall not preach in his town'. However, Wesley persisted in doing so, and when the elected town sovereign, a Mr Harcourt, interrupted him in person, Wesley was then invited by a wealthy merchant William McGeough to preach on his private property, at the site of the ancient chapel of St Columba.

194 *Opposite:* The slowly disintegrating red hats of former Cardinals hang in St Patrick's Roman Catholic Cathedral.

Wesley was small in stature, and Mr McGeough tactfully provided a chair on which he stood to preach. Incidentally the chair was preserved by the McGeough family, and was later donated to the National Trust at the Argory. Wesley visited Armagh again on nine occasions. On his next visit, almost two years later to the day, he again preached at McGeough's premises with considerable effect. He continued to preach in Armagh at regular intervals of about two years until 1775, and then there was roughly a twelve year gap until his next visit.

However, his popularity continually increased. The indefatigable Mrs Russell had rented a small thatched house in Thomas Street for Methodist meetings, and the growing fellowship built a Chapel. A neat and convenient meeting-house was built in Armagh, in 1786, by the Methodist society, in Abbey Street, a little above the spot where Mr Wesley had so often preached. It is attended by about 40 families. Their preacher inhabited a comfortable house, very near the building.[6]

The congregation soon grew to be too big for the church. When Wesley returned to Armagh on 17 June 1787 the house, then prepared by his friends, was found insufficient to contain half of the congregation, which had assembled to hear his discourse. Accordingly, they later built a new church on the site where Wesley first preached, and this remains the site of the present Church. On 16 June 1789, Wesley preached at Armagh, for the last time. He died two years later.

Before his last visit to the city, however, he had the satisfaction of knowing that his labours had not been in vain, in Armagh as elsewhere. The Methodist congregation in Armagh remained ever-aware of its historic foundation, and in 1988 it held a special Celebration to mark the conversion of John and Charles Wesley. Today the Methodist Circuit in Armagh and the

Harvest Festival in Armagh Methodist Church 1918. The Church was built in 1786, near the site where John Wesley had preached in 1767.

surrounding district has a congregation of around 100 families, and the circuit minister is the Reverend Ellen Whalley. Methodism has played, and continues to play, a distinctive role in the life of the city.

Presbyterianism in Ireland traces its roots to Plantation times when Scots settlers came to the Province. They set down roots mainly in Antrim and Down, but a number came to the Armagh area. There is a mention of a Mr Hope Sherrid ministering to Presbyterians in Armagh in 1659, but little enough is known about him. In May 1673, the Reverend Archibald Hamilton, who had been a minister at Benburb, received a call to Armagh, where he remained during turbulent times for Presbyterians. They were prohibited from holding public worship, and their Meeting-houses were closed by force.

When King William of Orange landed in Carrickfergus, the Presbyterians in Ulster appointed Archibald Hamilton, and the Reverend William Osborne of Dublin, to meet him at Belfast Castle and to reassure him of Protestant loyalty. Meanwhile, James II reached Armagh, as has been noted earlier, and Mr Hamilton fled to Scotland where he remained until 1692. On his return, however, he became the Presbyterian minister in Killinchy.[7]

The Reverend John Hutcheson, according to James Stuart, came to the city about the latter end of the year 1697. Previously there had been an unsuccessful attempt to appoint others, including a Mr Francis Fredell, from Donegore in Templepatrick. Mr Fredell successfully petitioned the

First Armagh Presbyterian Church at the Mall, c 1900. The small building to the left with the interesting spires is the Plymouth Brethren Church.

The Mall Presbyterian Church c1900. It bears the inscription Scotch Church, indicating the congregation's theological history.

Presbyterian Synod to reverse their earlier decision to appoint him to Armagh, on the grounds that "transportation from Donegore would be most gravanimous and crushing to him, both in body and spirit."[8]

During the ministry of Mr Hutcheson, a church was built in Abbey Street, near the ruins of the old monastery of St Peter and St Paul – the stones of which were used in the construction of the church. It is said that Dean Swift came across the masons smoothing a number of stones carved with heads and figures of cherubs and declared to his companion 'See these fanatical puritans are chiselling Popery out of the very stones!'[9]

Down the years, in the tradition of Presbyterianism, a number of different Ministers received a call to the Armagh Church. Some had a long ministry, like the Reverend John Maxwell who succeeded Mr Hutcheson in 1732 and served for thirty-one years. Others were less distinguished, though memorable for the wrong reasons. The Reverend William Henry who came from Stewartstown in 1791 was suspended from the ministry in 1795 for insobriety.[10]

Presbyterianism, then as now, exhibited a sturdy independence of mind, and the various claims of theologians, together with matters of conscience, were of paramount importance to clergy and laity alike. The evolution of

Presbyterianism in Armagh has been complex, partly due to disagreements and differing opinions on theology and politics. In Ulster some things never change.

At one stage there were three Presbyterian churches, and through amalgamation these became two, which are still in existence. Within the wider Presbyterian family in Armagh, there were a number of strong and colourful characters, and the city produced several Moderators of the Presbyterian General Assembly in Ireland, and a Moderator of the General Assembly in England.

The First Presbyterian Church in Armagh became embroiled in a number of religious controversies, including the row over Arianism which led to dissension within the congregation, and within the Synod of Ulster. This led to the formation of the Remonstrant Synod in 1829 and to the establishment, over a century later, of the Non-Subscribing Presbyterian Church.

For almost four years in the early nineteenth century, First Armagh was without a minister, and its affairs were transferred from the Armagh Presbytery to a committee of the Synod of Ulster. One of the ministers who preached for the vacancy in 1823 was the Reverend Henry Cooke, a leading figure in the Arian controversy. When he had finished preaching from his text "The door was shut", a member of the congregation was heard to declare "Aye, and the door of this church is shut against you."

Eventually a call was made out to the Reverend Pooley Shuldham Henry who was ordained and installed in First Armagh in 1826. From the start, Mr Henry was opposed by a section of his congregation and his involvement in politics and education only increased that opposition. This came to a climax in 1837 after a bitterly-contested Parliamentary election fought in a Tory stronghold. Some 60 families who were incensed by Mr Henry's Liberal views, memorialised (ie petitioned) the Armagh Presbytery to allow them to form another congregation.

This wish was granted. Although it was recognised officially as Third Armagh by the Synod of Ulster, it was known by its members as The Mall Presbyterian Church, the name it retains today. The development of The Mall Church, and of Second Armagh will be discussed later.

Meanwhile, the life and witness of First Armagh continued. In 1846 the Reverend P S Henry, who had not had an easy ministry in Armagh, resigned his charge on becoming the first President of the newly-established Queen's College, later Queen's University, in Belfast. The next incumbent of note, the Reverend Jackson Smyth, was installed in June 1859, the year of the great Ulster Revival in which he and others played an important part in the city.

He also played a significant role in the development of his own church, and during his ministry the congregation built a new church in The Mall, which was opened in May 1879. The former premises at Abbey Street were sold to the congregation of Second Armagh for £1,700. Just over a year later Dr Smyth was elected Moderator of the Presbyterian Church, which was widely regarded as an honour to himself, to his church and to the city of Armagh. He ministered at Armagh until his death in 1890, the year after the Great Armagh Railway disaster.

The Very Reverend Temple
Lundie, a former Presbyterian
Moderator and a former
Minister of First Armagh
Presbyterian Church.

It was nearly seventy years before the General Assembly elected another
Armagh minister as its Moderator. This time it was the Reverend A W Neill,
a native of Derry, who was installed in First Armagh in September 1928, and
who became Moderator twenty years later. Sadly he died half-way through
his year of office. His was, according to the *History of Congregations in the
Presbyterian Church in Ireland*, an outstanding Moderatorship.

The effect of his death was described by his successor the Reverend
George Temple Lundie in his short *History of First Armagh*. 'It came as a
profound shock to the congregation, the whole Church and the community
at large when Dr Neill passed away suddenly on the first Sunday in
November 1948, on a day when he was to have broadcast a Harvest Service
from the Church'.[11]

Dr Lundie was installed in First Armagh in 1949 and had a long and
fruitful ministry. He was a character in his own right, with a deep interest in
antiques, and a habit of using – on occasion – twenty words where ten would
suffice. But, as someone who knew him remarked, the twenty words were
always worth listening to! Dr Lundie could be incisive when he wanted to
be, and he, too, brought honour to himself, his church and Armagh by his
election as Moderator of the General Assembly in 1974.

His election as Moderator also maintained the distinctive record of First
Armagh in producing ministers who reached high office. Sadly, Dr Lundie's
successor , the Rt Rev Dr G F H Wynne, died in office in 1975, and Dr
Lundie had to undertake once again the onerous duties of the
Moderatorship. He resigned his pastorate in October 1978. Subsequent
ministers at First Armagh were the Reverend Philip Breakey, followed by the
Reverend James Sleith, and later the Reverend Tony Davidson, a Dungannon
man who had previously ministered in Limerick. He was installed in First
Armagh in 1994, and the congregation currently consists of some 300
families.

Mr Davidson describes First Armagh as a broad church, which seeks to
be inclusive. "Our people are proud of the traditions of First Armagh, and
they are aware that their Presbyterian roots in the city are deep. They are also
seeking to continue their Presbyterian witness in the best way possible into
the new Millennium."

Meanwhile, the congregation at The Mall Church flourished. On 13 June
1838, the Reverend John R McAlister was installed as its first minister and
this marked the beginning of a long and important period in the
development of the church. Mr McAlister served as minister for thirty-three
years, until his death in June 1871, at the age of fifty-five.

He had been deeply involved, like his fellow minister the Reverend
Jackson Smyth of First Armagh, in the 1859 religious revival in Ulster. He
recorded the effect on his Congregation: "the attendance upon public
worship has increased by one-third, the Sabbath School has doubled in
number and grown in spiritual life manifold; the Lord's supper has been
attended by one-third more than usual."

On his death, the congregation of The Mall recorded their appreciation
of him in a Memorial Tablet which they erected in the Church vestibule. It
stated, *inter alia*, "By his exertions this Church was built, a Manse, glebe and

The "Catch-My-Pal" Hall, 1912.
The Reverend Robert James Patterson, Minister of the Mall Church had strong temerance and helped to found the "Catch-My-Pal" total abstinence movement. Initially the members met at the Manse, and as numbers increased they moved to a corrugated iron hall.

daily schools provided and all left free of debt. To the discharge of his duties he brought singular energy and zeal. While his private life in all its relations, was a striking illustration of the power of gospel truth. He was an earnest pastor, and a faithful preacher, and the seals of his ministry were many".[12]

He was succeeded by the Reverend John Brown Meharry, who was installed in October 1871. He, too, was a man of exceptional gifts who consolidated the good work of his predecessor, but in 1875 he moved to a church in Newcastle-upon-Tyne, and later to London. He became Moderator of the English Presbyterian Church in 1906, and died on 20 January 1916.

Another notable incumbent in The Mall was the Reverend Robert James Patterson, who was installed in September 1892. He had strong sympathies for the work of the Temperance Movement. The Pioneer Movement, begun by a Roman Catholic priest in Dublin, had made an impact on the city of Armagh and surrounding districts. In 1909 Mr Patterson was stopped on his way home by a man who suggested that he should persuade his friends, standing around a lamp-post, to sign the pledge of total abstinence.

As a result they visited the Manse on the following evening, and agreed to sign the pledge. They further agreed to meet at the Manse the next week, and that each would bring a friend. This was the start of the Protestant Total Abstinence Union, more popularly known as "Catch My Pal". This organisation grew significantly, and in August 1910, the Reverend Patterson resigned from his ministry at The Mall to devote himself completely to the total abstinence movement.[13]

During the ministry of the Reverend David Graham, who was installed in May 1911, the Second and Third congregations were united on 1 April 1916, after much discussion, and became officially The Third, but still known popularly as The Mall. The complex origins of Second Armagh can be traced to a split in the Church of Scotland in 1733, when a number of ministers seceded, because they objected to the right of patrons to nominate ministers to congregations. This meant, in effect, that a minister could be imposed upon a congregation, contrary to the wishes of the majority of the people.

The rise of the so-called Seceders was welcomed by a number of Presbyterians in Ulster who had their own doctrinal problems. To add to the complexities, the Secessionists themselves were divided into two groups – the Burghers and the Antiburghers. There seems to have been some Seceder activity in Armagh around 1764, but little is known until 1786, when assistance was sought to build a meeting house in the city.

The congregation was without a minister until 1794 when a Reverend George Hamilton was ordained. Several years later, however, Mr Hamilton withdrew from the Burgher Synod and took many of the congregation with him. The Seceders continued, with difficulty, and eventually a Mr Samuel Oliver Edgar was installed as minister in 1811.

He was gloriously eccentric, and he dressed most colourfully compared to his more soberly-attired colleagues. A contemporary description of his dress tells us that "his coat was blue, his vest (waistcoats) white and his trousers, yellow, while his chest was adorned with watch chains and his fingers with rings".[14] He was an able student and writer, and he admitted that for some sixteen years, he studied – on average – for sixteen hours a day. His main interest, indeed obsession, was a study of *The Variations of Popery*.

During his ministry in Armagh, there were important developments among the Burgher and Antiburgher Synods. In 1818 the two branches of the Secessionists, which had quarrelled for some seventy years, formed the one Secession Synod. Even more important, in 1840, the Secessionists and other Presbyterians settled their differences, and the three congregations in Armagh became part of the one body – the Presbyterian Church in Ireland.

The colourful Dr Edgar died in June 1850, and his death was deeply felt in the whole city.[15] Only six months later his successor William Henderson was installed. He was a man of energy and enthusiasm, which was just as well – for he had much work to do. He soon discovered that the congregation consisted of few families, that attendance was irregular and that the church property needed repaired.

He set to work with zeal, and helped to breathe new life into the church. He started a morning Sunday School, and held an evening Sunday School in his own home. The congregation responded to his inspired leadership, and in 1852 they built the splendid Greenfield Manse on a hill along the Newry Road which still provides panoramic views of the city, and particularly of St Patrick's Roman Catholic Cathedral.

Two of the Reverend Henderson's brothers were newspapermen, like his father James who had been proprietor of the *Newry Telegraph*. One of his brothers succeeded his father in Newry, and the other became the proprietor of the *Belfast News Letter*, thus starting a family dynasty. The Reverend

Henderson died in 1868, unfortunately, at the age of forty-two.

The Second Armagh Church struggled during most of its existence, even though it moved from its Lower English Street premises in 1879 to the Abbey Street Church, when the First Armagh congregation took possession of its new church buildings. As the years went on, the small numbers in Second Armagh, and the consequent lack of finance, made amalgamation inevitable. Like many another Presbyterian church, then and now, Second Armagh tried to cling to its independence. By 1915 however, with only sixty-one families, its days were numbered. Late in that year, the congregation rejected a proposal to unite with First Armagh, and chose to amalgamate with The Mall instead.

The new united church progressed steadily. The incumbent minister Mr Graham served altogether some 28 years, and retired in 1939. His successor, the Reverend William Boyd, served for five years as an Army chaplain during the Second World War, mainly in the Far East. After the war he returned to The Mall, where he remained until 1950, when he accepted a call to First Lisburn. He was elected Moderator of the General Assembly in 1967.

During the ministry of his successor, the Reverend J C M Anderson, the name of Third Armagh was changed officially in 1953 to The Mall. Mr Anderson died in April 1980, and he was succeeded by the Reverend Dr John Lockington who was installed in January 1981. During his term of office, Dr Lockington wrote the *150th Anniversary History of The Mall*, which was published in 1987. Thirteen years later, he accepted a call to Gardenmore Presbyterian Church in Larne. In 1999 he was elected Moderator of the Presbyterian Church, thus maintaining the remarkable record of Armagh ministers, and former ministers, who reached the highest office of the Church.

The Very Reverend John Lockington, a former Presbyterian Moderator and a former Minister of the Mall Presbyterian Church, Armagh.

In 1990 Dr Lockington was succeeded by the current minister of The Mall, the Reverend Dr Joseph Thompson. He underlined the continuing sturdy independence of the Presbyterian ethos by pointing out that the present congregation, with some 335 families, had completed a suite of church halls several years ago at a cost of £650,000. The cost, he pointed out, had been fully paid-off and in a short time, without recourse to funds from the National Lottery. Presbyterians in general, unlike some Anglicans and others, do not approve of the policy of using National Lottery money to assist in the upkeep and development of church property.

Dr Lockington, who came to know Armagh well during his term of office in the city, noted that the Presbyterians were aware that they lived in a city with not only one but two Cathedrals. There was a feeling at times that they had to assert themselves, but personal relationships in general were good.

A former Presbyterian Moderator, the Reverend Dr John Dunlop, in his important study of Presbyterians and the conflict in Ireland, pointed out: "If the people of Ireland are to be understood, it is clearly necessary to understand the Presbyterians: who they are, where they are coming from, and how they see themselves.[16]

The same applies to their contribution to the history of Armagh. Presbyterians, no doubt, will continue to make a significant contribution to the ecclesiastical and community life of the city, just like the other traditions who owe so much to the mission of St Patrick and the Christian example down the ages.

NOTES

1 Alannah Hopkin, *The Living Legend of St Patrick*, published by Grafton Books 1989, pp.145-147

2 Elizabeth Shannon, *Up in The Park, published by Giland MacMillan, p.140.*

3 *Silver Linings – Travels around Northern Ireland*, published by Little, Brown and Company 2000, pp.211-212

4 Alf McCreary, *An Ulster Journey*, published by Greystone Books, 1986, pp.154-156

5 Stuart. Op. Cit. pp.483-484

6 Ibid. pp.501-503

7 The Reverend of Dr John Lockington has written a comprehensive account of the establishment of Presbyterianism in Armagh in his *Short History of The Mall Presbyterian Church* 1837-1987

8 Stuart, Op. Cit. p.486

9 Lockington. Op. Cit. p.6

10 Ibid. p.7

11 First Armagh Presbyterian Church 1673-1973, p.59

12 Lockington, Op. Cit. pp.16-19

13 Ibid. p.29

14 Ibid. p.47

15 Ibid. p.47

16 *A Precarious Belonging*, published by The Blackstaff Press, 1995, p.2

'I pray those who believe and fear God, whosoever deigns to look at or receive this writing which Patrick, a sinner, unlearned, has composed in Ireland, that no-one should ever say that it was my ignorance if I did or showed forth anything however small according to God's good pleasure; but let this be your conclusion and let it be so thought, that – as is the perfect truth – it was the gift of God. This is my confession before I die.'

These final words of St Patrick's *Confession* underline his transparent humility and his conviction that the vision for his mission, and the strength to sustain it, came directly from God. At the start of the Third Millennium, more than 1,550 years after the beginning of his mission, we have an historical vantage point from which to assess St Patrick's legacy. There are almost as many differing views about the significance of this legacy as there are Patrician scholars and others who have written about this wide subject.

For the purposes of this final chapter, however, I propose to focus on the legacy outlined at the end of the first chapter – namely Patrick's emphasis on the growth and witness of the Church, the development of education, and the evolution of better community relations, in the sense that he exhorted people to shun violence and to base their lives on the teachings of the Gospel.

There is no doubt that, numerically speaking, his mission was a spectacular success. As he states in his *Confession* "it was most necessary to spread our nets so that a great multitude and throng might be caught for God." The success of this mission in Ireland and its effect world-wide has been outlined earlier.

Despite the obvious success of St Patrick's mission, the reality today is that of a divided church – albeit with much in common, yet with significant differences in style and approach. The parting of the ways from Reformation times led to the growth of two sturdy branches of the same tree, though there are Protestants today who do not regard Roman Catholics even as Christians, as there are Roman Catholics who refuse to recognise the claims and status of the Reformed Churches.

In the centuries after the Reformation, there was little or no attempt to find common ground. The theological divisions were mirrored in the world of secular politics. The Roman Catholic Church was deeply associated with Irish nationalism, and the Protestant Churches became associated with Ulster unionism, most evidently in the years leading up to the Home Rule crisis.

These differing allegiances were clear at the highest ecclesiastical level.

The Anglican Archbishop of Armagh, Dr Crozier, was pictured at his Palace with Sir Edward Carson and Sir James Craig, the Ulster Unionist leaders, at the height of the Home Rule campaign. However when Northern Ireland came into being, Cardinal Logue declined to accept an invitation to the State opening of the Northern Ireland Parliament by King George V at Belfast City Hall on 22 June, 1921, as did Nationalists and members of Sinn Fein.

On that historic occasion, the King said "I speak from a full heart when I pray that my coming to Ireland today may prove to be the first step towards an end of strife amongst her people, whatever their race or creed." His heartfelt plea now seems immensely sad, given the legacy of bitter violence in Ireland during the rest of the 20th century, and beyond.

In 1931, for example, a mob in Cavan confronted an Orange gathering, and attacked an Orange Hall. Following anti-Catholic riots in Armagh, Portadown and Lisburn, Cardinal MacRory stated in December that "The Protestant Church in Ireland – and the same is true of the Protestant Church anywhere else – is not only not the rightful representative of the early Irish Church, but is not even a part of the Church of Christ." Predictably Orange resolutions during the subsequent marching season denounced "the unchanging bigotry of Rome" and also "the arrogant, intolerant and un-Christian pretensions fulminated by Cardinal MacRory."[1]

Even after the Second World war there was no real coming together. My personal recollection as a boy growing up in the mixed village of Bessbrook in South Armagh was that of Roman Catholics being "different". We went to different schools, though – happily – we played football together, and some of those early friendships have lasted a lifetime. But there was no concerted effort by either of the main denominations to find common ground.

In our village, the local Presbyterian minister and the Roman Catholic priest would exchange cordial greetings in the street and linger for a chat. But that was far as it went. There were no pulpit exchanges nor ecumenical services. The harsh reality was that a religious apartheid still existed. Mixed marriages with the blessing of both churches simply did not take place, and if a Protestant 'turned' by marrying a Roman Catholic he or she, in most cases, was ostracised by family and friends. Religious practice in the land of Saint Patrick still caused a great deal of heartache.

After Vatican II, the historic initiative announced by the visionary Pope John XXIII in 1959 and which opened in 1962 – it had also come about partly because of the more liberal thinking among leading Roman Catholic writers – the ice began to thaw, but not totally so. As the seismic shock of the Second Vatican Council worked its way through the Catholic body politic, there were Protestants in Northern Ireland who also saw the need for the churches to give a lead in bridge-building. Some of the early pioneers like the Reverend Dr Ray Davey, founder of the Corrymeela Community, the Reverend Dr Eric Gallagher, former President of the Methodist Church, the Very Reverend Dr Jack Weir, a former Presbyterian Moderator and others began the work of bridge-building that should have started several decades earlier.

When the Troubles erupted with fury in the late Sixties, the Churches –

Opposite: Cardinal Tomas O'Fiaich with Pope John Paul II.

like secular society – were unprepared for the magnitude of the task of guiding the warring tribes to a solution that would bring peace with justice. Many commentators, media, academic and others, criticised the Churches for their lack of preparedness to deal with the Troubles and to give a clear Christian lead throughout the years of crisis.

Such criticisms were both fair and unfair. Both main denominations have largely remained prisoners of political ideologies, but there have been individuals who have shown courage and vision in reaching out across the divide. Today there are church groups meeting in areas where this was once unthinkable. Roman Catholics and Protestants are engaged in the joint study of theology and in exploring what they have in common. These meetings do not make headlines, but this quiet bridge-building works better without the glare of publicity.

One welcome development has been the willingness of Church leaders to give a joint lead in public. In practice this means that the Protestant and Roman Catholic Archbishops, with tenure of office, enjoy more continuity than the Presbyterian or Methodist Church leaders who normally have only one year in post. Some of the latter have contributed to leadership, though the intensity of this commitment is variable, particularly in the Presbyterian Church which appeared at one time to elect progressive or conservative Moderators almost year about.

Though many initiatives have been undertaken by the leaders of the four main churches, in reality the perceived image of Church leadership has rested largely with the Protestant and Roman Catholic Primates, partly because of their continued appearance in the media, year after year. Armagh has set a good example in this respect. Cardinal Archbishop Tomas O'Fiaich, a distinguished scholar and former President of Maynooth, had a distinctive South Armagh style.

Unionists saw him as an unashamedly old-style "Nationalist" Catholic leader, and yet he was respected by Protestants who recognised his scholarship, frankness, and warm-heartedness. One former Moderator of the Presbyterian Church talks fondly of the warm hospitality of the parties in Ara Coeli where the Cardinal, at the right moment, could be persuaded to sing his party piece, "The Ould Orange Flute".

A good working relationship developed between the Primates in Armagh in recent years. Archbishop Robin Eames co-operated closely with Cardinal O'Fiaich, with his successor Cardinal Cahal Daly, and also with Archbishop Sean Brady, the current Primate. Dr Brady says "The symbolism of our joint presence is important, in the very fact of our being together and speaking together. In that way, we are being faithful to the spirit of St Patrick."[2]

The inspiration of St Patrick's example is also evident.

"He was a reconciler" says Archbishop Brady. "I am constantly amazed at his example of coming back to Ireland, to the people who had so mistreated him. It must have taken tremendous forgiveness on his part to do so, and this is most relevant to the challenges of reconciliation which face all of us today."

Archbishop Eames concurs: "St Patrick inspires me greatly. I find particularly in his *Confession* a great deal of language which can be updated and made relevant to the here and now. I believe that many people working

Cardinal Cathal Daly and Archbishop Robin Eames in the United States as part of a Church delegation. "There was surprise and amazement that we were together and that we were largely singing from the same hymn-sheet, without anyone being drastically out of tune".

in the field of reconciliation are doing so without realising, in fact, that they are doing his work. For me, personally, he is much more than a plaster-cast Saint."[3]

A good example of ecclesiastical co-operation, directly inspired by the example of St Patrick, was the year-long celebration "Armagh Together". It began, appropriately, on 17 March 1994, to mark the 1550th anniversary of St Patrick in Armagh. More than two hundred and fifty events were held, including conferences on subjects ranging from religion and conflict to science and the environment, and also Georgian architecture. The project had the full backing of the churches, including the two Archbishops.

Cardinal Daly, then Roman Catholic Primate, said

"St Patrick is very relevant to our times. It is sad that there are the wounds of pain and division between the Christian churches, but it is also an inspiration. We both feel proud of the heritage of St Patrick. We've become more conscious over the years, and particularly since the Second Vatican Council, of how much there is that unites us. In the past we have concentrated more on the things that have divided us."

In those days it was a different outlook, a different world. It was not that we were always in conflict with each other, but that we understood so little about how we respectively worshipped and what we respectively believed."

Archbishop Eames noted

"To set the present mood of co-operation in perspective, it is unthinkable that such progress would have been possible a generation back. We are doing things today that would not even have been dreamt of then. There were times when the Church of Ireland Archbishop and the Roman Catholic Archbishop were barely on speaking terms."

Both men travelled together on a Church delegation to the United States. Cardinal Daly reflected on the misconceptions abroad that the Irish problem is a "religious" conflict. He said

"It is seen now as a much more complex situation. There was surprise and amazement that we were together and that we were largely singing from the same hymn-sheet, without anyone drastically being out of tune."

It is important to emphasise, however, that – despite the greater understanding between both sides – fundamental differences about doctrine remain, a point summed up by Archbishop Eames:

"Cardinal Daly would be totally committed to the Irish nationalist outlook. Also he would find it difficult, I am sure, to accept my theology of the Church, just as I could not share his adherence to the Papacy, and to its power and influence. We can have very deep discussions – not arguments – about those things that divide us, as well as those we share in common."[4]

However, the critics of the Churches argue that despite the movement towards greater understanding, there remain shortcomings, including the lack of substantive movement on the vexed question of mixed marriages, the need for more dynamic leadership at all levels, the challenges within the Roman Catholic Church and its minority of errant clergy, the increasing secularisation with which the churches are grappling , and other issues.

That said, however, St Patrick's legacy in the creation of an active Christian church lives on today, with its human shortcomings as well as individual examples of courage, vision and forgiveness. Critics have continued to argue, with justification, that the Churches could have done more during the Troubles. It could be argued, also with justification, that the situation might have been worse, but for the example of the churches and the work of individual Christians during the long years of widespread violence.

The major blot on St Patrick's legacy, which would wound him greatly if he were alive today, is the continued divisions and misunderstandings. Nevertheless there is a growing awareness that the example of St Patrick transcends all such barriers. In an almost interminable debate in the letters column of the *Belfast Telegraph*, in which the differences between Protestant and Roman Catholic beliefs were debated in detail, the Reverend Patrick

McCafferty made the point about St Patrick's transcendence, and argued that while Patrick and the Celtic spiritual tradition would not have been anti-Rome.

> "He does ... rightfully belong to all the Christian traditions of Ireland, Britain and beyond. We can all find common ground in his burning love for Christ and his courageous faith as witnessed by his Confession and in the Letter to Coroticus."[5]

In the field of education, St Patrick's legacy led to the widespread development of scholarship, at home and abroad. The patron Saint who was so painfully aware of his own lack of education would be delighted today with the range of educational institutions that have been established at all levels. Reference has been made earlier in this volume to the flowering of Irish Christianity and scholarship which gave Ireland a deserved reputation the world over as "the land of saints and scholars". The work of Irish men and women in the mission field and in providing education overseas was part of that flowering in later centuries, even to the present time.

The stark fact remains, however, that education in Northern Ireland is divided into Protestant and Roman Catholic systems. In recent years there has been welcome co-operation between the two sectors, and people have a right to send their children to the schools of their choice, including, it should be said, the small number of integrated schools available.

Many people believe that the relative lack of integrated education is a major contributory factor to community conflict in Northern Ireland. That is not to argue that integrated education would be a panacea for all ills – the issues in Northern Ireland are much too complex to enable even such a radical development as that to bring a quick solution. It would seem obvious, however, that if Protestant and Roman Catholic children were encouraged to go to school together, this would help the young people (and the rest of their families) to move beyond the "them" and "us" mentality which has so polluted the religious, political and social life of Northern Ireland for so long.

Unfortunately, the Churches, the educationalists and the politicians have as yet been unable to lead society towards a more truly integrated view of education and of itself. Inevitably, St Patrick's legacy in education is flawed by divisions which fly in the face of the transcendent Christianity of the Patron Saint who was a reconciler as well as a pragmatist.

When one considers the legacy of St Patrick in the secular world, there are two dimensions to consider. There is what might be called the "fantasy world of Patrick", and also the world of the differing cultural and political traditions which have tried to bind Patrick to their cause. Each world, in a sense, is a blemish on the society which Patrick wished to create.

The so-called "fantasy world" of Patrick is that world of "Paddywhackery" which was always more Irish than the Irish. This included not just the various myths about his travels, his miracles and other supposed realities about his mission, but also the larger-than-life image of St Patrick as a benign old saint who loved a party, and who smilingly indulged the Irish love for a drop of the hard stuff. St Patrick may have had his lighter moments, which are not recorded, but his tough and difficult witness for Christ was a long way from the joys of the flesh, so evident in the late-winter festival celebrating St Patrick's Day.

A St. Patrick's Day
Blessing for You

St. Patrick's Day Wishes

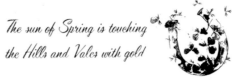

The sun of Spring is touching
the Hills and Vales with gold

St Patrick's Day celebrations have created a large market for greeting cards.

These include the widespread jollifications, notably in the USA but also elsewhere, in which the green beer flows liberally and anyone with a claim to even a drop of Irish blood in his or her veins embarks on a day of drinking and carousing that has nothing to do with the austere man who brought Christianity to Ireland. Some years ago I spent the week prior to St Patrick's Day in California. In San Francisco there were wonderful parties, which I thoroughly enjoyed, and in San Diego I noticed a pub sign for a party in "Murphy's Bar". The proprietor was Senor Jose Murphy, whose ancestral roots were in nearby Mexico! There is nothing wrong with a party on St Patrick's Day, but this is one aspect of the Patrician legacy which the Patron Saint might not readily understand.

The other dimension to the legacy of St Patrick in broadly secular society is altogether more serious, though in Ireland one can never totally separate the religious and the political. It centres around the attempts by one or other ecclesiastical or political tradition in Ireland, north and south, to include Saint Patrick in its ideology. The evolution of the celebration of St Patrick's Day itself is a classic example of this.

Professor Brian Walker, in his comprehensive account of this subject, points out that St Patrick is one of the most popular and most contested figures in Irish history, and notes the attempts by many Church writers – including James Ussher on behalf of the Church of Ireland and John Colgan representing the Roman Catholic Church in the seventeenth century, and others virtually up to the present – to trace the origins of their denomination

back to St Patrick.[6]

Armagh Together – St Patrick's Day parade.

Professor Walker further notes that in the last decade of the nineteenth century, St Patrick's Day was celebrated enthusiastically in many parts of Ireland, and that while it was clear that it was celebrated in the early 1900's more widely than at any time previously,

> "it is also evident that various groups valued the occasion in different ways." Under the influence of the Gaelic League the day became a focus especially in the South for Irish language enthusiasts, and while the majority of Protestants in the North "valued St Patrick's day as a holiday with a special Irish significance, they attached to it less of the religious, political and cultural importance given it by others."

Irish Dancing at a Fleadh in St Patrick's Cathedral.

Following partition, the differing attitudes to St Patrick's Day was more marked. In the Republic, St Patrick's Day became an annual holiday, and with the accession to power of Eamonn de Valera in 1932, the day took on a greater significance.

> "Links between Church and State were publicly emphasised by the annual procession on St Patrick's Day of de Valera and his Cabinet, complete with a cavalry troop, to the pro-Cathedral for Mass."

In Northern Ireland, St Patrick's Day was celebrated in a lower key. It was marked by well-attended Roman Catholic services, and by a much smaller number of Church of Ireland services, but there was by no means the widespread celebration by the whole community which took place in the South.

After the Second World War, the celebrations continued but the annual processions in the

213

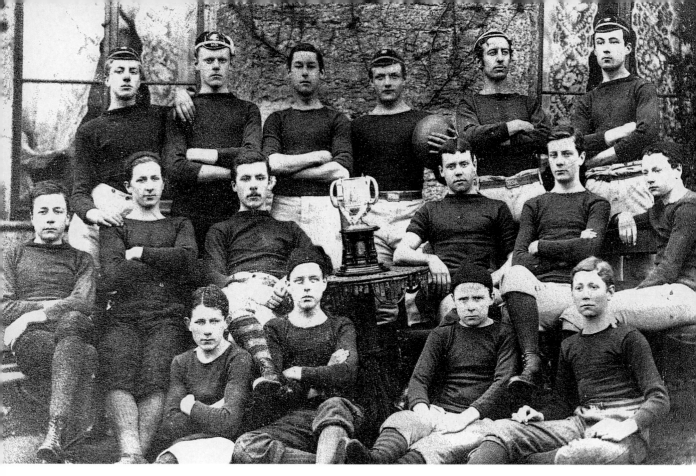

Schools' Cup Final: There is a tradition of playing the Rugby Schools' Cup Final at Ravenhill on St. Patrick's Day. Armagh Royal School won the inaugural competition seven times in the first ten years, including the 1880 team pictured here. Armagh Royal last won the Cup outright in 1977, just over a century after its first victory.

Republic of Ireland gradually lost their overbearing State-Church significance, and in Dublin the St Patrick's Day parade became more of a tourist attraction than a statement of political identity. In the North, however, St Patrick's Day continued to symbolise the differences between the two communities.

From my own experience, many Protestants were aware that their Roman Catholic neighbours and friends seemed to be having a better time than they were. At least they knew that it was a holiday, and they knew that there was something to celebrate.

In contrast, the Protestant celebrations seemed half-hearted. A number of Church of Ireland services took place, notably in Armagh and Downpatrick, but, to my knowledge, not in other Protestant churches every year. The only celebration on the Protestant side was the annual Schools Cup Rugby Final at Ravenhill, which mattered little to those who did not play rugby.

To many Protestants it seemed altogether most unsatisfactory. They were part of a community that somehow was afraid to show too much enthusiasm for St Patrick in case it could be regarded as "too Catholic". St Patrick's Day was not so much a deliberate take-over by Roman Catholics and Nationalists, but more the fact that Protestants and Unionists disenfranchised themselves. They were either too unsure, or too uninterested to claim what always had been a part of their heritage. St Patrick's Day, instead of being a reconciling symbol, was allowed to become the opposite.

The development of ecumenism was reflected in softening attitudes towards the celebration of St Patrick's Day. In 1964, the then Archbishop of Canterbury Dr Ramsey was invited to St Patrick's Day services held at Saul and Downpatrick. According to Professor Walker "This event was the occasion of one of the first ecumenical gestures when the local nationalist

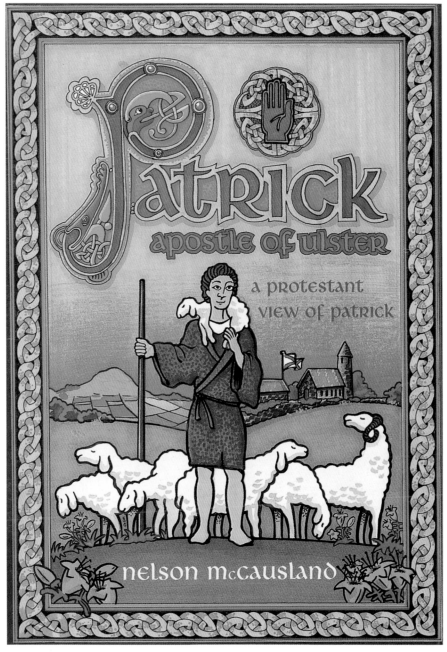

In 1997 the Grand Lodge of
Ireland published a booklet on
St. Patrick, with the sub-title
A Protestant View of Patrick

councillors turned up to greet the Archbishop at the cathedral, although they
felt unable to attend the service."[7]

On St Patrick's Day eight years later, Father Michael Hurley, SJ, became
the first Roman Catholic priest to preach in St Patrick's Cathedral Dublin
since the Reformation. Such interdenominational co-operation found
further expression later on, with the first joint Protestant-Roman Catholic
service in Down Cathedral taking place on 17 March 1985, and five years
later an ecumenical service was held in Armagh's Roman Catholic Cathedral
to commemorate the laying of the foundation stone there in 1840.

In the North, there was revived interest in St Patrick's Day among Roman
Catholics in the 1970's and 1980's. There was a St Patrick's Day parade on

the Falls Road, Belfast in 1974, and three years later a similar parade took place in Derry, after a lapse of a quarter of a century. Significantly there was also renewed interest in St Patrick among Orangemen. "In 1985 Belfast Orangemen took part in a St Patrick's Day parade along the Shankill and Newtownards Roads; in 1990 members from Belfast joined the brethren of St Patrick's Church Orange Lodge in Ballymena at their annual church service; and in 1994, St Patrick's flag flew over the Orange headquarters in Belfast for the first time on 17 March."[8]

In 1997, the Grand Orange Lodge of Ireland published a booklet titled *Patrick: Apostle of Ulster – A Protestant View of Patrick*. In the Foreword the Reverend Brian Kennaway, Convenor of the Grand Orange Lodge's Education Committee wrote "As we present this publication to the general public, we are conscious of the desire on the part of many in these days to 'listen to the other side'. It is our prayer that this publication may contribute to a better understanding of the Culture and Traditions of the majority population of the northern part of this island."[9]

The author, Nelson McCausland, noted that

"Unfortunately, many Roman Catholic writers and others persist in propagating the legends and myths which were invented by medieval writers, and many publishers persist in publishing such books. There is obviously a market for such material, and some people prefer the mythical Patrick to the historical Patrick."[10]

The author further claims that "the message Patrick preached in Ulster was a Biblical, Evangelical and Trinitarian message. It was the same message which the Apostles had preached four centuries before. It was the message which the Reformers preached a thousand years later and it is the message which evangelical Protestants still preach today. Patrick's name must go down in history with Paul, Augustine, Luther, Cranmer, Latimer, Ridley, Knox, Wesley, Spurgeon and all true preachers of the Gospel."[11]

McCausland asserts that Patrick's ministry "covered the length and breadth of Ulster and through his preaching many became Christians. Churches were built and men of God were ordained to minister in those churches." In essence he sums up "Patrick was God's man for Ulster, the Apostle of Ulster."[12]

Whatever may be made of this view, which narrows Patrick's mission down to Ulster even though many Patrician scholars feel that he travelled much further afield, it is significant that the Grand Orange Lodge actually published a booklet outlining its views on the subject. In doing so its members were accepting that, in their opinion, St Patrick was part of "the Culture and Traditions of the majority population of the northern part of this island". In other words, though they did not actually say so, they were underlining that St Patrick did not belong solely to the nationalist community.

St Patrick continues to remain part of this search for identity in Northern Ireland – or as some nationalists pointedly say "the North of Ireland" – at the beginning of the Third Millennium. After more than 30 years of community conflict is noteworthy, for example, that the Apprentice Boys in Londonderry organised a special St Patrick's weekend in March 2000. The aim was "to provide a positive contribution to commemorating St Patrick – something which Protestants can feel part of while at the same time offering something that everyone in the city can share and enjoy."

Alistair Simpson, the Apprentice Boys Governor, was quoted as saying

"The whole point of the Apprentice Boys of Derry organising this festival
weekend is to show that by thinking positively an organisation can work to the
benefit of its own community, yet still work to build bridges with others."[13]

Unfortunately the St Patrick's Day commemorations were less harmonious
elsewhere. In Belfast there was controversy over the St Patrick's Day parade
which was not supported financially by the City Council, and which was
claimed by some Unionists as being a Republican front – a claim which the
organisers angrily refuted. In Lurgan tensions were high as Unionist and
nationalist groups gave notice of their intention to hold a St Patrick's Day
parade in the town, with the inevitable newspaper headline "St Patrick's Day
march clash fear".

The Parades Commission decreed that members of the Apprentice Boys
would not be allowed to follow their chosen route in Lurgan on St Patrick's
Day, and that the parade of the Lurgan Martyrs Flute Band would also be re-
routed. A Sinn Fein Assembly member Dara O'Hagan welcomed the
decision to re-route the Loyalist parade but expressed puzzlement at the
restrictions placed on Republicans, a point echoed by spokesmen for both
sides following previous re-routings elsewhere. In the dark symmetry of
Northern Ireland politics it is impossible to please everyone.

The range of political and community attitudes to St Patrick was
mirrored in one of the early debates in the Northern Ireland Assembly on 7
February, 2000. A majority supported a motion calling on the Government
to declare March 17 a public holiday and for the flying of the Union Flag on
that day. Members from all parties paid tribute to the example of St Patrick
as a reconciler, but many then proceeded to score political points.

The proposer of the motion Kieran McCarthy of the Alliance Party noted

"Some workers, such as civil servants, bankers and indeed, Assembly Members,
will have the day off and can join in the celebrations. But many others, such as
the shipyard workers, the aircraft workers and other factory workers, will have to
plod on. Indeed, many children still have to go to school on St Patrick's Day."

The day, he further noted, was important for people throughout
Northern Ireland. "It celebrates the man who is historically associated with
bringing Christianity to Ireland. His importance is recognised by Protestants,
Catholics and many others. St Patrick is the great unifier."[14] Not surprisingly,
there were dissenting voices. Sammy Wilson, of the Democratic Unionist
Party, said that he did not consider himself as Irish and that he did not wish
to celebrate "Ireland's national day". He added "I do not wish to celebrate
the day on which Irish people celebrate their culture."[15]

However, his party leader, the Reverend Dr Ian Paisley, supported the
motion, partly on the grounds that he was refusing

"to hand St Patrick over to the Roman Catholic Church and the embrace of the
Pope, or to the IRA and Nationalists. He is a figure to be honoured and
remembered. He brought the Bible Gospel. In his works – the Confession, the
Epistle and the Hymn – one finds the simple Gospel of Jesus Christ."[16]

There was also humour during the debate. While Dr Paisley was in full
flow, a mobile phone started ringing. The Deputy Speaker reminded
Members about the prohibition on the use of mobile phones in the

Archbishop Sean Brady
"There's a great lesson in the forgiveness of St Patrick. He could have chosen to languish in recrimination, and to wallow in self-pity, but he opened himself to the grace of reconciliation."

Chamber. Dr Paisley apologised and explained that he had forgotten about the mobile phone in his brief-case. Another un-named member joked "Perhaps it is St Patrick on the telephone for you?", to which Dr Paisley replied "St Patrick has such a wonderful place in heaven that he would not return to a place like this!"[17]

The most significant point about the debate was the fact that it took place at all, and that there was broad agreement among the elected representatives on the transcendent example of St Patrick, even though – as has been noted – some indulged in political knockabout. Such an outcome would not have been possible a decade earlier, a fact which may point to some kind of progress in Northern Ireland.

The fact remains, however, that St Patrick is still used as a convenient badge by those who wish to substantiate their claim to express their particular culture or identity. To that extent, the legacy of St Patrick in bringing greater community understanding remains flawed. More than 1,550 years after his Mission deep divisions remain, despite the many attempts by groups and individuals to bridge the divide – some with notable degrees of success, and others less so.

Perhaps it is no surprise that in an imperfect world, the legacy of St Patrick remains flawed, despite the transcendent purity of his Christian witness which continues to inspire many Christians from all denominations not only in Ireland, north and south, but all over the globe. Although St Patrick is universally accepted as the patron saint of Ireland, and although his name adorns countless churches and cathedrals, and is the focus for multitudes of festivals and holy days – not least 17 March – the real Patrick remains for many a shadowy figure from the past, almost a refugee from a stained-glass window.

It is almost certain that the vast majority of people in Ireland, and beyond, have not had the time, nor the opportunity nor even the inclination to seek out the authentic historical figure from his writings and the times in which he lived. St Patrick, in the words of Archbishop Eames was "a real man for a real time saying real things", and not just a convenient figure from ancient history on which the Irish could build an identity, both ecclesiastical and secular.

Cardinal Daly says
"The real Saint Patrick has been insufficiently known in Armagh and all over Ireland. There has been a great deal of Patrician scholarship which has not been communicated to the people at large. If this happened, the general knowledge

about Saint Patrick would be much richer than the legends which are evidence of his popularity, rather than of devotion to his message. He was a model of Christian discipleship. I believe that in general we need a rediscovery of Saint Patrick for our times."[18]

Archbishop Brady concurs.

"We all know about St Patrick's Day but I don't think that many realise what an outstanding person Patrick really was. Hopefully people will look beyond the shamrocks and the green vestments and ask themselves 'What was he really like, what were his convictions, his faith, what he stood for, what he did, and, above all, what he was before he did anything?' He was someone who listened to God, he reflected on the Scriptures, he had a particularly rich prayer life, and he realised that God was calling him to do this special work. There was an important niche he was called by God to fill, and he filled it with outstanding success."[19]

A great deal of lip-service is paid to St Patrick. Archbishop Eames says "Everywhere I turn in my ministry, people want to relate Armagh to St Patrick. They want to relate the Armagh of the present to the Armagh that they perceive it to have been. But it is a struggle to get people at the beginning of a new Millennium to associate any significance to St Patrick's time. You actually have to go out on occasions and to draw people into special events to mark St Patrick's Day."[20]

Down the centuries of violence, of ecclesiastical division, and of community conflict in Ireland, it has been – and remains – difficult to hear the still, small voice of St Patrick in the midst of the storm. Archbishop Eames puts the point in a different way. He says:

"One could argue that all of us have let him down. The light of St Patrick has always been there, but it has burned the wick low in many instances. This is simply because we have not taken his message as seriously as we should have done. It shines brightest whenever people have the courage to witness the faith of Patrick and the courage also to say 'I want to help remove the bondage of violence and division from Ireland'. But at times the response to St Patrick's message is very dim."[21]

One of the most attractive characteristics of St Patrick was his humanity. Archbishop Daly comments:

"Patrick is a Christian whose humanity is better known than that of almost any other parallel figure, with the exception perhaps of St Augustine, who revealed his very soul in his Confession, which stands as perhaps a masterpiece of spiritual autobiography. Patrick's shorter Confession, which is not as well-crafted in style, is nevertheless a very intimate record of the feelings of Patrick's soul. In that sense we know more about what kind of man he was, as well as what kind of saint he was."[22]

A most fundamental and moving aspect of St Patrick's mission was his forgiveness of the Irish, the people who had made him a slave and who had treated him so badly. Archbishop Brady says

"It was by the Grace of God that Patrick came back, after so much suffering in Ireland. There's a great lesson in the forgiveness of Patrick, which is so often understated. When he escaped from Ireland and returned to his family they said, in effect 'Please stay with us, we don't want you to go back'. But back to Ireland he came. Just think of the humility of the man. He could have chosen to languish in recrimination, and to wallow in self-pity, but he opened himself to the grace of reconciliation."[23]

Archbishop Eames concurs

"Patrick did not see himself as a great prophet, or as a man who would manipulate or change history. He saw himself as a 'servant of servants' who was placed at a particular time in history when all the message that he needed to give was the message of the basic Gospel. I believe that in the times in which we are living St Patrick, if he were alive, would stress the importance of understanding the nature of forgiveness and of reconciliation, and that this begins on a one-to-one basis, from person to person, before it becomes institutionalised."

This remains the challenge of St Patrick today, for all the people of Ireland – north and south, religious and laity, politicians and people, Unionists and Nationalists, Loyalists and Republicans. Those who seek to claim the mantle of St Patrick, or take to themselves his name in their search for their identity and culture, cannot do so lightly without also taking on board the fundamental message of forgiveness and community tolerance which Patrick so eloquently expressed.

In that context, we have all failed. Yet in a society that is only slowly beginning to accept that St Patrick-and his example – belong to all of us, there is perhaps a basis on which to build a better future. This will be a future based not on the "Paddywhackery" of a jovial old saint for all seasons or a saint to suit all political ideologies, but on the austere example of a real man who knew pain, discomfort, violence and apprehension , yet who remained steadfast as a rock amid the swirling tides of the political violence and treachery of his times.

St Patrick himself stated in his Confession:

"Daily I expect murder, fraud or captivity, or whatever it may be: but I fear none of these things because of the promises of heaven. I have cast my myself into the hands of God Almighty who rules everywhere, as the prophet says 'Cast thy thought upon God, and He shall sustain thee'."

In our generation, and in generations to come, those who seek the real Patrick in a spirit of openness free from the myths of the past and the shibboleths of the present, will be richly rewarded. In doing so they will help to develop a greater awareness of the St Patrick who has deserved better from us but who can still inspire us to move through fear, violence and misunderstanding to build a society which we can all share and of which we can all be proud.

At the beginning of the Third Millennium, St Patrick remains a person for our time, saying real things to all of us. His challenge comes not only from his early mission in the city of Armagh but also as a man of God nearing the end of his life, and whose writings are as fresh as each new morning – but are we even prepared to listen? If we are not, the implications are obvious. The challenge from Patrick is still with us " ...if my own people do not know me, a prophet has no honour in his own country."

NOTES

1 Jonathan Bardon, Op. Cit. pp.536-538
2 Alf McCreary, in *Ireland of the Welcomes*, Vol. 47 No. 2, March-April 1998, pp.26-32
3 Ibid.
4 Alf McCreary in *Omnibus,* Summer 1994, pp.9-13
5 *Belfast Telegraph*, 23 March 1998
6 *Dancing to History's Tune – History, Myth and Politics in Ireland*, published by the Institute of Irish Studies at Queen's University, Belfast, 1996, pp.76-86
7 Ibid. p.83
8 Ibid. p.85
9 *Patrick: Apostle of Ulster*, p.5
10 Ibid. p.13
11 Ibid. p.371
12 Ibid. p.7
13 *News letter*, 16 March 2000, p.19
14 *Northern Ireland Assembly Official Report* (Hansard), Vol. 4 No. 9, 7 February 2000, pp.374-388
15 Ibid. p.382
16 Ibid. p.377
17 Ibid. p.376
18 Interview with Alf McCreary, 29 April 2000
19 Ibid. 3 August 2000
20 Ibid.
21 Ibid.
22 Ibid.
23 Ibid.

In 1932, the 1,500th anniversary of the arrival of St Patrick in Ireland was marked by the main churches. On March 17, a Pontifical High Mass was celebrated in St Patrick's Cathedral by Cardinal MacRory, assisted by six Bishops. This was the first Mass to be broadcast in Ireland.

The Church of Ireland also marked the anniversary with religious services, and a special Pageant at Castleward. William Conor, the distinguished Ulster artist, was commissioned to provide sketches for the costumes, and produced 15 beautiful water-colour drawings. Two of these are pictured here – depicting St Patrick as a young man and also as a mature Patriarch.

The drawings were purchased at the time by Archbishop D'Arcy, and presented to the Armagh Diocesan Office for display. In 2000 the drawings were put up for sale by the Diocesan Council partly to raise funds for church buildings and restoration.

They were purchased in the open market for £50,000 by Armagh Public Library, with substantial assistance from The National Lottery Heritage Fund and the Esme Mitchell Trust.

ST PATRICK'S WRITINGS
(from the translations of Dr Ludwig Bieler)

'Confessio'

I am Patrick, a sinner, most unlearned, the least of all the faithful, and utterly despised by many. My father was Calpornius, a deacon, son of Potitus, a priest, of the village Bannavem Taburnilae; he had a country seat nearby, and there I was taken captive.

I was then about sixteen years of age. I did not know the true God. I was taken into captivity to Ireland with many thousands of people – and deservedly so, because we turned away from God, and did not keep his commandments, and did not obey our priests, who used to remind us of our salvation. And the Lord brought over us the wrath of His anger and scattered us among many nations, even unto the utmost part of the earth, where now my littleness is placed among strangers.

And there the Lord opened the sense of my unbelief that I might at last remember my sins and be converted with all my heart to the Lord my God, who had regard for my abjection, and mercy on my youth and ignorance, and watched over me before I knew Him, and before I was able to distinguish between good and evil, and guarded me, and comforted me as would a father his son.

Hence I cannot be silent – nor, indeed, is it expedient – about the great benefits and the great grace which the Lord has deigned to bestow upon me in the land of my captivity; for this we can give to God in return after having been chastened by Him, to exalt and praise His wonders before every nation that is anywhere under the heaven.

Because there is no other God, nor ever was, nor will be, than God the Father unbegotten, without beginning, from whom is all beginning, the Lord of the universe, as we have been taught; and His son Jesus Christ, whom we declare to have always been with the Father, spiritually and ineffably begotten by the Father before the beginning of the world, before all beginning; and by Him are made all things visible and invisible. He was made man, and having defeated death, was received into heaven by the Father; and He hath given Him all power over all names in heaven, on earth, and under the earth, and every tongue shall confess to Him that Jesus Christ is Lord and God, in whom we believe, and whose advent we expect soon to be, judge of the living and of the dead, who will render to every man according to his deeds; and He has poured forth upon us abundantly the Holy Spirit, the gift and pledge of immortality, who makes those who believe and obey sons of God and joint heirs with Christ; and Him do we confess and adore, one God in the Trinity of the Holy Name.

For He Himself has said through the Prophet: Call upon me in the day of thy trouble, and I will deliver thee, and thou shalt glorify me. And again He says: It is honourable to reveal and confess the works of God.

Although I am imperfect in many things, I nevertheless wish that my brethren and kinsmen should know what sort of person I am, so that they may understand my heart's desire.

I know well the testimony of my Lord, who in the Psalm declares: Thou wilt destroy them that speak a lie. And again He says: The mouth that belieth killeth the soul. And the same Lord says in the Gospel: Every idle word that men shall speak, they shall render an account for it on the day of judgement.

And so I should dread exceedingly, with fear and trembling, this sentence on that day when no one will be able to escape or hide, but we all, without exception, shall have to give an account even of our smallest sins before the judgement of the Lord Christ.

For this reason I had in mind to write, but hesitated until now; I was afraid of exposing myself to the talk of men, because I have not studied like the others, who thoroughly imbibed law and Sacred Scripture, and never had to change from the language of their childhood days, but were able to make it still more perfect. In our case, what I had to say had to be translated into a tongue foreign to me, as can be easily proved from the savour of my writing, which betrays how little instruction and training I have had in the art of words; for, so says Scripture, by the tongue will be discovered the wise man, and understanding, and knowledge, and the teaching of truth.

But of what help is an excuse, however true, especially if combined with presumption, since now, in my old age, I strive for something that I did not acquire in youth? It was my sins that prevented me from fixing in my mind what before I had barely read through. But who believes me, though I should repeat what I started out with?

As a youth, nay, almost as a boy not able to speak, I was taken captive, before I knew what to pursue and what to avoid. Hence to-day I blush and fear exceedingly to reveal my lack of education; for I am unable to tell my story to those versed in the art of concise writing - in such a way, I mean, as my spirit and mind long to do, and so that the sense of my words expresses what I feel.

But if indeed it had been given to me as it was given to others, then I would not be silent because of my desire of thanksgiving; and if perhaps some people think me arrogant for doing so in spite of my lack of knowledge and my slow tongue, it is, after all, written: The stammering tongues shall quickly learn to speak peace.

How much more should we earnestly strive to do this, we, who are, so Scripture says, a letter of Christ for salvation unto the utmost part of the earth, and, though not an eloquent one, yet ... written in your hearts, not with ink, but with the spirit of the living God! And again the Spirit witnesses that even rusticity was created by the Highest.

Whence I, once rustic, exiled, unlearned, who does not know how to provide for the future, this at least I know most certainly that before I was humiliated I was like a stone lying in the deep mire; and He that is mighty came and in His mercy lifted me up, and raised me aloft, and placed me on the top of the wall. And therefore I ought to cry out aloud and so also render something to the Lord for His great benefits here and in eternity - benefits which the mind of men is unable to appraise.

Wherefore, then, be astonished, ye great and little that fear God, and you men of letters on your estates, listen and pore over this. Who was it that roused up me, the fool that I am, from the midst of those who in the eyes of men are wise, and expert in law, and powerful in word and in everything? And He inspired me - me, the outcast of this world - before others, to be the man (if only I could!) who, with fear and reverence and without blame, should faithfully serve the people to whom the love of Christ conveyed and gave me for the duration of my life, if I should be worthy; yes indeed, to serve them humbly and sincerely.

In the light, therefore, of our faith in the Trinity I must make this choice, regardless of danger I must make known the gift of God and everlasting consolation, without fear and frankly I must spread everywhere the name of God so that after my decease I may leave a bequest to my bethren and sons whom I have baptised in the Lord - so many thousands of people.

And I was not worthy, nor was I such that the Lord should grant this to his servant; that after my misfortunes and so great difficulties, after my captivity, after the lapse of so many years, He should give me so great a grace in behalf of that nation - a thing which once, in my youth, I never expected nor thought of.

But after I came to Ireland - every day I had to tend sheep, and many times a day I prayed - the love of God and His fear came to me more and more, and my faith was strengthened. And my spirit was moved so that in a single day I would say as many as a hundred prayers, and almost as many in the night, and this even when I was staying in the woods, and on the mountains; and I used to get up for prayer before daylight, through snow, through frost, through rain, and I felt no harm, and there was no sloth in me - as I now see, because the spirit within me was then fervent.

And there one night I heard in my sleep a voice saying to me: 'It is well that you fast, soon you will go to your own country.' And again, after a short while, I heard a voice saying to me: 'See, your ship is ready.' And it was not near, but at a distance of perhaps two hundred miles, and I had never been there, nor did I know a living soul there; and then I took to flight, and I left the man with whom I had stayed for six years. And I went in the strength of God who directed my way to my good, and I feared nothing until I came to that ship.

And the day that I arrived the ship was set afloat, and I said that I was able to pay for my passage with them. But the captain was not pleased, and with indignation he answered harshly: 'It is of no use for you to ask to go along with us.' And when I heard this, I left them in order to return to the hut where I was staying. And as I went, I began to pray; and before I had ended my prayer, I heard one of them shouting behind me, 'Come, hurry, we shall take you on in good faith; make friends with us in whatever way you like.' And so on that day I refused to suck their breasts for fear of God, but rather hoped they would come to the faith of Jesus Christ, because they were pagans. And thus I had my way with them, and we set sail at once.

And after three days we reached land, and for twenty-eight days we travelled through deserted country. And they lacked food, and hunger overcame them; and the next day the captain said to me: 'Tell me, Christian: you say that your God is great and all-powerful; why, then, do you not pray for us? As you can see, we are suffering from hunger; it is unlikely indeed that we shall ever see a human being again.'

I said to them full of confidence: 'Be truly converted with all your heart to the Lord my God, because nothing is impossible for Him, that this day He may send you food on your way until you be satisfied; for He has abundance everywhere.' And, with the help of God, so it came to pass: suddenly a herd of pigs appeared on the road before our eyes, and they killed many of them; and there they stopped for two nights and fully recovered their strength, and their hounds received their fill, for many of them had grown weak and were half-dead along the way. And from that day they had plenty of food. They also found wild honey and offered some of it to me, and one of them said: 'This we offer in sacrifice.' Thanks be to God, I tasted none of it.

That same night, when I was asleep, Satan assailed me violently, a thing I shall remember as long as I shall be in this body. And he fell upon me like a huge rock, and I could not stir a limb. But whence came it into my mind, ignorant as I am, to call upon Helias? And meanwhile I saw the sun rise in the sky, and while I was shouting 'Helias! Helias!' with all my might, suddenly the splendour of that sun fell on me and immediately freed me of all my misery. And I believe that I was sustained by Christ my Lord, and that His Spirit was even then crying out in my behalf, and I hope it will be so on the day of my tribulation, as it is written in the Gospel; On that day, the Lord declares, it is not you that speak, but the Spirit of your Father that speaketh in you.

And once again, after many years, I fell into captivity. On that first night I stayed with them. I heard a divine message saying to me: 'Two months will you be with them.' And so it came to pass: on the sixtieth night thereafter the Lord delivered me out of their hands.

Also on our way God gave us food and fire and dry weather every day, until, on the tenth day, we met people. As I said above, we travelled twenty-eight days through deserted country, and the night that we met people we had no food left.

And again after a few years I was in Britain with my people, who received me as their son, and sincerely besought me that now at last, having suffered so many hardships, I should not leave them and go elsewhere.

And there I saw in the night the vision of a man, whose name was Victoricus, coming as it were from Ireland, with countless letters. And he gave me one of them, and I read the opening words of the letter, which were, 'The voice of the Irish'; and as I read the beginning of the letter I thought that at the same moment I heard their voice - they were those beside the Wood of Voclut, which is near the Western Sea - and thus did they cry out as with one mouth: 'We ask thee, boy, come and walk among us once more.'

And I was quite broken in heart, and could read no further, and so I woke up. Thanks be to God, after many years the Lord gave to them according to their cry.

And another night - whether within me, or beside me, I know not. God knoweth - they called me most unmistakably with words which I heard but could not understand, except that at the end of the prayer He spoke thus: 'He that has laid down His life for thee, it is He that speaketh in thee'; and so I awoke full of joy.

And again I saw Him praying in me, and I was as it were within my body, and I heard Him above me, that is, over the inward man, and there He prayed mightily with groanings. And all the time I was astonished, and wondered, and thought with myself who it could be that prayed in me. But at the end of the prayer he spoke, saying that He was the Spirit; and so I woke up, and remembered the Apostle saying: The Spirit helpeth the infirmities of our prayer. For we know not what we should pray for as we ought; but the Spirit Himself asketh for us with unspeakable groanings, which cannot be expressed in words; and again: The Lord our advocate asketh for us.

And when I was attacked by a number of my seniors who came forth and brought up my sins against my laborious episcopate, on that day indeed was I struck so that I might have fallen now and for eternity; but the Lord graciously spared the stranger and sojourner for His name and came mightily to my help in this affliction. Verily, not slight was the shame and blame that fell upon me! I asked God that it may not be reckoned to them as sin.

As cause for proceeding against me they found - after thirty years! - a confession I had made before I was a deacon. In the anxiety of my troubled mind I confided to my dearest friend what I had done in my boyhood one day, nay, in one hour, because I was not yet strong. I know not, God knoweth - whether I was then fifteen years old; and I did not believe in the living God, nor did I so from my childhood, but lived in death and unbelief until I was severely chastised and really humiliated, by hunger and nakedness, and that daily.

On the other hand, I did not go to Ireland of my own accord, not until I had nearly perished; but this was rather for my good, for thus was I purged by the Lord; and He made me fit so that I might be now what was once far from me - that I should care and labour for the salvation of others, whereas then I did not even care about myself.

On that day, then, when I was rejected by those referred to and mentioned above, in that night I saw a vision of the night. There was a writing without honour against my face, and at the same time I heard God's voice saying to me: 'We have seen with displeasure the face of Deisignatus' (thus revealing his name). He did not say, 'Thou hast seen,' but 'We have seen,' as if He included Himself, as He sayeth: He who toucheth you toucheth as it were the apple of my eye.

Therefore I give Him thanks who hath strengthened me in everything, as He did not frustrate the journey upon which I had decided, and the work which I had learned from Christ my Lord; but I rather felt after this no little strength, and my trust was proved right before God and men.

And so I say boldly, my conscience does not blame me now or in the future: God is my witness that I have not lied in the account which I have given you.

But the more am I sorry for my dearest friend that we had to hear what he said. To him I had confided my very soul! And I was told by some of the brethren before that defence - at which I was not present, nor was I in Britain, nor was it suggested by me - that he would stand up for me in my absence. He had even said to me in person: 'Look, you should be raised to the rank of bishop!' - of which I was not worthy. But whence did it come to him afterwards that he let me down before all, good and evil, and publicly, in a matter in which he had favoured me before spontaneously and gladly - and not he alone, but the Lord, who is greater than all?

Enough of this. I must not, however, hide God's gift which he bestowed upon me in the land of my captivity; because then I earnestly sought Him, and there I found Him, and He saved me from all evil because - so I believe - of His Spirit that dwelleth in me. Again, boldly said. But God knows it, had this been said to me by a man, I had perhaps remained silent for the love of Christ.

Hence, then, I give unwearied thanks to God, who kept me faithful in the day of my temptation, so that today I can confidently offer Him my soul as a living sacrifice - to Christ my Lord, who saved me out of all my troubles. Thus I can say: 'Who am I, O Lord, and to what hast Thou called me, Thou who didst assist me with such divine power that to-day I constantly exalt and magnify Thy name among the heathens wherever I may be, and not only in good days but also in tribulations? So indeed I must accept with equanimity whatever befalls me, be it good or evil, and always give thanks to God, who taught me to trust in Him always without hesitation, and who must have heard my prayer so that I, however ignorant I was, in the last days dared to undertake such a holy and wonderful work - thus imitating somehow those who, as the Lord once foretold, would preach His Gospel for a testimony to all nations before the end of the world. So we have seen it, and so it has been fulfilled: indeed, we are witnesses that the Gospel has been preached unto those parts beyond which there lives nobody.

Now, it would be tedious to give a detailed account of all my labours or even a part of them. Let me tell you briefly how the merciful God often freed me from slavery and from twelve dangers in which my life was at stake - not to mention numerous plots, which I cannot express in words; for I do not want to bore my readers. But God is my witness, who knows all things even before they come to pass, as He used to forewarn even me, poor wretch that I am, of many things by a divine message.

How came I by this wisdom, which was not in me, who neither knew the number of my days nor knew what God was? Whence was given to me afterwards the gift so great, so salutary - to know God and to love Him, although at the price of leaving my country and my parents?

And many gifts were offered to me in sorrow and tears, and I offended the donors, much against the wishes of some of my seniors; but, guided by God, in no way did I agree with them or acquiesce. It was not grace of my own, but God, who is strong in me and resists them all - as He had done when I came to the people of Ireland to preach the Gospel, and to suffer insult from the unbelievers, hearing the reproach of my going abroad, and many persecutions even unto bonds, and to give my free birth for the benefit of others; and, should I be worthy, I am prepared to give even my life without hesitation and most gladly for His name, and it is there that I wish to spend it until I die, if the Lord would grant it to me.

For I am very much God's debtor, who gave me such grace that many people were reborn in God through me and afterwards confirmed, and that clerics were ordained for them everywhere, for a people just coming to the faith, whom the Lord took from the utmost parts of the earth, as He once had promised through His prophets: To Thee the gentiles shall come from the ends of the earth and shall say: 'How false are the idols that our fathers got for themselves, and there is no profit in them'; and again: I have set Thee as a light among the gentiles, that Thou mayest be for salvation unto the utmost part of the earth.

And there I wish to wait for His promise who surely never deceives, as He promises in the Gospel: they shall come from the east and the west, and shall sit down with Abraham and Isaac and Jacob – as we believe the faithful will come from all the world.

For that reason, therefore, we ought to fish well and diligently, as the Lord exhorts in advance and teaches, saying: Come ye after me, and I will make you to be fishers of men. And again He says through the prophets: Behold, I send many fishers and hunters, saith God, and so on. Hence it was most necessary to spread our nets so that a great multitude and throng might be caught for God, and that there be clerics everywhere to baptize and exhort a people in need and want, as the Lord in the Gospel states, exhorts and teaches, saying: Going therefore now, teach ye all nations, baptizing them in the name of the Father, and the Son, and the Holy Spirit, teaching them to observe all things whatsoever I have commanded you: and behold I am with you all days even to the consummation of the world. And again He says: Go ye therefore into the whole world, and preach the Gospel to every creature. He that believeth and is baptized shall be saved; but he that believeth not shall be condemned. And again: This Gospel of the kingdom shall be preached in the whole world for a testimony to all nations, and then shall come the end. And so too the Lord announces through the prophet, and says: And it shall come to pass, in the last days, saith the Lord, I will pour out of my Spirit upon all flesh; and your sons and your daughters shall prophesy, and your young men shall see visions, and your old men shall dream deams. And upon my servants indeed, and upon my handmaids will I pour out in those days of my Spirit, and they shall prophesy. And in Osee He saith: 'I will call that which was not my people, my people; ... and her that had not obtained mercy, one that hath obtained mercy. And it shall be in the place where it was said: "You are not my people," there they shall be called the sons of the living God.'

Hence, how did it come to pass in Ireland that those who never had a knowledge of God, but until now always worshipped idols and things impure, have now been made a people of the Lord, and are called sons of God, that the sons and daughters of the kings of the Irish are seen to be monks and virgins of Christ?

Among others, a blessed Irishwoman of noble birth, beautiful, full-grown, whom I had baptized, came to us after some days for a particular reason: she told us that she had received a message from a messenger of God, and he admonished her to be a virgin of Christ and draw near to God. Thanks be to God, on the sixth day after this she most laudably and eagerly chose what all virgins of Christ do. Not that their fathers agree with them; no - they often ever suffer persecution and undeserved reproaches from their parents; and yet their number is ever increasing. How many have been reborn there so as to be of our kind, I do not know - not to mention widows and those who practise continence.

But greatest is the suffering of those women who live in slavery. All the time they have to endure terror and threats. But the Lord gave His grace to many of his maidens; for, though they are forbidden to do so, they follow Him bravely.

Wherefore, then, even if I wished to leave them and go to Britain - and how I would have loved to go to my country and my parents, and also to Gaul in order to visit the brethren and to see the face of the saints of my Lord! God knows it that I much desired it; but I am bound by the Spirit, who gives evidence against me if I do this, telling me that I shall be guilty; and I am afraid of losing the labour which I have begun - nay, not I, but Christ the Lord who bade me come here and stay with them for the rest of my life, if the Lord will, and will guard me from every evil way that I may not sin before Him.

This, I presume, I ought to do, but I do not trust myself as long as I am in this body of death, for strong is he who daily strives to turn me away from the faith and the purity of true religion to which I have devoted myself to the end of my life to Christ my Lord. But the hostile flesh is ever dragging us unto death, that is, towards the forbidden satisfaction of one's desires; and I know that in part I did not lead a perfect life as did the other faithful; but I acknowledge it to my Lord, and do not blush before Him, because I lie not: from the time I came to know Him in my youth, the love of God and the fear of Him have grown in me, and up to now, thanks to the grace of God, I have kept the faith.

And let those who will, laugh and scorn - I shall not be silent; not shall I hide the signs and wonders which the Lord has shown me many years before they came to pass, as He knows everything even before the times of the world.

Hence I ought unceasingly to give thanks to God who often pardoned my folly and my carelessness, and on more than one occasion spared His great wrath on me, who was chosen to be His helper and who was slow to do as was shown me and as the Spirit suggested. And the Lord had mercy on me thousands and thousands of times because He saw that I was ready, but that I did not know what to do in the circumstances. For many tried to prevent this my mission; they would even talk to each other behind my back and say: 'Why does this fellow throw himself into danger among enemies who have no knowledge of God?' It was not malice, but it did not appeal to them because - and to this I own myself - of my rusticity. And I did not realize at once the grace that was then in me; now I understand that I should have done so before.

Now I have given a simple account to my brethren and fellow servants who have believed me because of what I said and still say in order to strengthen and confirm your faith. Would that you, too, would strive for greater things and do better! This will be my glory, for a wise son is the glory of his father.

You know, and so does God, how I have lived among you from my youth in the true faith and in sincerity of heart. Likewise, as regards the heathen among whom I live, I have been faithful to them, and so I shall be. God knows it, I have overreached none of them, nor would I think of doing so, for the sake of God and His Church, for fear of raising persecution against them and all of us, and for fear that through me the name of the Lord be blasphemed; for it is written: Woe to the man through whom the name of the Lord is blasphemed.

For although I be rude in all things, nevertheless I have tried somehow to keep myself safe, and that, too, for my Christian brethren, and the virgins of Christ, and the pious women who of their own accord made me gifts and laid on the altar some of their ornaments; and I gave them back to them, and they were offended that I did so. But I did it for the hope of lasting success – in order to preserve myself cautiously in everything so that they might not seize upon me or the ministry of my service, under the pretext of dishonesty, and that I would not even in the smallest matter give the infidels an opportunity to defame or defile.

When I baptized so many thousands of people, did I perhaps expect from any of them as much as half a scruple? Tell me, and I will restore it to you. Or when the Lord ordained clerics everywhere through my unworthy person and I conferred the ministry upon them free, if I asked any of them as much as the price of my shoes, speak against me and I will return it to you.

On the contrary, I spent money for you that they might receive me; and I went to you and everywhere for your sake in many dangers, even to the farthest districts, beyond which there lived nobody and where nobody had ever come to baptize, or to ordain clergy, or to confirm the people. With the grace of the Lord, I did everything lovingly and gladly for your salvation.

All the while I used to give presents to the kings, besides the fees I paid to their sons who travel with me. Even so they laid hands on me and my companions, and on that day they eagerly wish to kill me; but my time had not yet come. And everything they found with us they took away, and me they put in irons; and on the fourteenth day the Lord delivered me from their power, and our belongings were returned to us because of God and our dear friends whom we had seen before.

You know how much I paid to those who administered justice in all those districts to which I came frequently. I think I distributed among them not less than the price of fifteen men, so that you might enjoy me, and I might always enjoy you in God. I am not sorry for it – indeed it is not enough for me; I still spend and shall spend more. God has power to grant me afterwards that I myself may be spent for your souls.

Indeed, I call God to witness upon my soul that I lie not; neither, I hope, am I writing to you in order to make this an occasion of flattery or covetousness, nor because I look for honour from any of you. Sufficient is the honour that is not yet seen but is anticipated in the heart. Faithful is He that promised; He never lieth.

But I see myself exalted even in the present world beyond measure by the Lord, and I was not worthy nor such that He should grant me this. I know perfectly well, though not by my own judgement, that poverty and misfortune becomes me better than riches and pleasures. For Christ the Lord, too, was poor for our sakes; and I, unhappy wretch that I am, have no wealth even if I wished for it. Daily I expect murder, fraud, or capitivity, or whatever it may be; but I fear none of these things because of the promises of heaven. I have cast myself into the hands of God Almighty, who rules everywhere, as the prophet says: Cast thy thought upon God, and He shall sustain thee.

So, now I commend my soul to my faithful God, for whom I am an ambassador in all my wretchedness; but God accepteth no person, and chose me for this office - to be, although among His least, one of His ministers.

Hence let me render unto him for all He has done to me. But what can I say or what can I promise to my Lord, as I can do nothing that He has not given me? May He search the hearts and deepest feelings; for greatly and exceedingly do I wish, and ready I was, that He should give me His chalice to drink, as He gave it also to the others who loved Him.

Wherefore may God never permit it to happen to me that I should lose His people which He purchased in the utmost parts of the world. I pray to God to give me perseverance and to deign that I be a faithful witness to Him to the end of my life for my God.

And if ever I have done any good for my God whom I love, I beg Him to grant me that I may shed my blood with those exiles and captives for His name, even though I should be denied a grave, or my body be woefully torn to pieces limb by limb by hounds or wild beasts, or the fowls of the air devour it. I am firmly convinced that if this should happen to me, I would have gained my soul together with my body, because on that day without doubt we shall rise in the brightness of the sun, that is, in the glory of Christ Jesus our Redeemer, as sons of the living God and joint heirs with Christ, to be made comformable to His Image; for of Him, and by Him, and in Him we shall reign.

For this sun which we see rises daily for us because He commands so, but it will never reign, nor will its splendour last; what is more, those wretches who adore it will be miserably punished. Not so we, who believe in, and worship, the true sun - Christ - who will never perish, nor will he who doeth His will; but he will abide for ever as Christ abideth for ever, who reigns with God the Father Almighty and the Holy Spirit before time, and now, and in all eternity. Amen.

Behold, again and again would I set forth the words of my confession. I testify in truth and in joy of heart before God and His holy angels that I never had any reason except the Gospel and its promises why I should ever return to the people from whom once before I barely escaped.

I pray those who believe and fear God, whosoever deigns to look at or receive this writing which Patrick, a sinner, unlearned, has composed in Ireland, that no one should ever say that it was my ignorance if I did or showed forth anything however small according to God's good pleasure; but let this be your conclusion and let it so be thought, that - as is the perfect truth - it was the gift of God. This is my confession before I die.

Letter to Coroticus

I, Patrick, a sinner, unlearned, resident in Ireland, declare myself to be a bishop. Most assuredly I believe that what I am I have received from God. And so I live among barbarians, a stranger and exile for the love of God. He is witness that this is so. Not that I wished my mouth to utter anything so hard and harsh; but I am forced by the zeal for God; and the truth of Christ has wrung it from me, out of love for my neighbours and sons for whom I gave up my country and parents and my life to the point of death. If I be worthy, I live for my God to teach the heathen, even though some may despise me.

With my own hand I have written and composed these words, to be given, delivered, and sent to the soldiers of Coroticus; I do not say, to my fellow citizens, or to fellow citizens of the holy Romans, but to fellow citizens of the demons, because of their evil works. Like our enemies, they live in death, allies of the Scots and the apostate Picts. Dripping with blood, they welter in the blood of innocent Christians, whom I have begotten into the number for God and confirmed in Christ!

The day after the newly baptized, anointed with chrism, in white garments (had been slain) - the fragrance was still on their foreheads when they were butchered and slaughtered with the sword by the above-mentioned people - I sent a letter with a holy presbyter whom I had taught from his childhood, clerics accompanying him, asking them to let us have some of the booty, and of the baptized they had made captives. They only jeered at them.

Hence I do not know what to lament more: those who have been slain, or those whom they have taken captive, or those whom the devil has mightily ensnared. Together with him they will be slaves in Hell in an eternal punishment; for who committeth sin is a slave and will be called a son of the devil.

Wherefore let every God-fearing man know that they are enemies of me and of Christ my God, for whom I am an ambassador. Parricide! fratricide! ravening wolves that eat the people of the Lord as they eat bread! As is said, the wicked, O Lord, have destroyed Thy law, which but recently He had excellently and kindly planted in Ireland, and which had established itself by the grace of God.

I make no false claim. I share in the work of those whom He called and predestinated to preach the Gospel amidst grave persecutions unto the end of the earth, even if the enemy shows his jealousy through the tyranny of

Coroticus, a man who has no respect for God nor for His priests whom He chose, giving them the highest, divine, and sublime power, that whom they should bind upon earth should be bound also in heaven.

Wherefore, then, I plead with you earnestly, ye holy and humble of heart, it is not permissible to court the favour of such people, nor to take food or drink with them, nor even to accept their alms, until they make reparation to God in hardships, through penance, with shedding of tears, and set free the baptized servants of God and handmaids of Christ, for whom He died and was crucified.

The most High disapproveth the gifts of the wicked ... He that offereth sacrifice of the goods of the poor, is as one that sacrificeth the son in the presence of his father. The riches, it is written, which he has gathered unjustly, shall be vomited up from his belly; the angel of death drags him away, by the fury of dragons he shall be tormented, the viper's tongue shall kill him, unquenchable fire devoureth him. And so - Woe to those who fill themselves with what is not their own; or, What doth it profit a man that he gain the whole world, and suffer the loss of his own soul?

It would be too tedious to discuss and set forth everything in detail, to gather from the whole Law testimonies against such greed. Avarice is a deadly sin. Thou shalt not covet thy neighbour's goods. Thou shalt not kill. A murderer cannot be with Christ. Whosoever hateth his brother is accounted a murderer. Or, he that loveth not his brother abideth in death. How much more guilty is he that has stained his hands with blood of the sons of God whom He has of late purchased in the utmost part of the earth through the call of our littleness!

Did I come to Ireland without God, or according to the flesh? Who compelled me? I am bound by the Spirit not to see any of my kinsfolk. Is it of my own doing that I have holy mercy on the people who once took me captive and made away with the servants and maids of my father's house? I was freeborn according to the flesh. I am the son of a decurion. But I sold my noble rank - I am neither ashamed nor sorry - for the good of others. Thus I am a servant in Christ to a foreign nation for the unspeakable glory of life everlasting which is in Christ Jesus our Lord.

And if my own people do not know me, a prophet has no honour in his own country. Perhaps we are not of the same fold and have not one and the same God as father, as is written: He that is not with me, is against me, and he that gathereth not with me, scattereth. It is not right that one destroyeth, another buildeth up. I seek not the things that are mine.

It is not my grace, but God who has given this solicitude into my heart, to be one of His hunters or fishers whom God once foretold would come in the last days.

I am hated. What shall I do, Lord? I am most despised. Look, Thy sheep around me are torn to pieces and driven away, and that by those robbers, by the orders of the hostile-minded Coroticus. Far from the love of God is a man who hands over Christians to the Picts and Scots. Ravening wolves have devoured the flock of the Lord, which in Ireland was indeed growing splendidly with the greatest care; and the sons and daughters of kings were monks and virgins of Christ - I cannot count their number. Wherefore, be not pleased with the wrong done to the just; even to hell it shall not please.

Who of the saints would not shudder to be merry with such persons or to enjoy a meal with them? They have filled their houses with the spoils of dead Christians, they live on plunder. They do not know, the wretches, that what they offer their friends and sons as food is deadly poison, just as Eve did not understand that it was death she gave to her husband. So are all that do evil: they work death as their eternal punishment.

This is the custom of the Roman Christians of Gaul: they send holy and able men to the Franks and other heathen with so many thousand solidi to ransom baptized captives. You prefer to kill and sell them to a foreign nation that has not knowledge of God. You betray the members of Christ as it were into a brothel. What hope have you in God, or anyone who thinks as you do, or converses with you in words of flattery? God will judge. For Scripture says: Not only they that do evil are worthy to be condemned, but they also that consent to them.

I do not know what I should say or speak further about the departed ones of the sons of God, whom the sword has touched all too harshly. For Scripture says: Weep with them that weep; and again: If one member be grieved, let all members grieve with it. Hence the Church mourns and laments her sons and daughters whom the sword has not yet slain, but who were removed and carried off to faraway lands, where sin abounds openly, grossly, impudently. There people who were freeborn have been sold, Christians made slaves, and that, too, in the service of the abominable, wicked, and apostate Picts!

Therefore I shall raise my voice in sadness and grief: O you fair and beloved brethren and sons whom I have begotten in Christ, countless of number, what can I do you for? I am not worthy to come to the help of God or men. The wickedness of the wicked hath prevailed over us. We have been made, as it were, strangers. Perhaps they do not believe that we have received one and the same baptism, or have one and the same God as father. For them it is a disgrace that we are Irish. Have ye not, as is written, one God? Have ye, every one of you, forsaken his neighbour?

Therefore I grieve for you, I grieve, my dearly beloved. But again, I rejoice within myself. I have not laboured for nothing, and my journeying abroad has not been in vain. And if this horrible, unspeakable crime did happen – thanks be to God, you have left the world and have gone to Paradise as baptized faithful. I see you: you have begun to journey where night shall be no more, nor mourning, nor death; but you shall leap like calves loosened from their bonds, and you shall tread down the wicked, and they shall be ashes under your feet.

You, then, will reign with the apostles, and prophets, and martyrs. You will take possession of eternal kingdoms, as He Himself testifies, saying: They shall come from the east and from the west, and shall sit down with Abraham, and Isaac, and Jacob in the kingdom of heaven. Without are dogs, and sorcerers, ... and murderers; and liars and perjurers have their portion in the pool of everlasting fire. Not without reason does the Apostle say: Where the just man shall scarcely be saved, where shall the sinner and ungodly transgressor of the law find himself?

Where, then, will Coroticus with his criminals, rebels against Christ, where will they see themselves, they who distribute baptized women as prizes - for a miserable temporal kingdom, which will pass away in a moment? As a cloud or smoke that is dispersed by the wind, so shall the deceitful wicked perish at the presence of the Lord; but the just shall feast with great constancy with Christ, they shall judge nations, and rule over wicked kings for ever and ever. Amen.

I testify before God and His angels that it will be so as He indicated to my ignorance. It is not my words that I have set forth in Latin, but those of God and the apostles and prophets, who have never lied. He that believeth shall be saved; but he that believeth not shall be condemned, God hath spoken.

I ask earnestly that whoever is a willing servant of God be a carrier of this letter, so that on no account it be suppressed or hidden by anyone, but rather be read before all the people, and in the presence of Coroticus himself. May God inspire them sometime to recover their senses for God, repenting, however late, their heinous deeds - murderers of the brethren of the Lord! - and to set free the baptized women whom they took captive, in order that they may deserve to live to God, and be made whole, here and in eternity! Be peace to the Father, and to the Son, and to the holy Spirit. Amen.

(Permission to use these translations was kindly granted by Dr Bieler's daughter).

SUCCESSION OF ABBOTS, BISHOPS AND ARCHBISHOPS OF ARMAGH

In the following list a number prefixed to the name of a Bishop or Archbishop indicates the date of his appointment, or, if preceded by a dash, the date of the first known mention of him as Bishop of the See or Diocese. A number following a name indicates the date of voidance of the See. The cause of voidance was usually death, though where it is known to have been resignation or translation, these facts are stated.

ABBOTS AND BISHOPS

444	Patrick 461		-835	Forannan 852
	Benignus 467			MaelPatraic 862
	Iarlathi 481			Fethgna 875
	Cormac497			Cathasach 883
	Dubthach 513			Mochta 893
	Ailill 526			Maelaithghin
	Ailill 536			Cellach 903
	David O'Farnan 551			MelCiarain 915
	Carlean 588			Joseph 936
	Mac Laisre 623			MaelPatraic 936
-640	Tommene 661			Cathasach 966
	Segeni 688			Maelmaire 994
	Suibhne 730			Airindach 1006
-732	Congus 750			Maeltuile 1032
	Affiath 794		1032	Hugh O'Ferris 1056
-811	Nuadha 812			Maelpatraic 1096
-818	Artri 833		1099	Caincomrac

ARCHBISHOPS

1106	Cellach or Celsus 1129
1134	Maelmaedhog or Malachy O'Morgair
	tr. to Down
1137	GillaMac Liach or Gelasius 1174
	Gilbert O'Caran 1180
1181	Thomas O'Conor
-1206	Echdonn or Eugenius MacGillaweer 1216
1220	Luke Netterville
1227	Donat O'Fidhubra
[1238	Robert Archer, probably not consecrated]
1240	Albert, tr. to Pruscia
1247	Reynard or Raighned
1258	Abraham O'Connallan
1262	Mael Patraic or Patrick O'Scanlan
1272	Nicholas Mac Mael Isa

[1303	Michael MacLoughlin, not confirmed]
[1306	John Taffe, did not get possession]
1307	Walter Joyce, res.
1312	Rolland Joyce, res.
1324	Stephen Segrave
1325	David Mageraghty
1348	Richard FitzRalph
1362	Milo Sweteman
1383	John Colton, res., but died before his resignation had taken effect
1404	Nicholas Fleming 1415
1418	John Swayne, res.
1439	John Prene
1444	John Mey
1457	John Bole
1471	John Foxalls or Foxoles
1477	Edmund Connesburgh, res.
1478	Octavian de Palatio
1513	John Kyte, tr. to Carlisle
1521	George Cromer
1543	George Dowdall, deserted his diocese
1553	Hugh Goodacre
1553	George Dowdall (again) 1558
[1530	Donat MacTeague, not recognised by the Crown, 1562]
1563	Adam Loftus, tr. to Dublin
1568	Thomas Lancaster
1584	John Long
1590	John Garvey
1595	Henry Ussher
1613	Christopher Hampton

1625	James Ussher 1656
1661	John Bramhall
1663	James Margetson
1678	Michael Boyle
1703	Narcissus Marsh
1714	Thomas Lindsay
1724	Hugh Boulter
1742	John Hoadly
1747	George Stone
1765	Richard Robinson (Lord Rokeby)
1795	William Newcome
1800	William Stuart
1822	Lord John George Beresford
1862	Marcus Gervais Beresford
1886	Robert Knox
1893	Robert Samuel Gregg
1896	William Alexander, res.
1911	John Baptist Crozier
1920	Charles Frederick d'Arcy
1938	John Godfrey Fitzmaurice Day
1939	John Allen Fitzgerald Gregg, res.
1959	James McCann, res.
1969	George Otto Simms
1980	John Ward Armstrong
1986	Robert Henry Alexander Eames

(Listed in the *Official Guide to St Patrick's Church of Ireland Cathedral*)

A representation of a Celtic Cross, dating
from about the 11th century. It used to
stand in the Market Street on the Eastern
slope of Cathedral Hill. It was wantonly
destroyed on 2 July 1813, and the
fragments lay in the churchyard until
1916, when they were placed at the west
end of the aisle of St. Patrick's Church of
Ireland Cathedral
(Engraving from Stuart, 1819)

COMHARBAÍ PHÁDRAIG
(ST PATRICK AND HIS SUCCESSORS)

		Succeeded Cardinal	Died
1.	St Patrick	445	resigned
2.	St Benignus	455	467
3.	St Jarlath	467	481
4.	Cormac	481	497
5.	Dubtach I	497	513
6.	Ailid I	513	526
7.	Ailid II	526	536
8.	Dubtach II	536	548
9.	St David	548	551
10.	Feidlimid	551	578
11.	St Cairlan	578	588
12.	Eochaid	588	598
13.	Senach	598	610
14.	Mac Laisre	610	623
15.	St Tommine	623	661
16.	Seghene	661	688
17.	Flann-Febla	688	715
18.	Suibhne	715	730
19.	Congus	730	750
20.	Cele-Peter	750	758
21.	Ferdachry	758	768
22.	Cu-dinisc	768	deposed
23.	Dubdalethe I	778	793
24.	Faindelach (deposed and re-installed)	793	795
25.	Airechtach	793	deposed
26.	Connmach	795	807
27.	Torbach	807	808
28.	Nuada	808	812
29.	Flanngus	812	resigned
30.	Artri	823	833
31.	Eoghan	833	834
32.	Forannan	834 (dispute)	852

33.	Demot O Tighernan	834	852
34.	Fethgna	852	874
35.	Maelcobha	874	deposed
36.	Ainmeri	877	879
37.	Cathasach I	879	883
	Maelcobha (re-installed)	883	888
38.	Maelbrighte	888	927
39.	Joseph	927	936
40.	Mael-Patrick	936	936
41.	Cathasach II	936	957
42.	Muiredach	957	deposed
43.	Dubdalethe II	965	998
44.	Muirecan	998	deposed
45.	Maelmuire	1001	1020
46.	Amalgaid	1020	1049
47.	Dubdalethe III	1049	1064
	(Cumuscach) 1060-64		
48.	Mael-Isu	1064	1091
49.	Domnald	1091	1105
50.	Cellach (St Celsus)	1105	1129
51.	Murrough	1129	1134
52.	St Malachy	1134	resigned
53.	Gelasius	1137	1174
54.	Cornelius MacConcaille	1174	1175
55.	Gilbert O Caran	1175	1180
56.	Thomas O Conor	1181	1201
57.	Maelisu O Carroll	1184	1186
58.	Eugene MacGillaweer	1206	1216
59.	Luke Netterville	1217	1227
60.	Donat O Feery	1227	1237
61.	Albert Suerbeer, OP	1240	resigned
62.	Reginald OP	1247	1256
63.	Abraham O Connellan	1257	1260
64.	Patrick O Scanlan, OP	1261	1270
65.	Nicholas MacMaelisu	1272	1303
66.	John Taaffe	1306	1306
67.	Walter Joyce, OP	1307	resigned
68.	Roland Joyce, OP	1311	resigned
69.	Stephen Seagrace	1323	1333
70.	David Mageraghty	1334	1346
71.	Richard Fitz-Ralph	1346	1360
72.	Milo Sweetman	1361	1380
73.	John Colton	1381	1404
74.	Nicholas Fleming	1404	1416
75.	John Swayne	1418	resigned
76.	John Prene	1439	1443
77.	John Mey	1443	1456
78.	John Bole	1457	1470

79.	John Foxall, OFM	1471		1475
80.	Edmund Connesburgh	1475		resigned
81.	Octavian De Spinellis	1478		1513
82.	John Kite	1513		resigned
83.	George Cromer	1521		deprived
84.	Robert Wauchope	1539		1551
85.	George Dowdall	1553		1558
86.	Donagh O'Tighe	1560		1562
87.	Richard Creagh	1564		1585
88.	Edmund MacGauran	1587		1594
89.	Peter Lombard	1601		1625
90.	Hugh MacCawell, OFM	1626		1626
91.	Hugh O'Reilly	1628		1653
92.	Edmund O'Reilly	1657		1669
93.	St Oliver Plunkett	1669		1681
94.	Dominic Maguire, OP	1683		1707
95.	Hugh MacMahon	1714		1737
96.	Bernard MacMahon	1737		1747
97.	Ross McMahon	1747		1748
98.	Michael O'Reilly	1749		1758
99.	Anthony Blake	1758		1786
100.	Richard Reilly	1786		1818
101.	Patrick Curtis	1819		1832
102.	Thomas Kelly	1832		1835
103.	William Crolly	1835		1849
104.	Paul Cullen	1849	1866	translated to Dublin
105.	Joseph Dixon	1852		1866
106.	Michael Kieran	1866		1869
107.	Daniel McGettigan	1870		1887
108.	Michael Logue	1887	1893	1924
109.	Patrick O'Donnell	1924	1925	1927
110.	Joseph MacRory	1928	1929	1945
111.	John D'Alton	1946	1953	1963
112.	William Conway	1963	1965	1977
113.	Tomás Ó Fiaich	1977	1979	1990
114.	Cahal B Daly	1990	1991	Retired 1996
115.	Seán Brady	1996		

(Extracted in part from James Stuart's *Historical Memoirs of Armagh*. Listed in the Archdiocese of Armagh Directory.)

Anon:	*Armagh Cathedral Guide*; Derby, 1991
Bardon, J:	*A History of Ulster*; The Blackstaff Press, Belfast 1992.
Bassett, G.H:	*The Book of County Armagh*; Dublin 1888.
Bradley, T and Walsh J:	*A History of the Irish Church 400-700 AD*; Columba Press, Dublin 1991
Brett, C.E.B:	*Court Houses and Market Houses of the Province of Ulster*; Belfast, 1973.
Brett, C.E.B:	*Buildings of County Armagh*; Belfast, 1999.
Brown, C. J. & Harper, A.E:	*An Account of Excavations on the Cathedral Hill in 1968*: in "Ulster Journal of Archaeology". Series 3, Vol. 47, 1984.
Clarkson, L.A & Crawford, E.M:	*Ways To Wealth*, Belfast 1985.
Coleman, Rev. A:	*Historical Memoirs of the City of Armagh*; Dublin, 1900.
De Paor, M:	*The Relics of Saint Patrick*; "Seanchas Ard Mhacha", Vol. 4, No. 2, 1961–62.
Fitzgerald, D. & Weatherup, R:	*The Way We Were*; Belfast, 1993.
Gwynn, A:	*Brian in Armagh*; "Seanchas Ard Mhacha", Vol. 9, No. 1, 1978.
Hanson, R.P.C:	*St Patrick - His Origins and Career*; O.U.P, 1968.
Hopkin, A:	*The Living Legend of St Patrick*, Grafton Books, 1989.
Hughes, F. J:	*Eamhain Macha*; "Seanchas Ard Mhacha", Vol.1, No. 2, 1955.
Hughes, A. J. and Nolan, W. "et al":	*Armagh-History and Society*, Geography Publications, 2001.
Kilroy, P:	*The Society of the Sacred Heart in Armagh*; "Seanchas Ard Mhacha", Vol. 9, No. 2, 1979.
Leslie, J.B:	*Armagh Clergy And Parishes*; Dundalk, 1911.
Lewis, S:	*Topographical Dictionary of Ireland*; London, 1837.
Lindsay, E. M:	*The Story of Armagh Planetarium*.
Lockington, J.W:	*A History of the Mall Presbyterian Church, Armagh, 1837-1987*; Belfast, 1987.
Lundie, G.T:	*First Armagh Presbyterian Church Tercentenary*; Armagh, 1973.
Lynn, C:	*Account of Excavations at the Friary*; "Ulster Journal of Archaeology", Series 3, Vol. 38, 1975.
Lynn, C:	*Trial Excavations at the King's Stables, Tray townland, Co. Armagh*; "Ulster Journal of Archaeology", Series 3, Vol. 40, 1977.
Lynn, C:	*Excavations at Nos. 46-48 Scotch Street, Armagh*; in "Ulster Journal of Archaeology", Series 3, Vol. 51, 1988.

Lynn, J.M:	*A Short History of Wesleyan Methodism on the Armagh Circuit*; Belfast, 1887.
Macaulay, A:	*William Crolly, Archbishop of Armagh*; Four Courts Press, 1994.
McKinstry, R. "et. al":	*The Buildings of Armagh*; Belfast, 1992.
McKittrick, D. "et. al":	*Lost Lives*, Mainstream Publishing, Edinburgh and London 1999.
Mallory, J. P:	*Navan Fort, The Ancient Capital of Ulster*; Belfast.
Mallory, J. P:	*The Archaeology of Ulster from Colonization to Plantation*; Belfast, 1991.
Moody, T.W and Martin, F. X:	*The Course of Irish History*; Mercier Press, Cork 1967.
Moore, P:	*Armagh Observatory, 1790-1967*; Armagh, 1967.
Murray, R:	*A History of the Archdiocese of Armagh*; Editions Du Signe, Strasbourg, 2000.
O Fiaich, T:	*St. Patrick's Cathedral Armagh*; 1987.
Paterson, T.G.F:	*Harvest Home, The Last Sheaf*; Armagh, 1975.
Paterson, T.G.F:	*Old St. Malachy's*; "Seanchas Ard Mhacha", vol. 1, no. 2 1955.
Reeves, W:	*The Ancient Churches of Armagh*; Lusk, 1860.
Rogers, E:	Topographical Sketches in Armagh and Tyrone, 1874.
Rogers, E:	*Memoir of Armagh Cathedral with an Account of the Ancient City*; Belfast, 1876.
Rogers, E:	*A Record of the City of Armagh*; Armagh.
Simms, G.O:	*The Founder of Armagh Public Library*; "Irish Booklore", Vol.1, No.2, 1971.
Simms, G.O:	*The Real Story of Patrick*; The O'Brien Press, Dublin 1991.
Simms, J.C:	*Dean Swift in County Armagh*; "Seanchas Ard Mhacha", Vol.6, No.1, 1971.
Stuart, J:	*Historical Memoirs of the City of Armagh*; Newry, 1819.
Taylor & Skinner:	*Maps of the Roads of Ireland*; London & Dublin, 1778.
Walker, B and McCreary, A:	*Degrees of Excellance*; Institute of Irish Studies, Queen's University, Belfast, 1995.
Weatherup, D.R.M:	*The Armagh Public Library 1771-1971*; Irish Booklore, Vol.2, No.2, 1976.
Weatherup, D.R.M:	*Armagh, Historic Photographs of the Primatial City*; Belfast, 1990.
Woods, D:	*The Fateful Day*; Armagh, 1989.

ACKNOWLEDGEMENTS FOR ILLUSTRATIVE MATERIAL

The author and publisher gratefully acknowledge the assistance of all those who contributed or advised in the selection of suitable illustrations for *St. Patrick's City.* Our particular thanks to the following:

ALF McCREARY
Pages 4, 12, 21, 40, 63, 64, 97, Senate Seal 135, Burial Plaque 190

ARMAGH CITY AND DISTRICT COUNCIL
Pages 17, Franciscan Friary 50, 66, 85, 111, 138, 165, 171, 172, 174, 177 North South Council, 181, 194, 240

ARMAGH COUNTY MUSEUM
Page 116

ARMAGH OBSERVATORY
Pages 149, 150, 151

ARMAGH PUBLIC LIBRARY (The Governors and Guardians)
Pages 94, 147, 222

ARMAGH ROYAL SCHOOL
Page 214

BELFAST TELEGRAPH
Page 133

BENBURB VALLEY HERITAGE CENTRE
Page 77

BOARD OF TRINITY COLLEGE DUBLIN
Page 26

THE LINENHALL LIBRARY
Pages 39, 54, 58, 60, 61, 67, 68, 74, 100

THE McLAUGHLIN FAMILY
Pages 128, 131, 136

MICHAEL CAMPBELL
Pages 147, 173, Painting from Trian 190

NATIONAL LIBRARY OF IRELAND
Pages 112, 148, 197, 198

NORTHERN IRELAND TOURIST BOARD
Page 50 Strangford Lough, 164 Road Bowls

PATRICK CORVAN
Page 152 Planetarium at Dusk

QUEEN'S UNIVERSITY BELFAST
Pages 156, 157, 158, 160

ROYAL IRISH FUSILIERS MUSEUM
Pages 121, 134, Field Marshal Montgomery 135

THE STUDIO ARMAGH
Page 117

TOMAS O'FIAICH MEMORIAL LIBRARY AND ARCHIVE
Pages 21, 71, 78, 103, 207

THE ULSTER MUSEUM
Page 114

BRIAN LYNCH (Ireland of the Welcomes)
Pages 2, 16, 30, St. Patrick Death Carving 34, Lectern 92, 107, 186, 218

CHRISTOPHER HILL PHOTOGRAPHIC
Pages 113, 162, 175, 178, 180, 193, 209, 213

COLUMBA PRESS
Page 14

DARRYL HUTCHINSON
Page 142

IAN MAGINESS
Page 176 Prime Minister

JOHN HARRISON
Page 177 President Clinton, 184

JOHN B. VALLELY
Page 179

KELVIN BOYES
Page 176 Prince Charles

WILLIAM McCONNELL
Pages 8, 10, 16, 18, 19, 20, 24, 28, 31, 33, Mullaghbrack Mass Stone 34, 36, 38, 46, 47, 52, 70, 71, 72, 73, 75, 78, 79, 80, 84, 86, 87, 88, St. Patrick's Church of Ireland Cathedral 92, 93, 94, 101, 102, 103, 105, 106 Memorial, 140, Portrait 166, 188, 189, 191, 192, 195, 222

PUBLIC RECORD OFFICE OF NORTHERN IRELAND
PICTURES FROM THE ALLISON COLLECTION
Page 106 Cardinal Michael Logue
Pages 118, 119, 120, McCann's Shop 121, 126, 129, 130, 132, 145, 168, 196, 201

Corresponding PRONI catalogue numbers, under the General Prefix D2886:

A/2/14/14	Page 106	
A/2/12/16	Page 118	
A/2/4/18	Page 119	
A/2/5/78	Page 120	
A/1/6/36	Page 121	
A/2/4/14	Page 126	
A/1/6/58	Page 129	CB Cafe
A/1/6/56	Page 129	Woolworths
A/1/6/60	Page 130	Zweckers
A/1/6/2	Page 130	Lennox Shop
A/2/5/5	Page 132	
A/1/4/44	Page 145	
A/2/13/34	Page 168	
A/1/9/51	Page 196	
A/1/2/9	Page 201	

ARMAGH GUARDIAN (Mr Ted Trimble)
Page 131 – Newspaper Office

The Author and Publisher would also like to thank others too numerous to mention without whose assistance and encouragement this book would not have been possible. Finally, special thanks are due to the Dean and Chapter of St. Patrick's Church of Ireland Cathedral and the Administrator of St. Patrick's Roman Catholic Cathedral for the use of relevant illustrations.

INDEX

150th Anniversary of the Mall 203

Abercorn, Duke of 133
Act of Union 100
Aed, Bishop of Sletty 25
Ailild 35
Airgialla 18
Alexander, Dr 146
Allen, Philip 169
Allinson Photographic Collection 128
Amalgaid, Archbishop 44
Amathorex 23
Anderson, Rev. J.C. 203
Anglesea 5
Annals of the Four Masters 16
Annals of Ulster 35
Apple Blossom Festival 179
Apprentice Boys 216–17
Ara Coeli 106, 208
Archbishop's Palace *83*
Ardagh 32
Ardboe church 102
Argory, the 196
Armagh Bazaar 105
Armagh City and District Council 170
Armagh Guardian 128
Armagh Rhymers *180*
Armagh Together 209
Armstong, Charles *166,* 168
Armstrong, Dr John Ward 193
Astropark 153
Aughrim, battle of 73
Augustinian Order 35, 50, 67
Auxerre 8

Bagnall, Sir Henry 62
Bagot, Canon 112
Bailey, Prof. Mark E. *150,* 153
Bain, Prof. George *160*
Ballinderry church 102
Bangor 33
Bannavem Taberniae 5, *14,* 223
Bard of Armagh 78
Beckett, Prof. J.C. 157
Belfast Academical Institution 156
Benburb, battle of 68, 77
Benignus 35
Beresford, John George de la Poer, Archbishop of
    Armagh 90, *93,* 104, 109, 156, 143, 144, 147
Beresford, Lady Anne 94
Beresford, Marcus Gervais 95
Beveridge, Sir Gordon *157, 178*
Bieler, Dr Ludwig 223, 238
Black Death, the 55
Black, Heather *181*
Blair, Tony *176*
Blake, Anthony, Archbishop of Armagh 74
Blount, Charles (see Mountjoy, Lord)
Boa Island 30
Bobbio monastery 34
Boer War 123
Boer War Memorial *121*
Book of Armagh 15, 18, *19,* 20, 22, *26,* 34, 39, 71,
    94
Book of Kells 34–35
Book of the Angel 19, 26
Book of the Hours 173

Boru, Brian 22, *38,* 38–40, *39,* 43, 187
Boulter, Dr Hugh, Archbishop of Armagh *75,* 86
Boyd, Captain Alexander 114–15
Boyd, Rev. William 203
Boyle, Archbishop of Armagh 75
Boyle, Major 131
Boyne, battle of 73
Brady, Felim (see O'Donnelly, Dr Patrick), also
    The Bard of Armagh
Brady, Sean, Archbishop 145, 190, *218,* 219–20
Bramhall, Dr John 74
Brannigan, Pat 181, 182
Breakey, Rev. Philip 200
Brega, plain of 24
Brewer, Prof. John 160
Brocessa 146
Browne, Archbishop 57–58
Brownlow, Rev. Francis 22
Bruce, Edward 51, 53
Burke, Sir Bernard 94
Bushmills Distillery 141

Calpornious 5, 223
Campaign for Social Justice 137
Campbell, Major Alex 114–15
Campbell's mill 133
Carberry, Hugh 106
Carmelite Order 50
Carrickfergus Castle 51–*52*
Carroll, Roderick 168
Carson, Sir Edward 206
Cashel 32, 37, *42*
Cashel, Council of 48
Castleward 222
Cather, Lt. Geoffrey St George Shillington 122
Catholic Defenders 109
Catholic Emancipation Act 102
Catholic Reading Room 114
Caulfield, Captain 63
Cellach, Archbishop of Armagh 44–45, 86
Celsus, see Cellach
Celtic Warrior figure *33*
Chantrey, Sir Francis 91
Charles I, King 67–68, 70
Charles II, King 69
Charles, Prince *175*–76
Charters of Armagh 69, *79,* 85
Christian Brothers Grammar School 144
Cistercian Order 46
City Choir 179
City Hall 165
Clarkson, Prof. Leslie 97
Clayton, James *175*
Cleeland, James 117, 119
Cleeland, Margaret 117, 119
Clinton, Bill *177, 179, 184*
Clonard 33
Clones 25
Clonliffe College 105
Clonmacnoise 25
Clontarf, battle of 40, 43
Coalisland church 102
Coleman, Fr Ambrose 96
Coleraine 32
College of Further Education 146
Collins, Michael *126,* 127
Cologne 34

Conaing, nephew of Brian Boru 40
Confessio (St Patrick) 3–4, 6, 8–9, 12–13, *205, 223*
Connor, battle of 51
Connor, William 222
Conway, Cardinal *108,* 190
Cooke, Dr 95 ★★
Cooke, Rev. Henry 199 ★★ same?
Cooley, Thomas 83, 88
Corictic 23
Cormac, first abbot of Armagh 33, 35–37
Corn Market 94
Cornwallis, Lord 155
Coroticus 4–5, 235, 31
Corrigan, Peter 168
Corry, Isaac 142
Corrymeela Community 206
Cottingham, Lewis 91–92
County and City Club 114
County Golf Course 85
County Museum 175
Court House 85, 166
Craig, Sir James 206
Creagh, Richard, Archbishop of Armagh 60
Croagh Patrick 4
Crolly, William, Archbishop 111, 144, 156 *101,*
    102–104
Cromer, George, Archbishop of Armagh 57–58
Cromwell, Oliver 68–70
Crozier, Archbishop 122, 193, 206
Cullen, Cardinal Paul 105, 144
Cumberland, Richard 82

Daire, chieftain 25–26
Daire's Willows 135
D'Alton, Cardinal *108,* 130, *131,* 190
Daly, Cardinal Cathal 145, 160, *178,* 190, 208,
    209, 219
d'Arcy, Dr Charles Frederick 130, *131,* 193, *194,*
    222
Dartrey, Earl of 103, 106
Davenport, Dr William 148
Davey, Rev. Dr Ray 206
Davidson, Rev. Tony 200
Davison, Sir Joseph 132
Day, Dr John Godfrey Fitzmaurice 193
De Burgo, Richard, Earl of Ulster 51
De Courcy, John 49, 50
de Groot, Dr Mart 150
De Jorsey, Roland, Archbishop of Armagh 51
de Lacy, Hugh 48–49, 50
De Palatio, Octavianus, Archbishop of Armagh 55
Dearing Report on Higher Education 159
Dearing, Sir Ron 159
Deisignatus 227
Derry, Dr Edmund, Bishop of Dromore 74
Dervorgilla, wife of O'Rourke, Tiernan, King of
    Breifne 48
Devenish 25
Diamond, battle of 109
Dickens, Charles 165
Dixon, Dr Joseph 95, 105
Dobbin St 112
Doherty, Dr Charles 25
Dominican Order 50
Donaghmore church 102
Doncha, son of Brian Boru 40
Donnachadh, son of Flann 22
Donnelly (see O'Donnelly, Dr Patrick)
Dorset, Duke of 81
Dowdall, Archbishop of Armagh 58–59

Down Cathedral 215
Downpatrick 4
Downside Abbey, Bath 71
Dreyer, Dr J.L. 149
Drogheda 71
Druimsailech hill 89
Drumadd Barracks 177
Dubdalethy III, son of Maelmurry MacEoch 44
Dubhthach 146
Dublin 32, 37–38
Dublin City University 160
Dubtac 35
Duff, Thomas J. 104–105
Duke's Grove 135
Dunbar, George 94
Dundalk church 102
Dunkirk 134
Dunlop, Rev. Dr John 203
Dunsink Observatory 149
Durcan, Peter 123

Eames, Lord Robert 169, 191, 193, 208, *209,*
    210, *219*
Earnshaw, Thomas 148
Edgar, Dr Samuel Oliver 202
Edward VI, King 57, 59
Eglish church 102
Elizabeth I, Queen *54,* 57, 59–60, 62
Elizabeth II, Queen 177, *178*
Ellison, Rev. Dr W.F. 149
Emain Macha 15, *17, 18*
Eochod, King of Ulidia 47
Esme Mitchell Trust 222
Ewing, Gary 169

Faranan, Bishop of Armagh 37
Faughal 6
Faughart, Co Louth 31, 146
Ferdomnach 20
Fever Hospital 92
First Presbyterian church 199
Fiseole 34
Fitz Aldelm, William 49
FitzRalph, Richard, Archbishop of Armagh 55
Fletcher, Martin 187
Folly, The 135
Foxalls, John, Archbishop of Armagh 55
Franciscan friary *50*
Franciscan Order 50
Fredell, Francis 198

Gallagher, Rev. Dr Eric 206
Gaol 85, 177
Gaol Square 112
Gaul 7, 29
Gelasius, Archbishop of Armagh 46–47, 49
George I, King 75
George III, King 83, *84*
George V, King 127, 206
Germanus 23
Gillespie, Leonard 142
Gillis's mill 133
Giraldus Cambrensis 20
Girl's High School 143
Glastonbury 5, 34
Glenavy, Beatrice 30
Glendalough Round Tower *36*
Good Friday Agreement 177
Goodacre, Hugh, Archbishop of Armagh 59
Graham, Rev. David 202, 203

Graham, Robert 142
Grand Orange Lodge of Ireland 216
Granville, George 82
Great Armagh Railway Disaster 115–20, *116*
Great Bazaar 107
Great Northern Railways 117
Greenfield Manse 202
Green's Barber shop 183
Gregg, Dr John Allen Fitzgerald 193
Grew, Seamus 168
Grueber, Dr 142
Gulliver's Travels 172–73
Guy's bicycle shop 129
Gwynn, John 22

Hadrian's Wall 5
Hamilton, Paul 169
Hamilton, Rev. Dr James Archibald 148, 197
Hamilton, Rev. George 202
Hampton, Archbishop of Armagh 86
Hanson, Bishop 4, 8, 11
Harcourt, Mr 194
Hardcastle, Joseph A. 149
Helin, Elanor 'Glo' 153
Henderson, Rev. William 202–203
Henry II, King 48–49
Henry III, King 51
Henry of Lancaster 53
Henry VII, King 56
Henry VIII, King 54, 57–58
Henry, Rev. Dr Pooley Shuldman 157, 199
Henry, Rev. William 198
Heytesbury, Lord 156
Hill, John 79
Historical Memoirs of the City of Armagh 32, 96
History of Congregations in the Presbyterian Church in Ireland 200
History of First Armagh 200
Hoadley, Dr John, Archbishop of Armagh 76
Home Rule 120, 122, 206
Howells, Glen 175
Hurley, Fr Michael 215
Hutchinson, Brian *181,* 182
Hutheson, Rev. John 197

Iberia 29
International Astronomical Union 150
Iona 25, 35
Irish National Liberation Army 168
Irish Republican Army 136, 139, 165
Irish Volunteers 122
Irwin's City Bakery Café *129*

James I, King 79
James II, King 69, 72, 197
Jarlath 35
Jay, Richard 161
Jebb, Dr, Bishop of Limerick 100
John, King 50
Johnston, Francis 84, 88, 148
Johnston, William 167

Kells 30, 46
Kieran, Dr 105
Kildare 25
Kilmainham 40
Kinsale, battle of 63

Lady Anne's Cottage 94
Lambay 35

Lennox, Mr 113
Leoghaire, King 23–24
Lerins 8
Letter to Coroticus (St Patrick) 4, 235
Letter-Lunn, battle of 47
Liege 34
Life of Patrick (Muirchu) 19, 22, 25
Limerick 37
Lindisfarne 34
Lindsay, Archbishop 100
Lindsay, Dr Eric M. 149, *150,* 152
Lisnally 83
Lockington, Dr John 203
Lockwood, Sir John 157
Loftus, Adam, Archbishop of Armagh 59
Logue, Cardinal Michael *97, 106,* 122, 146, 206
Lombard, Peter, Archbishop of Armagh 62
Lost Lives 168
Louth 32
Lucca 34
Lundie, George Temple 200
Lydiat, John 141

Mael Maedoc (see St Malachy)
Mael Sechnaill, High King 43
Mael Suthain 43
Maelmurry Mac Eoch, Archbishop of Armagh 40, 44
Magherafelt 6
Magherafelt church 102
Maguire, Dr Dominic, Archbishop of Armagh 74
Makem, Tommy 179
Mall 85, 111, *112,* 114, 203
Mall Presbyterian church *198,* 199
Mallon, Seamus 170
Margetson, James, Archbishop of Armagh 86
Market House 112
Market Place Theatre and Arts Centre 175
Marsh, Narcissus, Archbishop of Armagh 75
Mary I, Queen 57, 59
Mason, Dr Tom *152*
Maxwell, Rev. John 198
Mayo 6, 32
MacAid, Nigel 45
Macan Asylum for the blind 93
Macan, Arthur Jacob 93
MacDomnald, Malachy, King of Ireland 44
MacDonald, Maurice 45
MacEoch, Archbishop Maelmurry
MacGauvran, Edward, Archbishop of Armagh 60–62
MacGorman, Torbac 35
Macha 15, *16*
MacMahon, Bernard, Archbishop of Armagh 74
MacMahon, Dr Hugh, Archbishop of Armagh 74
MacMahon, Ross, Archbishop of Armagh 74
MacMoyre, Florence 22, 71
MacMurrough, Dermott, King of Leinster 48
MacRory, Cardinal *108,* 190–91, *191,* 206, 222
McAlister, Rev. John R. 200
McArdle, Shane 169
McCafferty, Rev. Patrick 211
McCann, Dr James 193
McCarthy, James Joseph 105
McCarthy, Kieran 217
McCausland, Nelson 216
McCloy, Alan 169
McGeough, William 196
McGettigan, Daniel, Archbishop *102,* 105–106, 111

McLaughlin, Thomas 127, 130, *131*, 132–33, *136*, 137
McShane, Gavin 169
Meath 32
Meharry, John Brown 201
Meithlin, Prince of the Deisies 40
Mellifont Abbey 46
Methodist Circuit 197
Milford mill 133
Military barracks 86
Miliuc 23
Mill St 112
Milligan, Robert 128
Mitchell, Desmond *165*, 170–72, 179
Moel-Brigid, Archbishop 38
Moneymore church 102
Monserrat 147
Morrow, Robert 122
Mortimer, Roger 53
Mount Saint Catherine 145
Mountjoy church 102
Mountjoy, Lord 62–63
Mountnorris 141
Muircertach 38
Muirchu Moccu Machteni 22–25, 32
Mullabrack Mass stone *34*
Mundies Lending Library 147
Munro, General Robert 68
Murchard, son of Brian Boru 40
Murray, William 84
Museum of the Royal Irish Fusiliers 175
Myers, Kevin 171, 180

National Lottery Heritage Fund 222
National Museum of Ireland 31
National Trust 196
Natural History and Philosophical Society 114
Navan Centre 170
Navan Fort (see Emain Macha)
Neill, Rev. A W 200
Neilson, Dr James 102
Newcome, Archbishop of Armagh 90
Newry and Armagh Railway Company 115
Newry Magazine 96
Newry Telegraph 96
Newtownhamilton church 102
Nicholson, James *178*
Normans 43
Norse attack 38
Northern Ireland Housing Trust 135
Northumberland, Duke of 82, 85

O'Brien, Moriertach, High King 45
Observatory 85, *148–49*
O'Cahan, Manus 67
O'Connell, Daniel *100*
O'Corcoran, Thomas 49
O'Donnell, Cardinal *108*, 190, *191*
O'Donnelly, Dr Patrick 78
O'Dunan, Moelmurry 45
O'Fiaich, Cardinal Tomas 17, 32–33, 144–45, 190–91, *207*, 208
O'Hagan, Dara 217
O'Lochlin, Murtouch, High King 46–47
O'Melachlin, Dunchad, King of Meath 46
O'Neill, Capt. Terence 139
O'Neill, Eamonn 170
O'Neill, Hugh *60*, 62–63, 67
O'Neill, Owen Roe *67*, 68
O'Neill, Shane *58*, 59–60

O'Neill, Sir Phelim 67–68, *76*, 86
O'Nial, Con 58,
Opik, Dr Ernst Julius 150
Orange Order 109
Orangefield 135
O'Reilly, Michael, Archbishop of Armagh 74
O'Reilly, Richard, Archbishop of Armagh 74
Ornithological Society
O'Rourke, Tiernan, King of Breifne 48
Osborne, Rev. William 197
O'Scannail, Mael Patraic 51

Paisley, Rev. Ian 217–18
Palace Stables Heritage Centre 174–75
Pale, the 53
Palladius 3, 23, 29
Pangur Bán 20
Parades Commission 217
Paterson, T.G. 153, 155
Paton, William 79
Patterson, Rev. Robert James 201–202
Peep o' Day Boys 109
Penal Laws 73–74, 76
Penn, William 91
People's Democracy 165
Philharmonic Society 114
Philip II, King of Spain 60
Philip of Worcester, Lord Justice of Ireland 49
Pipers Club 179
Planetarium 152–53
Plantation of Ulster 65–67
Plunkett, St Oliver 69, *71*
Pollak, Andy 160
Popes:
    Benedict XV 71
    Celestine 29
    Clement VIII 62
    Innocent XI 74
    John Paul II *207*
    John XXIII 206
    Paul VI 71
    Sixtus V 55
Portadown 67
Portadown church 102
Portland, Duke of 155
Potitus 5, 223
Poynings, Sir Edward 56
Preston, Captain 118
Primate's chapel 84, 86, *87*
Princess Victoria's Royal Irish Fusiliers 123
Prosper of Aquitaine 29
Protestant Total Abstinence Union 201
Provisionals (see Irish Republican Army)
Public Library 85, 146–47, *147*, 175, 222

Queen Caroline *84*
Queen Charlotte 83, *84*
Queen's Colleges 155, 157
Queen's University Belfast at Armagh 85, 159
Queen's University Belfast 143, 153, 160
Quinn, Sean 168

Ramsay, Allan 84
Ramsey, Dr, Archbishop of Canterbury 214
Redmond, John 122
Reeves, Dr 22, 94
Regensburg 34
Reid, Joseph 167
Richard II, King 53
Richhill 83

Rinuccini, Nuncio 68
Robert II, King of Scotland 90–91
Robert, King of Scotland 51
Robinson Cup Anenometer 149
Robinson Memorial Refractor 149
Robinson, Dr Richard, Archbishop of Armagh 76, *80*, 81–88, 90, 109, 141, 144, 147, 155
Robinson, Dr Thomas Romney 148
Robinson, Sir William 86
Rodgers, W.R. 180
Rokeby, Lord (see Robinson, Dr Richard)
Rokeby, Yorkshire 81
Rome 8, 32
Royal Fusiliers 121, 134
Royal Irish Academy 22
Royal School 85, 141, *142*, 143
Rugby Club 114
Rural and Urban Council 174
Russell, Eleanor 194, 196
Ryan, Don 137, *138*, 139, 165, 171

Sacred Heart Convent 145
Sacred Heart Grammar School 145
Sacred Heart Secondary Intermediate School 145
Salzburg 34
Saul 4, 32
Schomberg, Duke of 72–73
Second Presbyterian church 203
Severus, Sulpicus 19
Seward, Nicholas 79
Shambles 112, 94
Shannon, Elizabeth 187
Sheridan, Dr 98
Sheridan, Noel *181*, 182
Sherrid, Hope 197
Silva Focluti 6, 226
Simms, Dr George Otto 11, 193, *194*
Simnel, Lambert 54–56
Simpson, Alistair 217
Sinn Féin 127
Sitric son of Amelanus 43
Skellig, Michael 35
Sleith, Rev. James 200
Slemish 4, 6, 23
Slieve Donard Hotel *134*
Smyth, Rev. Jackson 199
Somme, battle of 122
Speers, James *176, 182*
Spence, Charles 169
St Bernard of Clairvaux 45–46
St Bridget's Well 94
St Brigid 146
St Brigid's church, Kildare 25
St Brigid's High School 146
St Catherine's College *145*
St Ciaran's church, Clonmacnoise 25
St Columbanus 34
St Colum Cille's church, Iona 25
St Columba Abbey 40, 141
St Malachy 45–46, *47*, 190
St Malachy's church, *47*
St Mark's Church of Ireland church *192*
St Nicholas church, Carrickfergus 187
St Patrick, statue *8*
St Patrick, stained glass window *30*
St Patrick, carving *34*
St Patrick 3–15, 19–27, 141, 146, 181–83, 190, 210–11, 219–21
St Patrick's Breastplate 11–12
St Patrick's Cathedral, Dublin 215, 222

St Patrick's Cathedral, New York *12*
St Patrick's Church of Ireland Cathedral *20*, 30, *92*, 136, *140*, 185
St Patrick's College 102
St Patrick's Confession (see *Confesio*)
St Patrick's Day 24, 211–21
St Patrick's Grammar School 144–45
St Patrick's Roman Catholic Cathedral 10, 90, 95, 99, 103–108, *107*, 185, *186, 188–89, 194, 195*
St Patrick's Testament (see *also Book of Armagh*) 22
St Patrick's Trian *28, 31*, 33, 172–73, 175
Stevenson, William Ernest 133
Stone, Dr George, Archbishop of Armagh 76
Stopford, Edward Archdeacon 91
Strangford Lough 6, 38, *50*
Stringer, Peggy 98
Strong, family *168*
Strong(e), Norman 169
Strongbow 48
Stuart, Hon. William 112
Stuart, Imogen *21*
Stuart, James 96–97
Stuart, William, Archbishop of Armagh 90, 91
Swift, Jonathan 172–73, 198

Talana, battle of 123
Talbot, Richard 69, 72
Tandragee Man *24*
Tara 23–24, 32, 40
Taylor, John 166–67, *167*
Tennis Club 114
Thackeray, W.M. 92
Thompson, Rev. Dr Joseph 203
Times Book Club 147
Tirechan, Bishop 19, 25, 32
Trainor, Damien 169
Travelling Piper 179
Trier 34
Trinity College Dublin 70, 94
Troughton Equatorial Telescope *151*
Troughton, Messrs John & Edward 148
Trustee Savings Bank *166*
Tunis, Earl Alexander 134
Turgesius 37
Turlough the Great 47
Tyburn, London 71

Uí Néill, clan 18
Ulaid 18
Ulster Cycle of Tales 16
Ulster Defence Regiment 167
Ulster Railway Company 115
Ulster Schools Cup 143
Ulster Volunteer Force 122
Ussher, Dr James, Archbishop of Armagh 69, *70*, 71, 141

Vallely, Eithne 179
Vallely, John B. *179*
Variations of Popery 202
Vatican II 206
Vicar's Hill 86
Victoricus 8, 226
Vienna 34
Vikings 35

Wales, South 5
Walker, Prof. Brian 211–12
Walpole, Horace 82
War of the Roses 53

Warbeck, Perkin 53, 56
Waterford 37
Waterman, Dudley 17
Waucop, Robert, Archbishop of Armagh 58
Weatherup, Roger 15, 135
Weir, Rev. Dr Jack 206
Wellesley, Richard 142
Wellington, Arthur, Duke of 142
Wesley, John 194–96
Whalley, Rev. Ellen 197
Whitby 34
Wilkinson, Alexander 32
William Kennedy Piping Festival 179
William, Prince of Orange 65, 72–73, 197
Woburn Abbey, Donaghadee 94

Wood of Vocult (see Silva Foculti)
Wood, Charles *154*
Woodhouse, Helen 169
Woolworth's *129*
Workers Education Association 160
World War I 122
World War II 133, 143
Wurzburg 34
Wynne, Rev. Dr G.F. 200

Yellow Ford, battle of 62
Young Women's Christian Association 114
Young, Arthur 83

Zwecker's Hairdressers 129, *130*